The Reader's Brain

Have you ever found yourself rer̶
or five times and thought, "I shc
clueless as to why one paragraph just seems to flow" while you
simply can't recall the contents of another? Guess what: you are
not alone. Even the best writers fail to grasp why their writing
works. *The Reader's Brain* is the first science-based guide to writing, employing cutting-edge research on how our minds process
written language, to ensure your writing can be read quickly, assimilated easily, and recalled precisely – exactly what we need
to transform anyone into a highly effective writer. Using the five
Cs – clarity, continuity, coherence, concision, and cadence – this
book combines irreverent humor with easy-to-follow principles
that will make readers perceive your sentences, paragraphs, and
documents to be clear, concise, and effective.

YELLOWLEES DOUGLAS is Associate Professor of Management Communication at the University of Florida.

The Reader's Brain
How Neuroscience Can Make You a Better Writer

YELLOWLEES DOUGLAS, PhD
Clinical and Translational Science Institute and Center for Management Communication, University of Florida

CAMBRIDGE
UNIVERSITY PRESS

CAMBRIDGE
UNIVERSITY PRESS

University Printing House, Cambridge CB2 8BS, United Kingdom

Cambridge University Press is part of the University of Cambridge.

It furthers the University's mission by disseminating knowledge in the pursuit of education, learning and research at the highest international levels of excellence.

www.cambridge.org
Information on this title: www.cambridge.org/thereadersbrain

First published 2015

Printed in the United Kingdom by TJ International Ltd. Padstow Cornwall

A catalogue record for this publication is available from the British Library

Library of Congress Cataloguing in Publication data
Douglas, J. Yellowlees, 1962–
The reader's brain : how neuroscience can make you a better writer / Yellowlees Douglas, Ph.D. Clinical and Translational Science Institute and Center for Management Communication University of Florida.
    pages   cm
Includes bibliographical references and index.
ISBN 978-1-107-10039-8 (hardback : alk. paper) –
ISBN 978-1-107-49650-7 (paperback : alk. paper)
1. Reading – Psychology.   I. Title.
BF456.R2D677   2015
808.001′9 – dc23   2015003341

ISBN 978-1-107-10039-8 Hardback
ISBN 978-1-107-49650-7 Paperback

For my tireless, endlessly proactive, and visionary acquisitions editor – Rebecca Taylor at Cambridge University Press. Without her interventions, this book would have been consigned to oblivion – or Amazon's CreateSpace.

CONTENTS

ACKNOWLEDGMENTS

From the outset, I've silently thanked my initial round of anonymous psychologists, linguists, and neuroscientists, who provided spot-on advice on shifting the focus of *The Reader's Brain* – without a smidgen of the usual squeamishness academics exhibit at a reader-friendly approach in academic writing. Dr. Kenneth Heilman graciously provided me with a compelling narrative about a stroke patient, as well as references to two cases that proved integral to my thinking about writing, cadence, and the brain. And my credibility here would've been shot without the eagle eyes and superb suggestions for revision I received from Professors Gordon Pradl and Norman Holland. Both dramatically influenced the sensible side of my career and saved my bacon here. Finally, I owe an incalculable debt to Professor Sherrilene Classen, whose timely email enquiring after the availability of this book prompted me to submit the proposal one last time, after a decade of rejections. Without the enthusiasm both she and Rebecca Taylor displayed for the manuscript, this book would never have ended up in your hands.

CHAPTER 1

So much advice, so much lousy writing

Most people shun writing the way any chordate instinctively shuns pain. The task of writing is inescapably labor-intensive, no matter how facile a writer you are. Every blank page demands its lines of coherent sentences and cohesive paragraphs that ultimately amount to something like a rational, convincing argument. But our fear of writing reaches far beyond the hours we know we'll sweat over a keyboard, colonizing our blank screens with words. Instead, most of us are less afraid of the hard work than of grappling for hours with a complex system whose working parts we barely know. As a professor who has taught writing for more years than I'd care to publicly admit, I've heard thousands of confessions that gush out of students. *I'm a terrible writer*, they confess. Or, *Writing's my major weakness*. Strikingly, the majority of students who make these confessions are fairly strong writers – just as the students who assure me that they're good writers tend to create fresh paragraphs whenever they feel the reader needs to see a bit of white space, rather than from any sense of a paragraph as a coherent entity. Obviously, some sort of odd phenomenon must be at work here, when college students and even seasoned professionals have no idea whether their writing skills are adequate for a stringer position on the *New York Times* or barely pass muster as a child reporter writing for the *East Palatka Elementary Gazette*. Try making a similar analogy for reading or analytical skills, and you'll discover most people have a sound grasp of their abilities in these areas. But when the discussion turns to writing, a disconcerting number of us find ourselves at sea.

Three aspects of writing: micro, macro, middle

We struggle to even assess our writing ability because writing it-self is inherently complex. Most forms of writing demand simul-taneous attention to – along with at least some tenuous mastery of – three aspects of writing: argument, correct usage, and the con-stituents that make for clear, effective sentences and paragraphs. Unfortunately, the first two items have reaped all the press. Aristotle began a venerable, millennia-long history of writings on argument that continue today in classrooms the world over, des-pite Aristotelian notions of argument applying strictly to lengthy orations that ran to hours and were aimed at illiterate audiences with vastly different expectations and needs than any audience alive today. And, of course, the usage and correctness mavens are, as Christ described the poor, always with us – from the likes of H. W. Fowler through to William Bennett. But Fowler was a pub-lic school master, Bennett, a former Secretary of Education, and John Simon, another outspoken grammar maven, is a film critic. All of which proves you don't need any bona fide credentials as a linguist or researcher dedicated to the study of English to be a grammar maven – just muscular opinions about subjects like the correct use of *less* as opposed to *fewer*. You can master the art of using the colon correctly – one of the more recherché rules in the grammar canon – and also be on intimate terms with the difference between *logos* and *pathos* and even recognize an exor-dium when you see one, yet still write about as clearly as Forrest Gump. Why? Between the macro side of writing – the features of argument – and the micro side with its grammar and punctuation exists a vast middle ground, where virtually all the grunt work of writing occurs.

Ironically, the two ends of the writing spectrum collectively account for the majority of advice on writing and are probably responsible for the consumption of entire forests of virgin tim-ber over the centuries. But the vast middle ground has attracted relatively few experts. Moreover, to worsen matters, the handful of experts on this middle ground offer wrong-headed advice to writers. "Imitate published writers," advises Richard Marius in *A Writer's Companion.*[1] Unfortunately, this advice could land you in rather hot water when you channel James Joyce in your next performance evaluation. Or, even worse, as Marius puts it in Item 8 of his Fundamental Principles of Sentences: "Begin a Few Sentences with the Adverb *There*."

I happened to glimpse this particular gem in a writing manual I'd opened at random during a rant to a hapless sales assistant at a bookstore and waved the book at him, demanding to know if he realized this advice was the single worst recommendation you could make to any writer. Not surprisingly – given the wealth of misleading advice out there – he didn't. In fact, he probably considered steering me toward the Self Help section and recommending I browse the titles on anger management.

Even the most well-intentioned how-to-write manuals give us little concrete advice on all those burning questions that lie uneasily just below the surface as we hunch over keyboards and churn out sentences. How can you tell a good sentence from a bad one? What distinguishes a well-written paragraph from a crappy one? Are some word choices better than others? And how in the hell do you follow Principle #17 from that ever-present bible of writing advice, Strunk and White's *Elements of Style*, which counsels you to "Omit needless words"?[2] After all, how many people – outside of a few hundred thousand freshmen desperate to pad out a paper to a required word limit – have ever mused, "Oh, only a ten-word sentence – I'd better toss a couple of needless words in there"?

The reasons most writers have been struggling for years are actually pretty clear-cut. If you want to write well, you'll find a lot of contradictory advice in those helpful manuals on writing that attempt to address writing's middle ground and which clutter up the shelves at Barnes & Noble or Waterstones. Our libraries and bookstores are groaning with mostly consistent guidance on using punctuation and grammar and on crafting a convincing argument. But am I the only one who thinks Strunk and White's advice in *The Elements of Style*, "Find a suitable design and hold to it," is just a little too similar to a Buddhist koan? What about Sheridan Baker's exquisite description in *The Practical Stylist* of a paragraph as "a single idea…Like an essay itself, it has a beginning, a middle, and an end. The beginning and the end are usually each one sentence long, and the middle gets you smoothly from one to the other"?[3]

Whenever I read principles like these, I can't help recalling the episode of *Monty Python's Flying Circus* where Anne Elk defines a brontosaurus as being small at one end, rather large in the middle, then small again at the other end. Sad to say, Strunk and White's advice on building paragraphs is about as precise and helpful as Anne Elk's bit of wisdom. They seem to be telling us to be consistent – rather helpful advice in life as in writing. But our chief difficulty is then figuring out what the hell they mean by "a suitable design," which seems as elusive as the fine art of distinguishing necessary from unnecessary words. Does this strategy involve winnowing out those pesky, insignificant words like *in*, *to*, and *of*? Developing our vocabularies – or avoiding polysyllables at all costs? Or maybe they have something else entirely in mind: a paragraph that describes a complex topic, fat with sentences so long, they make Henry James seem like Hemingway – or the *New York Times* read like *The Sun*. And, while we're at it, does my paragraph have a beginning that falls into Baker's one-sentence definition, followed by a rather larger middle that gets tidily wrapped up by my concluding sentence?

If you're not quite confused yet, we could always obey Strunk and White's golden rule about suitable design, then follow *A Writer's Companion* and imitate the practices of published writers. If we just channel Henry Miller, Virginia Woolf, or ee cummings, we might get out of this particular rut,

although this

       might   not   be

a

good

       idea,   if   u

       think   about

              it.

The science of writing

Ultimately, all our problems with writing have a common source: precisely how all these experts arrived at the "principles" they claim lead to good writing. If you emulate what published writers have written – or, more accurately in many cases, got away with – you're not exactly treading a sure path to good writing. For instance, you run the risk of being mistaken for an ESL writer if you imitate the likes of Herman Melville. Writing researchers C. H. Knoblauch and Lil Brannon discovered this possibility when they slipped a swatch of *Moby-Dick* in with two student essays and asked teachers of writing to identify its strengths and weaknesses. The teachers' verdict: Melville's paragraphs had "some evident virtues, especially in [their] occasionally sophisticated word-choices…Sentence fragments abound, and the phrasing seems unnatural at times." The teachers decided Melville was probably an "advanced English Second Language student." Melville's masterpiece earned him a berth in a remedial writing class, not the impression one wants to make in applying for a job or writing a legal brief.[4] In addition, you will also never learn why some particular phrasings are better than others. Imitation works beautifully if you're learning the violin via the Suzuki Method. Imitation works for your average ten-year-old who can't read music but has parents with ambitions to produce the next Itzhak Perlman. However, imitation fails to work quite so well for a middle-level manager charged with writing a proposal. Come to think of it, unless you can locate a Warren Buffett rewrite of some thoroughly unintelligible bit of business prose, you'll have difficulty finding any stellar models of good writing in most professions, let alone for most of the kinds of writing our everyday lives require. Moreover, lore inherited from generations of not-particularly-helpful reference manuals on good writing is equally suspect. If you prefer active construction to passive, as so many books counsel, your writing *will* become more efficient and concrete. Yet virtually none of these experts explains why active construction works better than passive – or that this principle fails to apply in every situation.

Nearly all books on writing's under-explored middle ground deal merely with the surface, with messing around with words on the page, or with practices observed by what are usually arty writers with some credentials and a couple of books in print. But writing is always a transaction, a means to extend our convictions beyond the reach of the human voice, across time and space. At the receiving end: the hapless reader, confronted with the message you've sent. Even if you've written in English so plain you could put it on the label of a can of dog food, your readers have a fairly horrific amount of work to do – deciphering your meaning, minimizing ambiguities, pinning words into grammatical categories, filing your information away, comparing it against other information they already possess, and deciding which details merit transfer from fleeting short-term memory to more durable long-term memory.

Reading itself is a highly complex act. Until relatively recently, reading was what social scientists like to call a *black box*, a process where we know the inputs and the outputs but not the mechanism that translates one into the other. Back in the 1970s and 1980s, researchers in what was once the field of Artificial Intelligence, known familiarly as AI, pursued research on how readers understand written language, primarily because they were interested in building computers that could read. This research in psycholinguistics and cognitive psychology began shedding light on the mental processes that enable us to make sense of words on a page. By the early 1990s, however, most AI researchers were willing to admit that the field was something of a will-o'-the-wisp – building a machine that could think and read seemed like a good idea at the time. But after a few decades of watching computers still struggling to recognize speech or tell stories that could be handled with aplomb by an eighteen-month-old, most researchers moved on.

Despite the oomph and funding oozing away from AI research, research into the neuro-cognitive process of reading continued apace, in psycholinguistics, neuroscience, and cognitive and educational psychology, bolstered by new imaging technologies that offered glimpses of our reading brain. But this flourishing research on the act of reading remained utterly disconnected from research on writing, which seems like a puzzling omission, given just how eloquently psycholinguistic and neuro-cognitive studies on reading speak to what defines a clear sentence or coherent paragraph. However, in reality, this omission is hardly puzzling, given the way academics operate in discipline-specific silos that discourage them from venturing onto their colleagues' turf, not to mention the thoroughly daunting vocabulary required for the average humanist to wade through research results reported in the likes of *Science* or *Cerebral Cortex*. In addition, scientists rely on validated tests and expensive technologies from eye-tracking devices to functional magnetic resonance imaging (fMRI) to conduct research on the reading brain. In contrast, the humanists charged with teaching and researching writing have writing samples, questionnaires, and their own powers of observing fledgling writers at work. In terms of resources, the scientists might as well be Goliath, and the composition researchers and instructors, David – without the sling-shot.

The connections seem obvious between what neuroscientists and psycholinguists have learned about the reading brain and what writers need to know when they sit down with a blank page. Yet the science of reading and the teaching of writing end up as two conversations conducted in parallel – different audiences, tuned to entirely different channels. In fact, I dedicated a decade to studying research on the reading brain to gauge the impact of hypermedia environments on the act of reading, all while struggling to teach students to write and generally finishing each course feeling as though I should offer the students a tuition refund. I only realized I could leverage the research on reading to teaching writing when I accepted an invitation to spend a half-day teaching lawyers how to write readable legislation. Lawyers, I decided, would require hard data to change gems like the 290-word sentence on wire-tapping that appears in the California Penal Code Section 631a[5] into something resembling a string of sentences you could comprehend on the first, rather than the twelfth, reading. And, I realized, I had hard data in spades that I could translate into principles to guide writers.

Somewhat like music, writing is a system. Languages have rules about structure – where you put the subject, where you put the verb. Moreover, readers have an unconscious preference for certain types of sentences – a fact well established through decades of research into how brains process language. Put simply, when you write a sentence, your readers' brains will process that sentence in highly predictable ways, despite their blissful unconsciousness of all the cogs and wheels whirring as they scan the page. The same also holds true for groups of sentences, paragraphs, entire documents. So you ignore these predictable processes at your peril – and, unfortunately, also at your readers'.

This thumbnail history brings us, at last, to the good news. You can quickly and painlessly master the art of becoming a terrific writer. Or, at least, you, too, can be one of those hapless saps in the office who always gets lumbered with the job of writing documents simply because you do it so well. And the process is not only relatively simple; this method also works across virtually every field, profession, and type of non-fiction writing. In addition, this method uses a systematic, rules-based approach, well suited to the learning styles of engineers, scientists of every stripe, and everyone who prefers an approach to writing based on tangible data, rather than on instinct and verbal facility – or flailing around in the dark and hoping for the best. Follow most of the principles in *The Reader's Brain*, and your readers, your colleagues, and, more important, your superiors and clients will find your writing a model of precision and effectiveness. Best of all, this method stems from decades of scientific research in linguistics, cognitive psychology, and neuroscience. Moreover, I've road-tested this method for nearly a decade in writing courses for undergraduates in more than fifty disciplines, MBA students and mid-career executives, lawyers, engineers, and faculty in every branch of the biomedical sciences.

To paraphrase Scott Adams, the brains behind the American comic strip *Dilbert*, I'm writing from a position entirely different from the usual consultant or professor, mercifully insulated from the insults and challenges of workplace writing – a perspective Adams likened to "writing a first-hand account of the experience of the Donner party, based on the fact that you've eaten beef jerky."[6] Like Adams, I've gnawed some ankles. In fact, I've devoured some femurs while working as a copywriter for blue-chip clients and writing in the trenches in seventeen disciplines. I've tackled everything from white papers on vaccines for C-suite executives to articles straddling rheumatology, genetics, and cardiology. And my work tends to get accepted rapidly due substantially to the ease with which editors, executives, and reviewers can read it.

The pages that follow translate the research I've long relied on in psycholinguistics, cognitive psychology, and neuroscience into easy-to-follow principles that will enable you to

- construct sentences that efficiently convey your message, regardless how complex it is;
- understand where to place important information (and where to hide bad news to avoid unduly pissing your readers off);
- distinguish between good and poor word choices;
- create paragraphs that fit together seamlessly;
- introduce complex information without confusing the pants off your readers;
- make your sentences just seem to "flow" like an expert writer's.

The Reader's Brain uses five categories to promote clear, effective, and efficient writing, the five Cs: clarity, continuity, coherence, concision, and cadence. Practice most of these simple, easy-to-follow principles, and you'll not only become a good writer, you'll also become a pro at spotting – and fixing – even the worst writing disasters.

CHAPTER 2

The new science of writing

We owe a good deal of what we now know about the reading brain to a 1980s *idée fixe* – the scientific equivalent of padded-shoulder suits and even bigger hair: that computers could be taught to think, read, and play a mean game of chess. In retrospect, this sort of optimism is entirely understandable, since during the eighties, computers rapidly evolved from do-it-yourself Radio Shack-style jalopies with a fraction of the computing power of your run-of-the-mill modern cell phone to Maseratis capable of parallel processing. During the eighties and early nineties, computers progressed a generation in speed and capacity every two to three years. This trend tidily observed Moore's Law that predicted transistors and integrated circuits would double in capacity approximately every two years – a prediction that only proved uncannily apt, given that Moore made his prediction in 1965, the same year the first commercially successful mini-computer debuted.[1] Small wonder, then, that scientists in AI believed computers could also evolve in a matter of decades into the thinking creatures humans had taken millennia to become.

Now, not so many years later, we're ready to concede that HAL might not be around in 3001, let alone 2001, even though computers, it turns out, really *can* play a mean game of chess and even win at *Jeopardy*. In 1997, IBM's supercomputer Deep Blue won a six-game match against world chess champion Garry Kasparov – thrashing him so badly that the rattled Kasparov claimed the geeks behind Deep Blue were using a human chess master to control the computer's gambits. Still, however, computers cannot read – at least, not in the conventional sense of poring over lines of written symbols and arriving at an understanding of what Anna and Count Vronsky were up to in *Anna Karenina*. Nevertheless, for more than a decade, AI became the equivalent of the Klondike

Gold Rush, propelling scores of talented researchers and, more important, streams of research funding into studies of the reading brain. And the results, from our vantage point, proved more valuable than the equivalent of an *Anna Karenina*-reading HAL. The fruits of AI research into reading, as well as the neuroimaging studies of the reading mind that followed, have yielded a rich picture of how our minds process written language. With this picture, we can understand the characteristics that distinguish writing that can be read quickly, assimilated easily, and recalled precisely – exactly what we need to transform anyone into a highly effective writer.

Readability formulas: a non-narcotic sleep aid

As any teacher of technical writing will tell you, readability formulas are hardly new. Used for years in technical writing and editing, readability formulas rely on the sort of chestnuts that old-time editors with green eye-shades tended to pass out to cub reporters. Keep it simple. Keep it short. However, when these formulas were embodied in software style-checkers beginning in the late 1980s, they proved considerably less useful than a curmudgeonly editor. The simplest of these formulas relied on the one aspect of writing anyone could easily quantify – syllables in words and numbers of words in sentences. However, Flesch's Reading Ease score transformed that simple act of counting with an equation that appears more terrifying in its simplified form than the prospect of revising the 290-word nightmare sentence from the California Penal Code Section 631a (reproduced in its full glory in Chapter 1's note 5):

$$\text{Score} = 206.835 - (1.015 \times \text{Average Sentence Length}) - (84.6 \times \text{Average Syllables per Word}).$$

If you're hankering after something a bit less numeric and more user-friendly, you might turn to the Flesch–Kincaid score, which correlates the Flesch Reading Ease score to American standards for reading at grade levels and to the estimated percentage of the US adult population capable of reading at those grade levels. A score of 0–30 designated a document readable only by university graduates, while a score in the 90–100 range was readable by a fifth-grader, and, by extension, readable by over 93 percent of American adults by Flesch's reckoning. Perversely, the higher a Flesch Reading Ease score, the easier the reading of the sentence or passage. In contrast, lower scores on the Flesch–Kincaid indicate easier reading, with Dr. Seuss' *Green Eggs and Ham* scoring an improbable −1.3. This score suggests the ideal reader of *Green Eggs and Ham* is a fetus. However, if you break down the components of the actual text of Seuss' book, its Flesch–Kincaid score hints that the book's fifty words contain only eight polysyllabic words, all of them the word *anywhere*. If a negative grade level for reading is difficult to picture, American readers might prefer to recall a member of the US Congress filibustering by reading *Green Eggs and Ham* aloud at the sort of speed a teacher might adopt for a class of not-terribly-bright kindergartners.

However, Flesch and Flesch–Kincaid scores hardly resemble the handy formula that tells you how to compute your maximum heart rate (220 − [your age] = maximum heart rate). As a result, researchers tried a simpler formula, now embodied in Gunning's FOG Index:

> Grade Level = 0.4 (average sentence length
> + hard words of more than two syllables).[2]

If you feel an overwhelming urge to run and drink something alcoholic after struggling to apply these formulas to your writing, you have plenty of company. Moreover, you're also giving in to a thoroughly sane impulse. Flesch, Flesch–Kincaid, and the FOG scores are excellent at ensuring reading prompts in an experiment are all more or less comparable in their demands on readers' educations and brains. However, none of these formulas provides much in the way of insight into the challenges your sentences throw at readers. For starters, the number of syllables in a word isn't a reliable gauge of its difficulty. Specifically, *praxis* and *model* have the same number of syllables, but few fifth-graders would have a nodding acquaintance with *praxis*, for all its two-syllable length.

Moreover, readability formulas are deceptive, as they rely on a relentless counting of syllables and words to arrive at a sense of how challenging a reader might find any sentence or document. Yet a brief sentence can prove more demanding on your readers' brains than a sentence of three or four times its length. For example, consider this sentence, drawn from *The New Yorker*, a magazine that famously boasted three full-time grammarians on staff, none of whom seems to have been on duty the day this gem went to press:

> *What those of us who know Agee's criticism almost by heart read over and over, however, is the reviews that appeared in* The Nation.[3]

The sentence runs to a mere twenty-four words, of which nine are polysyllabic, if not exactly the "hard" words of Gunning's FOG Index. However, the sentence's structure or *syntax* is so complex that writer David Denby himself was a bit fuzzy on which word represented the sentence's grammatical subject – apparently, the same confusion that afflicted the skeleton staff of *The New Yorker*'s vaunted grammarians. The sentence's grammatical subject is a noun clause, the most subtle of the clauses to detect in English, with a prepositional phrase and an adjective clause wedged between the subject of the noun clause and its verb. Noun clauses tend to fly under readers' radars for two reasons: (1) they lack clear-cut cue words and (2) they rely on strings of nouns and verbs to represent a single noun. Confused? You ain't seen nothing yet. Look again at the detail the reader's brain must grasp as a whole to understand the grammatical subject of the sentence: *What those of us who know Agee's criticism almost by heart read over and over.* Denby has written a sentence that begs to be re-read and not in the savoring-the-words way one uses on the closing sentences of *The Great Gatsby*. Instead, we reread Denby's sentence because we've experienced what linguists call a "garden path" moment where our initial predictions about what we're reading – the meaning of the words, phrases, and clauses based on parts of speech – have led us totally astray. In this sentence *What* is paired with the verb *read*, with the modifying adjective clause *who know Agee's criticism* rearing its head confusingly between the subject and verb. In addition, readers process sentences most easily when the verb closely follows the grammatical subject, while Denby's sentence chucks ten words between the subject *What* and its verb *read*. For the record, according to the text analytics on my writing software, Denby's twenty-four-word sentence scores 62.6 on Flesch, 10.5 on Flesch–Kincaid, and 12.9

on FOG. In other words, the sentence we just stumbled over would pass most editors' sniff tests for readability. As *Dilbert* readers might say, "Go figure."

Compare the burden of reading Denby's sentence to this sentence, drawn at random from Lynne Truss' *Eats, Shoots & Leaves*, a paean to punctuation:

> *Using the comma well announces that you have an ear for sense and rhythm, confidence in your style and a proper respect for your reader, but it does not mark you out as a master of your craft.*[4]

Even though Truss begins with a gerund phrase, *using the comma*, acting as a grammatical subject, and the sentence runs to thirty-eight words, the readability analytics give her sentence a thorough drubbing, with a Flesch score of 50.3, a Flesch–Kincaid of 15.7, and a FOG of 17.3.

Bewildered by gerunds and grammar generally?

If you find yourself equating gerunds with rare, tropical diseases, consult the Supplement, "Everything You Ever Wanted to Know about Grammar, Punctuation, and Usage – and Never Learned," for a thorough, demystifying discussion of gerunds and the roles they play in English, along with the other parts of speech and of sentences, as well as a brief guide to the vagaries of English punctuation.

By all readability measures, Truss' sentence is more difficult than Denby's, even though most readers can run through it quickly and understand it without feeling as though they had hacked their way through the dense verbiage characteristic of a fund prospectus for your 401(k). In fact, along with its irreverent wit, the sheer readability of Truss' prose contributed to the surprise bestseller status of *Eats, Shoots & Leaves*. The problem with the reliability of readability formulas is similar to the challenges facing computer scientists attempting to simulate reading with a machine. Counting will only get you so far.

Pity the poor writer who actually pores over these textual analytics, attempting to make her sentences more readable. At worst, the analytics might prove as illuminating as the software in David Lodge's novel *Small World*, which helpfully told a famous working-class author of the Angry-Young-Men stripe that his most commonly used word in every novel was *greasy*. (Unsurprisingly, after that revelation, Lodge's fictional and formerly prolific writer found himself utterly blocked, seeing *greasy* taunting him in every line.) At their most useful, readability formulas can encourage writers to prefer shorter sentences to longer ones. But if, God forbid, you slavishly adhere to the guideline of sentences optimally containing an average of twenty words, an entire document containing sentences of such a uniform length will put your readers to sleep. You will end up creating not a highly readable, compelling article or proposal but, instead, the perfect non-narcotic sleep aid for anyone squeamish about relying too heavily on Ambien to help them drift off.

In contrast, readability characteristics come to us via decades of research into the way our minds process written language. Studies measure eye movements or *saccades*, borrowing from the French term that literally means "jerks," an accurate description of the way your eyes skip across a printed line. By examining readers' saccades using eye-tracking devices or other imaging technologies, researchers can determine the efficiency with which readers comprehend sentences. Electrical impulses recorded at the scalp measure the brain's reactions to lines of print in milliseconds and microvolts. Magnetic imaging captures the brain processing paragraphs. Even studies that fail to use any sexy imaging technology still effectively record reading times, comprehension, and recall of a variety of paragraphs, sentences, and choices of words. With this rich body of research, spanning disciplines from linguistics to neurology, we can gain a full-fledged picture of precisely how readers transform black marks scattered on a white page into, say, details of the hurricane-force winds forecasters are predicting to hit your locale in the next 24 hours.

Imaging the reading brain

Scientists today use five different neuroimaging technologies as a window on the reading brain. The oldest technology, electroencephalograms or EEGs, measure low amplitude electrical activity at the scalp. Positron emission tomography or PET scans display blood flow as the brain processes information. But newer technologies like functional MRIs (fMRIs), magnetoencephalograms (MEGs), and diffusion tensor imaging (DTIs) offer far greater precision and resolution in the images of the working brain that they produce. Nevertheless, each neuroimaging method, even fMRIs, MEGs, and DTIs, has its drawbacks. EEGs generate such weak signals – less than the equivalent of a flashlight battery – that researchers need to average results over multiple trials to arrive at what they call "event related potentials" or ERPs. In addition, ERPs only register signals from the cerebral cortex, independent of the involvement of deeper brain structures. Similarly, PET and fMRI scans lack the time resolution to capture events as fleeting as the brain recognizing a word. DTIs, for all they yield in terms of high-resolution, three-dimensional imaging of the brain, provide minutely detailed maps of neural connections but only give us insight into the brain's white matter (the glial cells and axons that forge connections) and not its gray matter (the parts of the brain current research clearly links to cognitive processing). Currently, only MEGs have the capacity to capture brain activity at the level of milliseconds. But, like most new technologies, MEGs are prohibitively expensive and, as a result, are currently rarely used in research. Consequently, most studies tend to rely on multiple forms of neuroimaging to compensate for the shortcomings of individual technologies.

The mechanisms of reading: see Jane read. Read, Jane, read

The more researchers study reading, the more surprised they are by its sheer complexity. Reading comprehension is a multi-stage process, all researchers agree, although few studies have established definitively precisely how many stages actually occur between your eye falling on an article containing an astrologer's prediction in *The Sun* and the moment you finish it and begin wondering whether you should book that Christmas holiday in Mexico if the world is slated to end before October 31st.

Not surprisingly, the first stage, agreed on by all researchers, involves recognizing words. Using eye movements, scientists have tracked the length of time our eyes stop or fixate on individual words and linked it with EEG activity, measuring the amount of brain activity, or *cognitive load*, involved in identifying a word. Skilled readers, the sort who down entire issues of *The New Yorker* with coffee, pause on words for only 300 milliseconds, a mere fraction of the blink of an eye. This sort of speed translates into 400–500 words per minute and, in readers trained to take in entire sentences in a single eye fixation, up to a staggering 1600 words per minute – or one word every 40 milliseconds.[5] But the speed of our eye movements depends entirely on the context surrounding the word. The more specific the context, the more constraint those surroundings put on the individual word, and the fewer meanings we're likely to attach to it. Since most languages tend to assign multiple meanings to a single word, even the meanings of individual words are never completely certain. Moreover, words that sound like other words – the old homonyms like *principle* and *principal* that continue to dog most of us well past our twelfth birthdays – complicate the identification process, causing more brain activity and slowing down the speed with which our eyes move across the page.

While scientists measure eye movements and EEG microvolts, other researchers use neuroimaging to pinpoint the areas responsible for the two primary phases of the reading process. Here, again, EEGs and fMRIs reveal different areas in the brain tackling the two phases. Wernicke's area, the area of the brain responsible for processing both spoken and written language, has been identified as central to word recognition. But evidence also points to interaction with the bulge behind Wernicke's area, the angular gyrus, which borders regions that handle visual, spatial, and language skills. The angular gyrus may be involved in the second phase of reading: relating individual words to the words that surround them in a sentence. This process, however, must also involve Wernicke's area, since our recognizing individual words hinges on our ability to narrow their range of meaning according to the context.

In the blink of an eye

Readers take, on average, 200–300 milliseconds to identify a printed word. But experienced readers, in studies that exposed them to partially blacked-out words in brief flashes, were able to begin the process of identifying words within 50 milliseconds.[6]

If you're still not convinced that reading the gossip column in the *New York Post* is the mental equivalent of doing the 100-meter butterfly, you might want to reconsider because the second phase of reading involves multiple types of processing. Readers rely on *syntactic processing* to assign meaning to words based on their place in the sentence's structure or syntax. For example, many words in English act like baseball's utility players: the most flexible of them can act as nouns or verbs or, with some additions like *-ed* or *-ly*, adjectives or adverbs. Even words that we tend to treat as simple verbs like *throw* can also easily act as nouns: *That throw was lousy.* Moreover, some words, while handily inflected in speech to indicate their status as noun or verb, remain ambiguous on the page. *Rebel* can serve as a noun – *He's a rebel* [REBel] – and, of course, as a verb, *He's about to rebel* [reBELL].

We make sense of words during the syntactic phase of processing the same way we recognize words on the page. We rely on surrounding words to anticipate how the sentence will structurally play out. And we anticipate what's coming next, as with so many other operations in the brain, by projecting the most common, most predictable scenarios. Here, the brain's tendency to anticipate the most common scenario dovetails rather neatly with the old chestnut beloved of professors in medical school: *When you hear hoofbeats, think horses, not zebras.* In other words, anticipate what you're most likely to see in context, which, unless you happen to be standing on a Kenyan savannah, will tend to be horses. As a result of our brains' continually anticipating the familiar, readers of English expect to see the main noun of any sentence before they encounter its main verb. So our brains expect and process easily *I dodged the bullet*, but not *The bullet I dodged,* which, while actually still comprehensible, tends to sound as if the sentence belongs more to the realms of poetry than reportage.

Still, in a simple sentence, this sort of syntactic departure is a curveball our brains handle easily, as we can sort out the relationships between subject, verb, and object without too many machinations, especially since the content is equally straightforward. Consider, however, a sentence where the complexity of the content is mirrored by the equally gnarly sentence structure, a scenario more typical of most writing we encounter than *The bullet I dodged*:

> *Thirteen of the 27 genes significantly up-regulated at short reperfusion but not at long reperfusion encode for known transcription factors or inflammatory cytokines, suggesting roles in gene transcription and regulation at this early reperfusion time point.*

This sentence, written by a faculty member in medicine, puzzled the other faculty in my writing course because the faculty expected to see the first likely culprit for the sentence's main verb early in the sentence, not far behind the sentence's subject. Instead, the sentence led us down a garden path similar to the one in Denby's sentence in *The New Yorker*. In my writing course, we all battened onto *up-regulated* as the sentence's verb, a tactic which played out beautifully until we hit *encode*, the sentence's real main verb. Since *up-regulated* was accompanied by *but not at long reperfusion*, our predictions seemed momentarily confirmed, as *but not* tends to be paired with verbs in most sentences we encounter. Yet, in this instance, the arrival of the real verb, *encode*, promptly destroyed that prediction and made a hash of our comprehension of the main part of the sentence: its subject and main verb. This development required us to soldier on to the end of the sentence, attempting to make sense of it, and then to reread the sentence. Or we could begin the sentence over again with a different prediction of its structure. The rereading and new prediction should reveal that *up-regulated* is actually part of a modifier referring to *genes* – not a verb at all.

While not terribly common, garden path sentences reveal several key features of our word- and sentence-level processing. First, the meanings of words are inextricably linked with their situation within any sentence's structure. *Up-regulated* as a verb is a rather different animal than *up-regulated* the adjective, despite the verb's seemingly narrow and highly technical use in an article on genes and lung transplants. Second, when your readers hear hoofbeats and expect horses, introducing them to a herd of zebras might be a handy means of snagging their attention when you're creating a work of art but is generally disastrous in any other form of communication. Efficiency and clarity in writing, as in most forms of communication, result when writers and readers rely on the same sets of expectations. We process sentences most efficiently, requiring less brain activity and less time for reading, with only brief eye fixations, when the sentence conforms to our predictions. In these instances, when words look like verbs, they also act like them.

Prediction is, after all, not only a key element in the process of reading but also a typically uni-directional affair. Backtracking on predictions means only one thing: you were wrong. Reading requires us to generate hypotheses, then test them, sentence by sentence. This process remains subconscious only as long as our predictions play out, and we keep moving forward on the page. Similarly, readers must backtrack in sentences whenever their predictions about word meaning and sentence structure fail to play out. But reading, like prediction, should also be uni-directional. Reading requires a substantial cognitive load merely in completing the process of identifying, predicting, and confirming. Reading is only efficient when the process is looking forward, not bogged down in backtracking, especially since the process also requires a further step that links word- and sentence-level predictions.

Inference building: see alligator chomp. See Jane run

Obviously, recognizing the meanings of words and understanding the roles they play within a sentence's structure represent only two steps in the reading process. To comprehend, assimilate, and recall written language, however, we need a further phase in the reading process: inference building. Beginning readers, like the first-graders who run their fingers under the words as they read, focus on word and syntax processing. But once you leave behind the *See Jane read. Read, Jane, read* stage to start reading about hobbits, the NYSE, and deficit spending, your reading process must encompass inference building to convert nouns and verbs into actions, abstractions, and theories. Consider, for example, the demands placed on us when we read even the short sentence, *Horace knew he was going to have to break the lock to get free.* To make sense of this sentence, we have to envision a scenario, one that involves identifying exactly what kind of lock Horace is struggling with. If we already know Horace is doing time at San Quentin or Wormwood Scrubs, we immediately perceive *lock* as a metal object that prevents inmates from escaping their cells. But if we know that Horace is a wrestler, struggling to qualify for the Olympic team, the word *lock* takes on a very different meaning – signifying the sort of hold an opponent has on Horace.

As even this simple example illustrates, all three phases of processing work in concert. First, we identify the words and their meanings, relative to their role in the sentence's structure. Then we confirm their accuracy by also measuring them against the contents of our long-term memories. Specifically, we access our long-term memories to verify what we read against what we know of the world. According to some researchers, we build inferences by drawing on our long-term memory to compare the sentences we read to what we know of the world around us, relying on as many as five categories to turn sentences into scenarios: time, space, actor, cause, and intention. Or, put more simply: who, when, where, why, and how. In addition to being staples of journalistic enquiry, the words *who, what, when, where, how,* and *why* enable readers to see sentences as tightly connected. Readers use inference-level processing in making sense of sentences, but they also tend to rely on explicit inferences more heavily in seeing sentences as connected. In addition, we read faster and recall content better when sentences use transitions that explicitly flag causation.[7] For example, consider this simple, concrete scenario:

> *Suddenly, John fell to his knees and began retching violently, as if the pizza were poisoned. Mary screamed.*

Nearly everyone would automatically assume that Mary screams in reaction to John retching on the floor – either in horror at the possibility he's been poisoned or in genuine fear at the damage he's about to inflict on her precious Persian rug. But, in fact, causation is the unseen glue that holds most sentences together. We assume that sentences that follow each other contain events that also follow each other. John retches first, then Mary screams. Our brains, once again, are opting for the obvious, the usual connection. This bias stems from the rarity with which we encounter sentences from two entirely different scenarios, involving totally different casts of characters, that nevertheless follow one another sequentially. The same holds equally true for nearly any sequence. If I begin to count 1, 2, 3, 4, 5, you're certain to assume the next number will be 6 rather than 79 or 4586.

Space and time

Researchers have established that readers assume that sentences that follow one another inevitably reflect events that follow one another, what linguists have dubbed the *iconicity assumption*.[8] In other words, we unconsciously assume, as we read, that order on the page reflects the order in which events unfolded. This assumption probably reflects our brains' predilections for perceiving events in sequences that play out in terms of causes and effect.

If you ask cognitive psychologists like Jerome Bruner, causation is not simply glue for binding sentences together. Causation, in his view, enables stories to exist.[9] After all, stories happen because something – a misplaced letter, a lottery win, a car wreck, a loaded glance in an elevator – throws the status quo seriously out of whack. What happens next is invariably a reaction to that cause, which causes a long train wreck of reactions until the story finally reaches a new status quo and The End. Moreover, for forty years psychologists have demonstrated just how centrally cause and effect figure in human perception, observing the ability to detect cause and effect in infants as young as six months.[10] When you think about it, the ability to detect cause and effect is not only central for learning – touch the stove and toast your fingers – but also central for survival. Get too close to the alligator, and you might end up serving as lunch.

But cause and effect never exist in a vacuum. Instead, they are always embedded in a scenario that enables us to actually see cause and effect in action. After all, John retching and Mary screaming, even in a scene as minimal as those two sentences sketch out, needs to be embedded in a setting that includes time, place, actor, and intention. For us to link John heaving with Mary shrieking, we have to assume they're both in the same place, re-acting in roughly the same time frame. We need to understand that John is the main actor and that John's holding his sides and gasp-ing theatrically are the product of having eaten bad pizza rather than, say, the product of his seeing just how effectively he can tor-ment Mary. Without those assumptions about time, space, actors, and reasons for acting, we cannot begin to see cause. In fact, we cannot begin to understand how the sentences relate to one an-other or perhaps even what they mean. But even if someone had supplied instructions to us about time and space and intentions in asides as we read – "Assume John's actually got salmonella, and Mary's an incurable hypochondriac" – we'd fail to grasp what the sentence meant unless we had some knowledge about food poisoning or what retching looks like. In other words, we need something cognitive psychologists call *schemas*, to comprehend just about anything we read.

Schemas: no such thing as an immaculate perception

Both syntactic and inferential levels of processing rely on frame-works for understanding, known to cognitive psychologists as *schemas*. Schemas are the building blocks of comprehension, pat-terns that enable us to make sense of what we see and hear, even directions on how we should act in specific situations.[11] Every day, we use dozens of schemas to make our way in the world. For example, whenever we enter a restaurant and sit down, we rely on a schema that tells us that waiters will arrive at our tables bearing menus of food available for order and await the nitty-gritty on how we want our prime rib cooked. Restaurant schemas subtly inform us that asking about blood work on a sick cat is not standard restaurant behavior and would, in any case, net zero results, since waiters tend to know the condition of the day's specials but never the shape Fluffy was in when you left home. Moreover, schemas seamlessly underlie our everyday comprehension. Schemas tell us that objects that appear smaller are, in fact, farther away from us. In the same way, a schema also reassures us that the railway tracks before our train really do remain parallel, despite our eyes telling us that the tracks converge in the distance. Without schemas, we're unable to recognize what we see. In fact, as art historian E. H. Gombrich argued, we're unable to see anything without having a schema that enables us to perceive and process what our eyes tell us.[12]

If this concept sounds far-fetched, consider the case of a man who had something close to Gombrich's waggish immaculate perception, Virgil, the blind massage therapist in Oliver Sacks' *An Anthropologist on Mars*.[13] At age fifty, Virgil regained his sight but relied on his sense of touch to decipher the bewildering images he encountered. Without a visual schema, Virgil remained what Sacks calls "mentally blind" because he failed to understand the visual inputs his eyes and brain sent him. Ironically, even once Virgil regained his sight, he continued to use his fingers and hands to orient himself and to make sense of the world.

But even mild mismatches with existing schemas can derail our comprehension of what we think we already understand. In one instance, a New Yorker recounted passing a security guard's radio on September 11, 2001, on his way into work: "I thought my Spanish was passable, but that dude's radio just said a plane flew right through the World Trade Center." He calmly went about his work for the rest of the day, convinced his Spanish was at fault, rather than the possibility that a plane had actually flown through one of the towers at the World Trade Center, an event which confounded any conventional schema.

Like our brains, our schemas seize on default conditions – the standard configurations, characteristics, and outcomes that characterize an object or scenario. For all their helpfulness in enabling us to perceive the world, understand what we see, and act on it, schemas nevertheless remain fairly blunt instruments that require us to make inferences. In a sense, schemas act like inference-generators that establish our expectations for how a situation or transaction will play out. Schemas lay out possibilities for actions and interpretations, and we make inferences about the way sentences will play out based on our understanding of the larger context. But schemas also provide us with a feedback loop. We can confirm the accuracy of the schema we've unconsciously chosen to guide our interpretation of an article in the *New England Journal of Medicine* by checking the way it fits with the local details we encounter at sentence level.

On the written page, cues for schemas abound. For example, a *Wall Street Journal* article generally promises a focus on business and finance. So we'd be jarred to instead stumble across, even on the Op-Ed pages, a breathless exposé worthy of the US supermarket tabloid *The Sun* on a woman giving birth to a black lamb after accidentally being inseminated with ram semen. Similarly, the titles of articles or books, their author names, and other details, as we'll see in Chapter 3, also cue schemas that help us narrow considerably the range of inferences we need to make as we read.

Not surprisingly, individual articles or chapters themselves need to cue schemas as early as possible to provide readers with a clear blueprint of exactly where all those printed pages are headed. Even before the days of online publishing and fine-toothed search engines, abstracts served as an excellent look-ahead to readers, providing thumbnail sketches of the territory covered by the article. Ditto introductions to articles and books, which generally provide detailed road maps to readers, and even, as we'll see in Chapter 5, the beginnings of paragraphs. Ultimately, schemas even intervene in our syntax-level processing, guiding us to latch onto the first suitable candidate for a verb – as in the *up-regulated* garden path sentence earlier – based on our experiences with millions of previous sentences. As a result, a familiar schema can speed our comprehension at all three levels of the reading process: lexical, syntax, and inference processing.

Similarly, departures from schemas can be the readerly equivalent of a knuckle-ball, as I. A. Richards once discovered when he required his Cambridge undergraduates, supposedly seasoned scholars of literature, to interpret poems from which Richards had removed both titles and authors' names. The result: his students floundered, thrashed around in their interpretations, and, generally, behaved like total incompetents. Disgusted, Richards used this experiment as the pretext for developing the approach to understanding literature he introduced in *Practical Criticism*, a work which gave rise to one of the major schools of literary criticism in the twentieth century, the so-called New Criticism. But Richards, had he known anything about the cognitive process of reading, would have found a simpler explanation right under his nose. By removing the titles and names of famous poets, Richards also removed valuable schematic clues that his readers needed for syntax- and inference-level processing, setting them the task of interpreting complex pieces of writing without knowing what they were reading.

Imagine trying to understand any complex piece of writing – a feasibility study, a shareholders' report, an article from *Nature*, a blog entry – without having any knowledge of who wrote it or for what purpose. You'd expend a good deal of energy casting around for likely schemas to throw into the breach, then hastily revising your guesses and trying on other schemas. Or imagine going to the cinema to watch a film without knowing its title, director, or even the type of film you're watching. A character fleeing pursuit by rattling down the stairs into a murky basement is one matter in a slasher flick, another in a horror film, quite another in a thriller – and an entirely different animal in a romantic comedy. No immaculate perception, indeed.

Putting it all together: readability outcomes

Reading, as the phases in this complex process reveal, is bloody hard work, even if we perform most of it unconsciously. Generally, when we read something that's well written, the complexity of the process and its cognitive demands are invisible. If, however, you're reading something that's poorly written – and this list can include everything from a featured article in *Nature* to the documentation for Microsoft Word, and the writings of too many philosophers – you suddenly become aware of the cognitive overhead. Reading becomes difficult. Recent research on the reading process is particularly valuable because, from it, we can easily separate good writing from the difficult and the truly execrable. Well-written documents lend themselves to easy reading, swift processing, and good memorability. In other words, good writing is writing that follows the contours of the processes our minds use to interpret and absorb it. In contrast, lousy writing bucks them – at their writers' and readers' peril.

By using cognitive research on the reading process, we can arrive at readability outcomes that enable us to make concrete decisions in our writing that lead to papers, memos, briefs, in fact, any kind of non-fiction document, that our audience reads quickly with apparently little awareness of effort and recalls promptly and easily. For starters, we know that reading always relies on projection and verification, a process that constantly looks forward. As a result, clear writing requires word choices and sentence structures that avoid our needing to backtrack when we read. So clarity involves our choosing, as we'll see in detail in Chapter 3, concrete words over abstractions, words that have definite, relatively fixed meanings. Ideally, we should choose words that make clear their role in both the structure and action of the sentence. The sentence about Horace and the lock, for example, would read more clearly if it read *head-lock* or even *hold*, rather than simply *lock*, since those other two terms make immediately apparent exactly the sort of situation Horace finds himself in. Similarly, the more concrete the terms and the more apparent their roles in the sentence structure, the more efficiently readers can fix their sights on an appropriate schema, and the easier the task of inference building.

The chapters that follow leverage neuroscience research into the workings of the reading brain to supply writers with five easy-to-follow categories to make informed decisions about which words to use, how to structure sentences, how to jam readers' tendencies to skim overly dense paragraphs, and even where to stash information they need to disclose but would rather their readers forgot. In the chapters that follow, you'll find simple, concrete principles that work across a myriad of writing tasks and situations, all summarized at the end of each chapter.

Takeaways for good writing: what you need to remember about readability outcomes

For those of you who like to flash your science at doubting colleagues or scoffing friends, you can summarize readability outcomes pretty easily and still come across like a PhD:

- Clarity: Words are concrete and boast relatively fixed meanings that are immediately obvious from their position in the sentence structure.
- Efficiency: Sentences rely on common sentence structures, introducing grammatical subjects (see Chapter 3) and verbs close to the beginnings of sentences, to aid in immediate inference building. Sentences also provide clear, linguistic cues that make causation and continuity between sentences apparent.
- Effectiveness: Paragraphs and entire documents front-load overviews of contents at their beginnings, enabling readers to fix on helpful schemas that speed the comprehension process. Paragraphs and documents also provide as many cues as possible about the contents that follow, using concrete titles and subheadings to provide further schematic cues.

CHAPTER 3

Choosing words and structuring sentences
The first C: Clarity

In this chapter you will learn how to
- create sentences readers process most easily
- choose the best possible subjects
- ensure your verbs work for you
- make your sentences both lean and mean – shorter and clearer.

According to neuroscience research, we're hard-wired to register cause and effect. In the 1940s, researchers showed volunteers animated films of circles, squares, and rectangles shuffling around the screen. The film was hardly the equivalent of an animated *Gone with the Wind*, but, when researchers asked their subjects to describe what they had seen, the men and women related charged scenarios involving not only causation but intention and even, for multiple participants, conflict between two men pursuing the same woman.[1] In a later version of the same experiment, study participants repeatedly reported that the circle had been chasing the square – or the rectangle was pursuing the circle. More surprising, the subjects seemed inordinately hung up on cause and effect – what they described was invariably a full-fledged story.[2] Later, studies with infants as young as six months similarly revealed the same fixation with cause and effect.[3] Obviously, an inborn ability to perceive cause and effect would be rather handy, especially to early hunter–gatherers out scrounging around for dinner amid lions, tigers, or bears. That same ability today stops us from lovingly laying our hands on a stove burner or fondly running a finger along the sharp edge of a whacking great knife.

This same innate tendency can also explain our attraction to stories – even our hard news is delivered in the form of stories – and our ability to recall small, throwaway details when they're embedded in a story. Similarly, readers devour and recall easily sentences that include cause and effect. Make a sentence into a miniature narrative, and your readers will easily remember what you've written. In addition, they'll also mentally process your writing more quickly and with little awareness of the hard work that goes into reading.

In fact, reading itself is the equivalent of hard labor. Even someone caught up in the most formulaic scene of the schlock-iest Harlequin Romance is busily multitasking. As we read, we ferret out the meanings of words and create connections between sentences, then compare what we read to our own experience of the world and of other novels. We also squirrel away juicy details for later recall. And we relate the meaning of the immediate detail to the overall story – say, the significance of that near-grope in a packed elevator to the plight of a hapless, single fledgling attorney with a serious thing for her boss. All this effort also explains why reading the instructions for programming a universal remote control for your flat-screen TV can feel like the equivalent of digging a grave. Or why you feel as if you're in dire need of a brain transplant if, God forbid, you need to actually read any of those helpful instructional manuals that rely on triple negatives and sentences you'd need to recruit a linguist to interpret. And you'd also need to resign yourself to the linguist throwing up her hands in defeat.

Clarity invites us to read – and keeps us happily reading. Clarity always distinguishes good writing from the jungly thickets of dead sentences that you couldn't recall five minutes after reading them, if someone held a loaded gun to your head. I once took only a single, skinny book by an academic hottie – who shall remain nameless – for a flight from London to New York, convinced that surely the lack of any other form of reading matter at 39,000 feet would force me to digest this little academic treatise on modern life. In mid-flight, I staggered to the john, then returned to my book, which I hadn't bookmarked. For the next 90 minutes, I reread the sixty pages I'd just plowed through, without the slightest jolt of recognition…until I stumbled across my own scrawl in the margins. Ten years before this moment, I would've blamed my education (*Michigan is a state school, after all!*), booze (*I shouldn't have had that fourth glass of cheap champagne!*), or my lack of attention or sleep or brain-power. But now I knew better. My blood-alcohol was zero, and years of research had taught me that my total lack of comprehension – let alone bloody recall – was the author's fault, not mine. Nearly every sentence was passive, stuffed with abstractions, chocked with memorable subjects like *it*. Worse, virtually every sentence was so long that, by the time I reached its end, I wondered what the hell the beginning of the sentence had been about. In short, the academic hottie had committed every imaginable sin against clarity.

An extremely short history of English

English is a mongrel, a Johnny-come-lately to world languages descended from Old Norse, Anglo-Saxon, Latin, and French, a result of the 1066 Norman Conquest of what later became England. Typically, English tends to happily mug whatever scraps of languages it happens across and, as one wag put it, rummage around in the pockets of its victim for loose bits of grammar. Like a hustler sporting an array of diamond Rolexes and stainless Tag Heuers all massed together on one wrist, English also traditionally makes little attempt to integrate the words and phrases from the languages it absorbs into language that obeys the rules of standard written English. In France, you get words like *le blue-jean*; in English, you get *schadenfreude*.

As a result, even to this day, English's Latin and French vocabulary is clearly distinct from the words Anglo-Saxons used before 1066. Words that come to English from Latin and French tend to begin with prefixes like *de-, dis-, in-, im-, non-,* and *un-* and to end with suffixes like *–ion, -ate, -ive,* and *-ity*. Moreover, both Latin- and French-based terms are more abstract and longer than words with Anglo-Saxon counterparts. In contrast, nearly all Anglo-Saxon words refer to concrete objects and have a single or few syllables. And, perhaps not surprisingly, all the four-letter words US broadcast networks still charmingly bleep out, lest they pollute American family values, come from good old Anglo-Saxon.

For decades, expert writers have been exhorting readers to stick to that Anglo-Saxon vocabulary. In "Politics and the English Language," George Orwell indulged himself in a lengthy harangue on avoiding the corrupting influence of Frenchified English. Orwell argued that, for example, the public found easier to swallow *elimination of unreliable elements* than its concrete, Anglo-Saxon counterpart: "People are imprisoned for years without trial, or shot in the back of the neck or sent to die of scurvy in Arctic lumber camps." Unfortunately, Orwell phrased much of his jeremiad in the same abstract, polysyllabic Latinate language he was urging readers to avoid at all costs, in addition to falling back on the passive construction he advised writers to shun in favor of active construction. But Orwell had a point. The more concrete your language, the more easily readers can picture, grasp, and recall your meaning. In addition, concrete language is infinitely better at telling mini-stories than Latin-heavy, abstract words can ever be. And the more complex your topic, the greater your need to use concrete language to describe it.

TERMS YOU'LL NEED TO KNOW

While diagramming sentences belongs among the practices banned by the Geneva Conventions, if you want to write anything well, you actually do need to identify the function of words in a sentence.

A *noun* refers to a person, place, thing, or idea. Nouns include words like *thoughts, dogs, skies, actors,* and *Mormons.*

Pronouns, on the other hand, stand in for nouns and always refer to another noun in a sentence or in the preceding sentence. Pronouns include *I, you, me, they, us, we, him,* and *it.*

Grammatical subjects are the main noun or pronoun in a clause or sentence, always paired with the main verb.

A *verb* portrays action or describes a state of being. Action verbs include *launched, imitated,* and *gawped,* while non-action verbs – known as intransitive verbs – include all forms of *to be.*

Adverbs tend to end in *–ly* and usually modify verbs, although they can sometimes modify another adverb. Examples of adverbs include *quickly, reluctantly, crudely, deviously,* and *winningly.*

Prepositions are words that can fit in the formulaic sentence teachers bludgeoned into students in grade school: *The mouse ran* _____ *the box,* plus the word *during.* Prepositions include *in, on top of, through, without, around, beneath, over,* and *throughout.*

Not surprisingly, prepositions make up the beginning of every *prepositional phrase,* little clumps of words that indicate relations between things in space or time. Each prepositional phrase includes a preposition, followed by a noun, often paired with a couple of descriptive words that modify the noun, known as *adjectives.*

Think of *nominalizations* as castrated verbs, sapped of their livelihood by serving as nouns. Every nominalization once had its origins in a verb before it acquired the Latin-sounding endings that transformed it into a noun. Nominalizations include *evaluation, dispensation, utilization,* and *creation.* Generally speaking, if you can turn the noun into a verb – and even solid old Anglo-Saxon words like *life* and *freedom* can be turned into verbs, if you think about it – you're looking at a nominalization.

Together, a noun and a verb make up a *clause. Major clauses* are complete sentences that can stand by themselves and still make sense, even in isolation from the rest of the sentence. A *minor clause,* however, will sound incomplete or like a sentence fragment if you subtract it from the rest of the sentence. In the sentence, *Do it because I said so! Do it* is the major clause, since it makes sense even when isolated from the rest of the sentence. On the other hand, *because I said so* sounds incomplete when hacked off from the complete sentence, making it a minor clause.

For a complete guide to everything you never learned about grammar, in addition to punctuation, see the Supplement on page 164.

Reading is a three-step dance

Reading is actually a heavy slog, as we saw in Chapter 2, the reason why the passenger in the seat next to you on your long-haul flight is more likely to be working away at Sudoku or staring at a film rather than reading even that cheesy mass-market paperback destined to end up in the seat-back pocket when you all disembark. Assisted by eye-tracking devices, EEG, and fMRI technologies, researchers identified three distinct levels of cognitive processing involved in the act of reading even a paragraph in *People* or *Hello!* magazines, not exactly the equivalent of reading *Finnegans Wake:* lexical, syntactic, and inferential, all of which are relevant to clarity.

The first level, lexical processing, begins when readers recognize individual words and assign them a fixed meaning, based on familiarity with the word from prior encounters. Using saccades, scientists have tracked the length of time our eyes linger on individual words and linked these saccades to EEG activity, measuring the amount of brain activity involved in identifying a word. But in English the speed of our eye movements depends entirely on the context surrounding a word. In English, neither the position of the word in the sentence nor the way the word ends clearly tells us whether *hope* is a noun (*Please do not flush your unrealized hopes and dreams down the toilet*, to quote the instructions on the toilet on a Virgin train in the UK) or a verb and a noun (*I hope I didn't flush my unrealized hopes and dreams down the toilet*, as one passenger told me, on emerging from the same loo). And, if you're reading the work of a writer untutored in the correct use of the hyphen – which includes a substantial chunk of the US population – "hope" might even be an adjective, as in "hope inducing," rather than "hope-inducing," where the hyphen helpfully tells the reader that at least the verb and noun forms of the word are out of the running. Even the word *writing* itself can act as a noun, verb, or even an adjective, as in *I'm writing [verb] this writing [noun] on a writing [adjective] tablet*, a sentence demanding readers disambiguate the three different parts of speech occupied by the same word, even with correct punctuation.

As a result, the interdependence of the meanings of words and their positions in a sentence inextricably links the first and second levels of processing. Readers make sense of words during the second, or syntactic, phase of processing the same way they recognize words on the page. We use surrounding words to anticipate how the sentence will structurally play out.[4]

Generally, these first two levels of processing occur together, with readers relying on the third level, inferential processing, only when the sentence's contents fail to make sense. As we saw in Chapter 2, we make inferences based on schemas we've acquired to make sense of the world. When sentences correspond to familiar schemas, we read their contents more rapidly and recall them more easily than when we encounter an altogether unfamiliar schema.[5] Ultimately, we unconsciously rely on all three levels of cognitive processing as we read: lexical, syntactic, and inferential. And, given the roles cause and effect play in our perceptions of the world – as we saw in Chapter 2 – when you write sentences that embody cause and effect, readers read them more swiftly and easily than sentences that fail to explicitly link actors and actions causally. This complex, three-step dance explains the first principle to writing clearly, why readers will perceive your writing as clear and easy to read if you rely on active, rather than passive, construction, along with the other three clarity principles we'll explore in detail below.

Try to visualize the concrete details in the following examples:

Example A:
Panting from the pursuit, Tucker ducked around a corner and huddled under a honeysuckle bush, while his would-be captors raced past.

Example B:
The would-be captors were evaded by Tucker, who ducked around a corner and huddled under a bunch of vegetative assemblages.

While you might find both sentences to be fairly similar, researchers have repeatedly proved that you'd be more likely to recall Example A than Example B. For starters, have you ever tried to picture a vegetative assemblage? Multi-syllable words, a legacy of the good old Norman Conquest, entered English either directly from Latin itself or in a watered-down Latinate form via French. Crack open your *Webster's*, put your finger on any polysyllabic word, and you'll discover a Latinate term that is generally an abstraction. *Vegetative assemblages* will send your average reader scrabbling for a dictionary. And that nice little scrap of terminology will also force your readers' brains into twists and turns worthy of a contortionist. Is a vegetative assemblage a honeysuckle bush? What about multiple honeysuckle bushes? Or do honeysuckle grouped together with guavas, trumpet vines, and juniper count as a bona fide set of vegetative assemblages? Incidentally, if you're convinced this term is so patently ridiculous that no one would ever be caught dead using it, think again. Several years ago, a group of engineering students submitted a proposal for the design of a campus conference center, a plan heavily dotted with what the proposal identified as *vegetative assemblages.* The students meant *shrubs.*

Clarity Principle #1:
Prefer active to passive construction

If you glance again at Example A, you'll notice that Tucker is performing the actions in the sentence in chronological order. First he runs, then he hides while his pursuers lope past. In this sentence, action originates with an actor at the beginning of the sentence, *Tucker.* The sentence then dramatizes the action through the verbs *ducked* and *huddled,* with the result that his would-be captors run past him, arriving at the end of the sentence. Note how this sentence neatly conforms to readers' assumptions that the order in which events occur linguistically in a sentence mirrors the order in which they unfold in the world.

But in Example B, the sentence distorts the order in which the actions occurred. The action flows back-asswards, so to speak, with the outcome of Tucker's action – evasion – conveyed passively. In this version, even though Tucker clearly initiates the main action in the sentence, in grammatical terms, he's relegated to the equivalent of walk-on Second Spear Carrier.

If you actually learned a smattering of English grammar – a process that, in America, usually means you were taught by (a) nuns, (b) teachers born before 1934, or (c) parents who were high-school English teachers – you'd know that Tucker in Example B is actually the object of a preposition, one of those annoying little throwaway bits of grammar that clutter up sentences. Prepositions and their full-blown counterparts, prepositional phrases, are grammatically insignificant. In fact, if the nuns insisted you parse sentences into parts of sentence, as well as parts of speech – a process that still strikes terror in the hearts of even arrogant English

PhDs with a bit of dust on their credentials – you'd discard entire prepositional phrases, crossing them out to distinguish them from the meatier parts of the sentence.

In Example B, the verb is the ever-dynamic *was evaded*. Note how the presence of forms of *to be* (*is, was, was being, was seen to be*) shoves the action into the wings. You're no longer witnessing an event unfolding. Instead, some unseen being is narrating the event *ex post facto*, hardly edge-of-the-seat stuff, let alone the things stories are made of. But, while non-action verbs sap the vigor from sentences, they don't always signify a passive sentence or what's known as *passive construction*. Non-action verbs are merely a symptom of a sentence that might be passively constructed. You can have a non-action verb and an actively constructed sentence, but not an action verb and a passively constructed sentence. For instance, *Tucker was furious at his pursuers* relies on a form of *to be* but is nevertheless an actively constructed sentence. Why? *Tucker*, the grammatical subject, clearly is also experiencing fury. In contrast, *Tucker, an overweight Jack Russell, was pursued by a pack of feral cats*, is passively constructed, despite action seemingly promised by the verb *pursued*. If you decouple the sentence's meaning from its structure, Tucker isn't an actor, despite his being the grammatical subject. Instead, he is the object of pursuit by feral cats. As in all passively constructed sentences, the sentence fails to mirror the unfolding chronology of events.

To root out passive construction, try using zombies

Confused? Try this acid test. Insert the phrase *by zombies* into the sentence after the verb: *The would-be captors were evaded by zombies*. If the sentence makes sense with zombies in it – with zombies representing the implied actors – then you're looking at a passively constructed sentence. In contrast, *Panting from the pursuit, Tucker ducked around a corner by zombies* makes no sense, not merely because we've yet to encounter a zombie outside a film or television. The zombie, vampire, or superhero acid test, I've discovered, works nearly instantly with everyone, including students who've never had to think about clauses and grammatical subjects.

Why is active construction such a big deal?

Our brains process active sentences more efficiently than passive sentences for four reasons. First, most psychologists agree that cause and effect – exemplified in the sequences of images that made babies' heart rates and blood pressure jump – power human perception. In study after study, researchers have found that readers process sentences containing causal relationships more quickly than they do other kinds of sentences.[6] Second, causal order involves active construction, which reproduces the chronological order of events. If I say *I lobbed the cookies at his head*, the sentence preserves the order of events in which I chucked a batch of chocolate chip cookies at my victim's head. But if I say *The cookies were lobbed at his head by me* – virtually the same sentence, different word order – the result of the tossing precedes *me*, the actor who actually tossed those lumps of baked dough. Moreover, readers implicitly expect the order of items in sentences to replicate the order in which events unfolded, as we saw earlier in this chapter. And this inverted order requires readers to understand the action by reassembling the pieces in order. Third, readers' brains take longer to process passive construction but tend to speed through active. Fourth, readers misinterpreted implausible sentences one-quarter of the time when sentences relied on passive construction like *The dog was bitten by the man*. Readers committed this error presumably not because they could visualize a scenario in which a neighbor assaulted, say, a corgi minding its own business, but because the passive construction obscured agency. Or readers made this error because they required substantially more time to make sense of the passive, implausible sentence than either the active, implausible sentences or the passive, plausible sentences. And, finally, active construction builds on the default order of sentences in English – subject–verb–object.[7]

In fact, in nearly every language in the world, subjects normally precede objects and nearly always come before verbs. Psychologist Steven Pinker notes in his popular book *The Language Instinct: How the Mind Creates Language* that most languages have either a subject–verb–object (SVO) order or a subject–object–verb (SOV) order, both natural orders for depicting cause and effect. In fact, the majority of the world's languages have either an SVO or SOV order.[8] But English's subject–verb–object order reflects causation so strongly that it may hijack newly developing languages. In the 1970s, when linguists in South America discovered people in Guyana speaking a new, weird kind of Dutch, they discovered the speakers of the language, now known as Berbice Dutch, formed sentences with subject–verb–object order. Yet the languages Berbice Dutch evolved from – Dutch and an African language called Ijo – both place verbs at the ends of their sentences. In spite of its origins, Berbice Dutch evolved from two subject–object–verb languages into a subject–verb–object language order most likely because this order more closely replicates the way we perceive events in the world.[9] First we encounter the actor, then the action, then the result. Just like life – at least most of the time.

Exceptions to the rule

"Aha," you think, "so much for giving writers some hard-and-fast rules to cling to." Most of us not-so-secretly long for rules, especially if we've put off the dreaded act of writing a paper or grant until the deadline looms mere hours away. Rules, after all, constrain the myriad decisions that plague us when we write, making them particularly handy during the small hours when you feel as though you need lashings of caffeine and toothpicks to prop up your eyelids. However, the exceptions to the rule on passive construction are mercifully few, based on studies of readers' brains and recall of sentences.

1. Use passive construction when entire sections of documents, like the methods sections of studies, employ it, as our brains can process substantive chunks of continuous passive construction nearly as efficiently as we can actively constructed sentences.[10] In addition, passive construction in this setting conveys the gist of a methodology more efficiently than continually reiterating, "We excluded … We tested … We evaluated …" and a barrage of sentences all beginning with the same grammatical subject, *I* or *we*.

2. Use passive construction when the actor performing the action is unknown or less important than the outcome you're describing.

Why these two particular exceptions? Readers read and interpret passively constructed sentences efficiently when the emphasis shifts to the outcome of an action, a condition common to both of these two exceptions. For methods sections in reports of experiments, the focus is uniformly on the outcome, not on the actors. Similarly, in the second condition, the outcome assumes greater importance than the actor – or the actor is irrelevant or even unknown.[11] In making memorable speeches, politicians make exemplary use of this exception, Franklin Delano Roosevelt did in his famous speech following the Japanese attack on Pearl Harbor on December 7, 1941.[12]

    3. Use passive construction when you wish to avoid assigning agency to anyone in particular, to avoid legal liability.

If you're an American, you will likely have thought of this exception already. In the United States, I've heard a seven-year-old threaten a school administrator with a lawsuit for pulling him off the unfortunate child he was busily pummeling during recess. I've also encountered an undergraduate who used his litigious father – a lawyer, of course – to sue a university instructor because she failed to point out the student left his $250 textbook behind in a classroom heaving with other students. In contrast, in the UK, when I once threatened to sue the company that left my house without a source of heat or hot water for three weeks in the chilly, damp dead of winter, I received only icy silence in response. In countries outside the United States, most writers are less mindful of litigious agency and methods for avoiding liability by falling back on passive construction.

    If you're a solicitor, barrister, or attorney, however, you might want to reconsider this particular exemption, as courts have sometimes found in favor of plaintiffs because passive construction obscured who did what.[13]

Corollary: Beginning a sentence with There is or There are is ALWAYS a bad idea

Unless you're angling for a Booker, Pulitzer, or Nobel in Literature, writing poetry, song lyrics, or graffiti, the same handy *There is* or Adverb + [ANY FORM OF *TO BE*] is thoroughly lethal to readers' comprehension. While ubiquitous in speech and writing, this construction belongs strictly in speech, which is notoriously rife with inefficiencies and redundancies. In speech, we rely on *There is* and other less-than-efficient ways of phrasing things to ensure our audience gets the point of the sentences we hear, despite weird accents, rapid-fire speech, and wandering attention spans. And *There is* comes in handy for stretching out rhythmic lines in song lyrics to match the music. Take, for example, that timeless Animals' "House of the Rising Sun" lyric which begins, "There is a house in New Orleans, they call the Rising Sun," that stems from an old oral tradition of blues songs. The song, probably created in Kentucky mining camps, eventually found its way to the determined musicologist Alan Lomax, who, armed with a primitive tape recorder, first captured the lyric from a backwoods teenager. Woody Guthrie later heard it and recorded his rendition before The Animals created the version Baby Boomers tend to recall fondly.[14]

There is-type constructions most likely come to us from French, courtesy of the Norman Conquest, where literate Normans swarmed over the illiterate Anglo-Saxons in what is now England. Unsurprisingly, Latin and French trumped Anglo-Saxon, especially since writing enabled the Normans to claim written titles to English property formerly held by the Anglo-Saxons, who needed trusty men who swore oaths to attest to their ownership.[15] In French, *il y a* is a useful construction for representing shifts in time or setting. In oral English, that old Norman phrasing persists stubbornly. Artifacts like *there is* peskily hang around, long after their utility has vanished, because recording language in writing slows its evolution. Bring in the printing press and mass-produced copies of a standardized language, and you petrify it.[16]

Why is *there is* and its relatives so detrimental to clarity? When you begin a sentence with *There is*, you turn the natural order of English sentences upside down. Since *there* is a lowly adverb – the sort of word nuns would've insisted you cross out on your homework – *there* hogs the spot where your readers would normally expect to see the all-important subject of the sentence. Worse, the verb *is* shoves its way in front of the actual subject of the sentence, which really jams your readers' radar. Readers begin making predictions about the way a sentence will play out beginning with its first words, enabling them to make sense of whether *rebel* is a someone upsetting the apple cart or an action that upsets the apple cart. Those predictions sharpen when we identify the sentence's grammatical subject and end after we identify the main verb. When you insert an adverb in the slot where readers unconsciously expect to spot the subject and you place the verb before the grammatical subject, you flummox readers' expectations. You also create atypical sentence structure, since English's default order is subject–verb–object and only verb–subject–object in the rare, inverted question form. Atypical sentence structure slows down readers' processing of the sentence's components and their meaning.[17] In the meantime, you also lumber your readers with passive construction – as we've just seen, not a brilliant strategy – and a non-action verb, which we'll explore in detail shortly.

In short, there is nothing redeeming in *there is* constructions on the page, unless you're aiming for a conversational style, aping Hemingway, or tweeting about something. Or aiming to piss readers off by committing the selfsame sin you've just exhorted them to avoid on pain of death.

Once, when I was teaching a writing course for clinicians in a college of medicine, one of my students announced proudly that she'd eliminated every last instance of *There is* and *There are* from her article on pediatric diabetes. My eye fell on the first page of the article, first paragraph: *There are*. By the time the rest of the class finished prospecting for those pesky little constructions on her first page alone, we'd counted eight. And yet the endocrinologist had proofread her article diligently. Because we're used to seeing these buggers littering up sentences, most of us have difficulty spotting them. So, before you finish any piece of writing, use the "Find" command in your writing software and type in *There is* or *There are*. When you happen across one of these constructions, revamp the sentence. Instead of saying *There are three ways we can think of this*, write, instead, *We can think of this dilemma in three ways.* As we'll see in the next chapter, this reshuffled order will also help focus your readers' attention on the most important content in the sentence.

Clarity Principle #2:
Make your verbs portray action whenever possible

Reading through sentence after sentence of non-action verbs is about as interesting as curling up with the instructions for programming a universal remote to operate your TV, the kind that require you to try fifty different codes to pair the remote with your flat-screen, after your dog chewed the original that handily came with the TV. Reading non-action verbs is the sort of exercise that only my ex-father-in-law could appreciate, a man who thoughtfully videotaped every page of his Australian tax return and generously sent the tape, complete with monotone voiceover narration, to his grandchildren as his first communication with them in years. Yet, page through just about any document that bores you stiff – academic journals, instructions for connecting your TiVo, pages of legalese from your divorce proceedings – and you'll stumble across the mother lode of non-action verbs. Deprive lawyers and professors and researchers of non-action verbs, and you'd condemn these hordes to decades of Hoover Dam-sized writers' block.

Non-action *verbs*, remember, are not of the same magnitude of crime as passive *construction*, not exactly a lethal crime against writing. Nevertheless, non-action verbs can be nearly as deadly to the clarity – not to mention the liveliness – of any sentence as passive construction.

From a psychological perspective, action verbs considerably simplify the act of reading by performing two valuable functions. First, they clarify relationships within the sentence in a who-is-doing-what-to-whom sort of way, clearly pinning causation to a verb and thus clarifying which noun is performing the action and which noun, receiving it. For those inclined to slog through fMRI or EEG studies of the reading brain, this clarification speeds reading and also proves less taxing on readers' brains.[18] Second, action verbs immediately help readers grapple with the lexical demands reading places on our brains. By clearly fixing the action and identifying actor and outcome, a sentence using action verbs eases readers' identification of the parts of speech each word represents. This fixing of action remedies the challenges of reading English, a language in which neither the order of words nor their form dictates their meaning absolutely. Instead, in English, context, syntax, and plausibility constrain the array of meanings we could attribute to each word. As a result, the action verb alone helps readers identify causation and, as we've seen earlier, more easily determine the meaning of each word. When you use action verbs, you handily tackle the demands of both lexical (word) and syntactic (the part of speech or role played by each word) process-ing simultaneously.[19]

Moreover, non-action verbs have other notable drawbacks. For starters, non-action verbs act as mere place markers – bookmarks rather than sentences telling the story. Use a non-action verb like *is, was, appears, constitutes, represents,* or *has been*, and your sen-tence no longer tells a story. In fact, your sentence will probably read about as dynamically and memorably as instructions for whip-ping up tomato soup from a can of Campbell's. Your sentences, propped up by non-action verbs, simply convey static states, which can prove about as interesting as watching paint dry. These non-action verbs also result in readers spending more time pondering the relationships between nouns in your sentences, partly demon-strated in a study of transitive (which we've called *action*) versus intransitive (which we've called *non-action*) verbs.[20] Non-action verbs leave us wondering who did what to whom. Researchers explored the challenges to readers' brains in identifying lexical and syntactic meaning via neuroimaging studies where subjects read sentences with explicit versus implicit causation.[21] If you fall back on ye olde non-action verbes, your readers are going to spend more time wrestling with the issue of who did what to whom than if you use action verbs, which clearly attribute agency (the actor) by embodying action.

Second, non-action verbs are also dull and unmemorable. In contrast, *sneezed, yawned, barfed,* and *chundered* might be intransitive, merely reporting a state of being, rather than portraying an action with an outcome. Nevertheless, *shrugged, chuckled,* and *sank* remain colorful and action-oriented verbs, whereas non-action verbs fail to capture action concretely. If you want to lull your readers to sleep, salt your sentences liberally with verbs like *has been* and watch your readers' eyelids start drooping. Non-action verbs in a string of sentences read mon-otonously and also tend to create abstract sentences, making them difficult for readers to remember. In a 1976 study of 200 action verbs, researchers discovered that the more concrete the verb, the easier readers' comprehension and more precise their recall of the sentences.[22] Concrete verbs help clarify the mean-ing of even abstract nouns within the same sentence, while also helping readers fix the meaning of words and the roles they play within the sentence, the old dance between lexical and syntactic processing that reading inevitably entails at the sentence level. Moreover, even when verbs seem to represent action, they can fail to embody the sentence's primary action. When writers use "light" verbs, they convey action only via a direct or indirect object. In English, the verbs *made*, *give,* and *take* become light verbs when they appear in *made a deal, give me a break,* or *take a hike.*[23]

Finally, and most importantly, non-action verbs are the equivalent of couch potatoes who call for someone to hand them the remote if it ends up being more than two feet away. They simply occupy space. They never carry their weight. And they need other forces to prop them up and keep everything together. Because non-action verbs merely indicate a state of being, rather than dramatizing action, writers must insert other words to carry the load the verbs should be shouldering. As a result, writers must festoon sentences with non-action verbs with more words: adverbs to pump some color into the action and prepositions to indicate relationships between things in space and time. In fact, non-action verbs necessitate the use of prepositions so consistently that, if you spot a short sentence sporting more than three or four prepositional phrases, you can be certain you're dealing with either a non-action verb or passive construction – or both.

Scads of prepositional phrases are nearly always a symptom of an inefficient and unclear sentence. When you're writing your sentences, think about making your verbs pull their weight. Use action verbs like *powered, catered, provided, annoyed, acted, protested, convinced.* Your sentences will not only read more concretely and be more interesting to your readers, they'll also be much shorter and more efficient than sentences that rely on non-action verbs.

Compare, for instance, Examples A and B below:

Example A:
Chess Aviation has an excellent concept. The idea of catering any service to the extremely wealthy has always been a viable idea. Airline service is necessary for most high-level executives of corporations, businessmen, and wealthy individuals. The airline service that is provided by commercial carriers is extremely poor.

Example B:
The management team has built Chess Aviation around an excellent concept: catering to the extremely wealthy. Many high-net-worth individuals fly frequently, including wealthy businessmen and high-level executives of corporations. However, commercial air carriers tend to provide poor service, falling far short of what affluent people expect.

While the topic is hardly edge-of-the-seat stuff – particularly given the nosedive the aviation industry suffered in the wake of 9/11 – Example A, written in a business plan by an MBA student, is vague and relies entirely on the verbs *is* and *has*. In Example A, *catering any service to the extremely wealthy* remains an idea, an abstraction. But, when readers encounter Example B, they won't have any difficulty in picturing executives boarding planes and flying. Example B is both more concrete and clearer. This example is also more interesting to read and easier to recall than Example A, fixing actor and action easily in readers' brains, even though the two examples convey nearly identical content.

Corollary: Avoid nominalizations!

Aside from being an obnoxious, difficult-to-pronounce word that can make you want to run for your dictionaries – or run, period – nominalizations are the villains of sentences because they steal the action from the verb. You might think of nominalizations as neutered verbs that convert concrete action into an abstract noun: *utilization* (from *use*), *development* (from *develop*), *communication* (from *communicate*), *punishment* (from *punish*). As we've already seen, the more concrete and causal your sentences, the more easily readers move through lexical and syntactic levels of reading. Moreover, as scholars have noted, nominalizations – the word itself is a hideous transformation of the already-Latinate verb *to nominalize* – obscure action, agency, and even meaning in sentences.[24] Take action away from the verb, and, most of the time, you can kiss goodbye your chances of writing a sentence that anyone other than a doting mother would want to read. Moreover, if you're a basic scientist writing about heatshock protein 70, for God's sake, avoid mirroring the complexity of your topic with linguistic complexity. And nominalizations tend to be complex, abstract, and difficult to picture, with the notable exceptions of words like *life, hope,* and *love,* all of which are nominalizations of the verbs *live, hope,* and *love.*

Unfortunately, nominalizations are sneaky, flying stealthily beneath our radar because they crop up in so much of what we read. Just because other writers routinely get away with using nominalizations, however, doesn't mean that using them is a good idea. If you've written a sentence that seems sluggish or even dull, check for nominalizations that rob your verbs of get-up-and-go. On the other hand, if you stumble across one of those rare nominalizations – like *transformation* in the examples below – that's simply lying innocuously in your sentence, letting the verb do its thing, leave it alone. That sort of nominalization isn't harming anything.[25]

Spot the nominalization

How do you spot a nominalization? Simply ask yourself if the noun can also be changed to a verb. Sometimes, as with the nominalization *liberty,* the words themselves look pretty innocuous – no Frenchified polysyllables there. But not all nominalizations have multiple syllables or end in the telltale *-ion.* So ask yourself if you can squeeze a verb from the noun: *liberate.* If the answer is "yes," you're staring squarely at a nominalization. Now look at the verb closest to the nominalization. Is the verb also just lying there, failing to depict any action whatsoever? If the nominalization occurs near verbs like *has been* or any form of the verb *to be,* you need to get rid of the nominalization.

How do you get rid of nominalizations?

Fortunately, getting rid of nominalizations is less difficult than pronouncing the word itself. Getting rid of nominalizations, however, requires you to also think about active construction and action verbs. And you were probably hoping for a quick fix. Unfortunately, you also must observe our next principle, which involves choosing the right subject for your sentence. First, though, you have to spot the nominalization, as in the following sentence:

There was first a review of the transformation of the market for mouthwash.

Now, if you've been paying any attention to this chapter – as opposed to reading it while mouthing the lyrics to a song on your playlist or half-watching TV, you should've spotted three clarity issues that virtually scream out from the page. Give up? First, the sentence begins with *There was*, a violation of what should be the First Commandment of Writing: Thou Shalt Not Use *There is, There was, or There are* in any sentence. Second, the short sentence also boasts no fewer than three prepositional phrases, a dead giveaway of a sentence in dire need of a clarity tourniquet. And, third, the sentence also contains the word *review*. *Review*, in case you'd merely skimmed over this seemingly innocuous word, is one of those dreaded nominalizations – in this instance, one that's sucking the life out of the verb. While *review* is a noun, you can also turn it into a verb, *review*, as in *we reviewed the market*.

Is *review* just an innocent bystander in the sentence? After all, the word doesn't even end in one of those nasty-sounding *-ion* endings, right? Okay, proceed to Step 2 and look at the verb. Is it depicting action?

In fact, the verb in the example is non-active, and the sentence omits any explicit actor, let alone including one helpfully in the grammatical subject. Flummoxed? Try the *by zombies* test: *There was first a review of the transformation of the market for mouthwash by zombies.* Now you know you really have to overhaul the sentence. This patient needs a tourniquet and sutures, so stop thinking you can simply put a bandage on the sucker and sidle off. For starters, you have to ditch *There was* and the passive construction. To achieve this change, however, you need to cast around for a likely suspect for your subject. A good candidate in this instance would be something like *department* or that other likely suspect, *researchers*. Both are good candidates because both words represent actors – groups of people capable of making something happen. Now change the nominalization *review* into your verb, which makes both the sentence and verb active:

> *First, the department reviewed the transformation of the market for mouthwash.*

Personally, I'd be fairly happy with this version. But the anally retentive among you might have spotted yet another nominalization skulking in even our revised sentence: *transformation*. If you want to ensure your readers come away from this sentence with a highly concrete picture of exactly what occurred, you might want to change this nominalization back to a verb, like *changed*, and also scrounge around for another likely actor-subject, such as *companies:*

> *First, the department reviewed how companies had drastically changed the market for mouthwash.*

I'd lay serious money, however, on no one grousing over the quality of your writing if you leave *transformation* intact. In fact, as you can see, the third version of the sentence is slightly longer than the second. When nominalizations aren't bleeding the life out of your verbs and making your sentences passive, they're not entirely bad things. Sometimes, they even let you say things more efficiently than you otherwise could, as with the slight difference in length between the second and third versions of the sample sentence above.

Turning passive sentences into active involves choosing the right subject

All right, we're ready for a trial run at observing Clarity Principles 1 and 2. Let's say you're struggling over an irate letter to City Hall, complaining about the sudden, nosebleed-inducing hike in your property assessment. As you reread your magnum opus, however, you stumble across the following sentence:

> *My property's assessed value has been doubled in the past year, despite the fact that it got walloped by hurricanes Frances and Jeanne.*

"Uh, oh," you think, feeling a vague realization that the writing's not quite as stellar as it could be. Okay, *has been* could be a non-action verb. But how can you really be certain that the entire sentence is passive? Then you remember the *by zombies* test. So you plug the phrase *by zombies* in here, so the sentence becomes *My property's assessed value has been doubled in the past year by zombies*. Oops. Well, presumably, your local officials would like to attribute anything nasty to hordes of zombies, rather than themselves, humble civil servants who can get the sack or chucked out of elected office, but they rather inconveniently can't blame anything on zombies. At least, not yet.

Now you need to locate a possible culprit – uh, actor: the property appraiser. Your property cannot really do the doubling. If it did, you would just have to resign yourself to a fate at the hands of some obscure market forces, rather than insinuating that, say, the property assessor has a serious case of the envies where your house is concerned. You're writing to City Hall because you feel someone has made a human error, right? So the actor performing the doubling is a property assessor, or someone in the tax collectors' office, not your property or zombies.

Now we need an action verb:

> *The property appraiser has doubled the assessed value of my home in the past year, despite the fact that it got walloped by hurricanes Frances and Jeanne.*

Not bad. However, that last clause, everything after *past year*, is still pretty kludgy, especially *the fact that it got*, a passive construction that doesn't exactly trip off the tongue like iambic pentameter. Try to locate a suitable actor, in this case, the hurricanes, which are unfortunately capable of actions that produce effects, as the residents of Florida, New Orleans, and New York can attest. Then pair the actors with an action verb:

> *The property appraiser has doubled the assessed value of my home in the past year, despite hurricanes Frances and Jeanne damaging the house.*

Your sentence is now not only City Hall-ready, you might even get approached for a job writing for your local bureaucrats. Most people, after all, can recognize good writing, even if they can't quite pull it off themselves.

Not entirely coincidentally, our revision of the City Hall sentence brings us rather nicely to our third clarity principle.

Clarity Principle #3:
Use actors or concrete objects as your grammatical subjects

Actors are individuals, groups, even abstractions that are capable of action. Words like *I, she, we, he,* and *they* all make for solid actors, as do *researchers*, *Verizon*, *Maggie Smith*, *Ford*, *Special Forces*, *the marketing department*, *my Jack Russell*, *the football team*, *our investment club*, and even abstractions like *The White House*. In fact, even words like *a recent study*, *the site proposal*, *my letter*, and the *New York Times* all also qualify as good actors because these terms are all capable of effecting a change or of acting on a situation or influencing people's opinions.

Actors make the best subjects
Good actors make for the strongest possible subjects for your sentences. Why? Actors always clearly perform actions, which have results. When you begin sentences with actors, you also rely on action verbs – and active construction. As a result, your sentences will read like miniature stories, mirroring the cause–effect bias our minds display in perceiving the world around us.[26] If you fail to find a likely actor lurking somewhere toward the tail end of your sentence and you can't invent a likely suspect, try casting around for a concrete object, something your readers can easily picture. Avoid, at all costs, abstractions as your grammatical subjects, unless you absolutely must focus your sentence on an abstract concept. In fact, when you turn the page, you'll discover that I've used abstractions like *language* and *ambiguity* as subjects, even though neither word is an actor, because these concepts represent the main ideas in each sentence. Later, in our next chapter, we'll discover how to turn this occasional difficulty with abstract subjects into a strategy that can help bind your sentences together.

Actors avoid ambiguity
Language can be wretchedly ambiguous. Take, for example, the time I was relating to my best friend the news that another friend's

mother, who could slip comfortably into a Size 0, had appeared with D-sized breast implants.

"It was awful," I told my friend. "He said they felt horribly fake."

My friend was aghast. "He felt *his mother's breasts*?"

Fortunately, since we were chatting via mobile phone, I could quickly correct her, telling her that my friend said he could feel the implants when he hugged his mother, not by playing with her chest.

But, if I had, instead, put those details into writing, that ambiguity would go uncorrected, could even queer my friend's entire reading of the event, let alone of my other pal's character. Spoken language seldom remains ambiguous for long because we can always halt the conversation and swiftly correct our conversational partners. But writing enables us to extend our thoughts and experiences. Writing extends our ability to persuade others, beyond the reach of the human voice, across space, across time. But writing also ensures we're seldom around to correct someone when what seemed patently transparent to us seems about as clear to our readers as mud.

Hence, to write is to tango with ambiguity at every step. Your readers may shade a word like *inconsequential* with a connotation that never occurred to you. Or your reader might mistake your meaning completely, mistaking the word *jazz*, for example, for a men's cologne and not a form of music. I discovered this particular bit of ambiguity when I asked my ex-husband, while he was watching the Harlem Gospel Choir on TV, "Is that Jazz?" I meant the cologne he was wearing. Instead, he replied, exasperated at my presumed ignorance, "No, it's *gospel*." Ambiguity is why lawyers can turn a transaction as simple as buying a house into a sixty-page nightmare, then earn 200 bucks an hour for reading through the same sort of contract. Writing is a constant battle against ambiguity, a struggle to cement clear meaning into place on the page, regardless of who reads it.

So avoiding ambiguity is paramount in writing – another reason why choosing an actor or concrete object for your subjects is such a good move. For example, even a sentence as simple as *This is a good idea* is rife with ambiguity. To begin with, what on earth does *this* refer to, anyway?

In case you dozed through that day in grade school English –
or, worse, you were burdened with a student teacher – pronouns
ostensibly refer to a noun, situated either in the same sentence
or in an earlier sentence. Since, however, *this* is the first word in
the sentence, you need to backtrack into the preceding sentence
to happen on the noun to which *this* refers. Unfortunately, pronouns like *this* seldom refer to specific nouns. Instead, they tend
to reference the content of a part of a sentence, sometimes even
the entire sentence. This situation saddles your readers with two
difficulties. First, they have to determine exactly what you mean
by *this*, seldom an easy task. Second, and worse, your readers
must backtrack from the sentence they've just read to coax out
the true identity of *this* so they can figure out what you're saying. And any time you require readers to backtrack, as a writer,
you're dead. Why? Prediction is the engine that enables lexical
and syntactic comprehension. Moreover, readers take more time
identifying pronouns – even definite pronouns like *she* – when the
pronoun referent was situated two sentences earlier than when
the culprit, er, referent, occurred in the end of the sentence immediately preceding it.[27]

Remember, readers generally work their tails off to make sense
of even the instructions on a box of Jell-O. They're busily sorting
out the meanings of words, putting content together and comparing it with their store of knowledge, recalling what they've just
read, figuring out where your drift is taking them. As a writer,
you must make that task seem as effortless as you possibly can –
which means you should avoid anything that might ever force a
reader to backtrack. As a result, you should avoid using isolated
pronouns as your subjects – words like *this, that, these, it,* and
those, which always rely on other words to express their meaning
explicitly.

EXPERT TIP: Avoid using isolated pronouns as your grammatical subjects
Avoid using isolated pronouns like *this, that, these, those,* or *it* as your
grammatical subjects. If you must use a pronoun at the beginning of a
sentence, ensure you pair it with a noun. Turn *This seems like a mistake*
into *This tactic seems like a mistake.*

Corollary: *Avoid using phrases and clauses as your grammatical subjects*

An MBA student once raised his hand toward the close of class and got straight to the issue that had been making him writhe in his seat for an hour.

"I'm really concerned," he said, "about Devon's over-reliance on gerundial phrases as his grammatical subjects."

While the rest of the class wanted to bash him, I had to fight down the impulse to high-five him. His classmate, Devon, should have been concerned. In fact, a surplus of gerund phrases like *listening to Devon's endless gerundial phrases* and *watching market fluctuations* put Devon in the same company as ham-fisted writers, researchers who completed PhD degrees, and analytic thinkers who actually read something other than the crawl at the bottom of the news. Devon saw ideas as connected in an endless chain, precisely the sort of thing that graduate programs encourage in their students. Unfortunately, that kind of thinking, so handy in writing a grant, can make your writing read like those tortuous sentences written by German philosophers. Worse, your sentences slow down your readers' speed, trigger needless cortical activation – the equivalent of your car's engine roaring as you labor up a steep incline – and can even cause your hapless reader to slog through the entire bloody mess of a sentence again.

Why? Gerunds, in particular, pose three challenges to readers. Gerunds are words inviting us to interpret them as verbs, since they are essentially verb forms that end in *-ing*. But, instead of conveying action, gerunds sneakily occupy the role of a noun in a sentence. As a result, gerunds first invite us to misinterpret the role they play in the sentence, since readers often need to read to the end of the gerund phrase to identify what roles the gerund (and gerund phrase) perform in the sentence: *Interpreting the gerund phrase interpolated between the subject and verb made us misread the sentence.* Second, gerunds seldom do anything as innocuous as occupying a simple part of sentence, as in the sentence *I like swimming.* In this example, *swimming* is acting as a noun (the part of speech) and also playing the role of the direct object of *like*. Instead, gerunds tend to insinuate themselves into sentences at the head of noun clauses. And, third, gerunds also have a pesky way of encouraging writers to lard those noun clauses with embedded phrases, or, worse, clauses:

> *Integrating the fragments gleaned from a sentence into a vast mental database to be recalled at a later point when they become useful could tax even a brain like Einstein's.*

Note, before you begin tearing out bits of hair, that this sentence both represents and accurately describes a phenomenon linguists have established in multiple studies. To make sense of the sentence, the reader's brain must place each element in the sentence into an existing framework. In a subject–verb–object ordered language like English, the put-upon reader of this sentence must hold *Integrating the fragments gleaned from a sentence into a vast mental database to be recalled at a later point when they become useful* in suspension until she reaches the verb *could tax*. Along the way, she must avoid seizing on potential verbs like *gleaned, recalled,* and *useful,* all of which will eventually make a hash of the sentence's meaning. In addition, she has to wend her way through thickets of phrases and clauses worthy of late Henry James' syntax. First, the sentence unfurls with the gerund phrase, *integrating the fragments,* which would be easily comprehensible if only the writer had inserted the major clause's main verb directly after the gerundial phrase – in addition to crafting a sentence that made sense. Instead, though, he plugged in a participle, *gleaned,* then two prepositional phrases, *from a sentence* and *into a vast mental database.* To inflict still further pain and suffering on his readers, he followed these phrases with an infinitive phrase, *to be recalled,* then another prepositional phrase for good measure, *at a later point,* and closed with an adjective clause *when they become useful.* This final clause is particularly knotty, as adjective clauses generally begin with *that* or *which,* rather than *when,* usually associated with adverb clauses. However, in this sentence, *when they become useful* clearly modifies *point,* making the clause an adjective clause.

Confused? You should be. After all, the reader has to hold all those complex parts of sentence in a comprehensible framework prior to reaching the verb. To make comprehension still more challenging, the sentence strings together different types of phrases and clauses.[28] Unsurprisingly, when readers slog through sentences like that gerund-led gem, they display multiple signs of cognitive overload. In studies, readers were slower at detecting blips flashed on a screen while reading the sentence and also struggled to keep lists of words accurately in their memories. In addition, their EEGs showed the high cortical activation emblematic of cognitive heavy lifting.[29]

EXPERT TIP: If you are unable to avoid using a phrase or clause as your grammatical subject, keep it short

Readers can avoid garden path moments and cognitive overload if you make brief that gerund or infinitive phrase or noun clause which you insist on using as your grammatical subject.

Clarity Principle #4:
Place grammatical subjects close to the beginnings of sentences and the verb as close as possible to the subject

Okay, now you've nailed your actor or object for your subject, I'm going to tell you where to put them. Politely.

Readers are impatient suckers – they need to be. Guessing what comes next is actually the mechanism that propels reading along, enabling us to interpret and comprehend what we read. Once we know the context of an article or a novel, we can begin weighing everything we read. Contexts serve us like maps of unfamiliar terrain: we measure what we see and guess our whereabouts based on the larger picture the map provides. Maps help us project what comes next. And the more detail we receive from our immediate surroundings, the better our projections, and, the better our projections, the easier the navigation.

Back during the Artificial Intelligence craze, researcher Roger Schank attempted to design a computer that read like a human being – and the primary mechanism that powered the computer's reading was projection.[30] So, unsurprisingly, the more detail you provide readers with up front, at the outset of any sentence, the easier the task of reading. Readers naturally expect to encounter what a sentence is about, its main actor or subject, in the grammatical subject. Moreover, unconsciously, readers begin comprehending sentences only after they reach the grammatical subject. Once they locate the subject, the comprehension process begins, resembling – let's say, for the sake of visualization – an intake of breath. After readers encounter the subject, they hold that virtual breath until they stumble across the verb, completing the main action, the core of any sentence. Then they exhale, ready to take in further details, modifications, the little niggling hedges academic writers are so fond of larding their sentences with.[31]

As a result of this mechanism, readers fail to notice or recall much detail placed either before the subject or between the subject and verb, the two things that form the nub of the context for any sentence. Pile lots of hedges or little positioning clauses at the outset of any sentence, and you're almost guaranteeing your readers will have to plod dutifully back through the sentence again in a vain effort to tease out its meaning. Shoehorn more than a line of detail between your subject and verb, and you ensure the content will become fodder for instant amnesia. Moreover, you also set your readers up for a second troll through the sentence, as they attempt to piece together the relationship between the subject and verb.

The next time you encounter a sentence that seems more like a trek through the Oriente rainforest than a stroll down a sidewalk, try the following test. First, draw a line under the opening words in the sentence. If you have to plow through more than five or six words before you hit the subject, the writer has probably erred by packing in too much modifying detail before she provides you with the goods you actually need to modify. Worse still, all that detail can derail your readers' ability to even understand the sentence's meaning.

You can, of course, begin sentences with the occasional short phrase like *After that last hang-over* or *On my way to the Humane Society* without unduly taxing your readers. Similarly, you can even salt the beginnings of some sentences with short clauses like *Although the Lexington Avenue Local was running late, as always*. Just don't make a habit of it. Think: subject first, then verb, then...the deluge of details.

Consider this gem, written by a faculty member in prosthodontics:

> *The short longevity of most common restorations and*
> *especially those of resin-based composite materials calls for*
> *detailed studies of factors which may lead to an extension of*
> *the lifetime of restorations.*

Try picturing *short longevity*, then count the number of words, many of them wretchedly Latinate, between the grammatical subject, *short longevity*, and the verb, *calls*, which readers must first differentiate from other potential verb-candidates in the sentence, *studies* and *lead*. You staggered through eleven words between the subject and verb, if we count *resin-based* as a single unit. Now look at the same prosthodontist's revision, the week after my course bludgeoned her with the clarity principles you've just encountered:

> *Resin-based composite materials fail to last long.*

In the revised sentence, *materials* occurs within two words of the sentence's beginning, while *fail* crops up immediately after the subject. Note that, for all its impenetrability, the original version relies on active construction and an action verb, a good demonstration of why writers should try to use most of the four clarity principles, rather than concentrating on just active construction. And note that, in the revised version, the sentence employs both active construction and an action verb.

EXPERT TIP: Start sentences with a subject and follow with a verb
Start most sentences with the subject at the outset, followed closely with a verb.

Putting clarity principles into practice

Before you start attacking the sample sentences below with your newly discovered clarity chops, let's pause to put them together by examining differences between two examples. Consider the differences between Example A and Example B, below. Before reading, prepare to time yourself as you read each one, then cover the example with one hand and attempt to paraphrase it, keeping track of how long your paraphrase takes. Then compare the times for reading and paraphrasing Example A to Example B. Be certain to tackle Example A with Example B covered, for reasons I'll explain when you're finished.

Example A:

The permanent neurological impairment typical of chronic inflammatory demyelinating disorders of the central nervous system (CNS), such as multiple sclerosis, is due to the axonal loss resulting from recurrent episodes of immune-mediated demyelination. So far, experimental cell therapy for these disorders has been based mainly on the transplantation of myelin-forming cells, or their precursors, at the site of demyelination. Although such an approach can trigger functional recovery and restore axonal conduction, the limited migration of lineage-restricted, myelin-forming cells through the brain parenchyma highlights the beneficial effect of transplantation to the site of the injury. This raises critical issues regarding the therapeutic use of focal cell transplantation to treat diseases in which multifocal demyelination is the main pathological feature. Such issues are compounded by the poor expansion capacity of myelin-forming cells in culture, which greatly limits their availability and further hampers their prospective application in clinical settings.[32]

Example B:

Multiple sclerosis affects nearly one million people worldwide, subjecting people from young adulthood onwards to repeated immunological attacks on the brain and spinal cord. Twice as many women as men are afflicted with the disease. The effects vary depending on where exactly in the nervous system the attacks occur, but paralysis, blindness, loss of sensation, and lack of coordination are among the types of devastation wrought by an immune system gone awry. Until now, treatment strategies have generally been aimed at blocking

the autoimmune attacks and reducing the amount of
collateral damage caused. Pluchino et al. (2003) describe
a complementary approach – repairing some of the harm
already done.[33]

Now consider the irony behind these two passages, the first of which took you significantly longer to read or paraphrase. They both describe the same study. The difference? Scientists wrote Example A – probably delegating the writing to the lowest-ranking member of the research team, usually the least experienced member of the lot, which seldom guarantees good writing. In contrast, an editor at *Nature*, ever-mindful that the journal reaches a generalist audience of science wonks, wrote the readable Example B, a summary of the study for *Nature*'s introductory pages, the ones that make the full articles at least marginally comprehensible to non-specialist readers.

Takeaways for clarity: what you need to make your sentences easy to read

Whenever you can, you should
- make your sentences active
- use action verbs
- choose actors or concrete objects as your subjects and
- place both actor and verb as close to the beginning of sentences – and to each other – as possible.

CHAPTER 4

Putting sentences together
The second C: Continuity

In this chapter you will learn

- where to place information you want readers to remember
- why long sentences are so difficult to read
- how to make your sentences hang together tightly
- how to help your readers absorb even complex information easily.

Let's say you're doing what no undergraduate in his or her right mind does: bothering to read your university's mission statement:

> *Teaching – undergraduate and graduate through the doctorate – is the fundamental purpose of the university. Research and scholarship are integral to the education process and to expanding humankind's understanding of the natural world, the mind and the senses. Service is the university's obligation to share the benefits of its knowledge for the public good.*

You reach the second paragraph, quoted in italics in the paragraph above. How many times do you have to read it? I'm guessing, if you were trying to figure out what the paragraph actually meant, you probably had to read it at least twice. Why? After all, the paragraph's sentences are reasonably short. And the information the sentences convey ain't exactly rocket science. Actually, you're unlikely to glean any factual information from this sort of generic, mission-statement-ese that seems to say something while really saying next to nothing. Moreover, the language itself isn't terribly complex. Actually, the sentences are even active, even if the grammatical subjects are all abstractions. So what's the matter with this paragraph?

Mind the gap!

The answer actually lies *between* the sentences. Look at the gaps between each sentence carefully. Each sentence exists in splendid isolation from the sentence that precedes or follows it. The first sentence is about teaching, the second, about research and scholarship. And the third is about service. No words act as transitions to guide readers from one sentence to the other. And each sentence fails to provide so much as a suggestion of what links its concepts to the contents of neighboring sentences. In fact, only a college faculty member could probably read this paragraph, pause, and still correctly recall its content because only faculty understand that careers at big universities involve teaching, scholarship, research, and service – at least in theory, on annual reports, and during usually beady tenure and promotion performance reviews. Unfortunately, universities seldom write mission statements for people contemplating careers at a university. Instead, mission statements ostensibly target would-be students. Or, in some cases, the parents who plan on footing the bill for their kid's tuition and want to know something about the place that threatens to eat their entire retirement savings. As a result, the academics who could understand this paragraph easily are unlikely ever to read it. Ironic, isn't it?

Look carefully at this paragraph again, a paragraph written by a professional, probably in exchange for a paycheck. Yet this professional writer made the same mistake that virtually all beginning writers make – *taking for granted what readers know*. You can provide all sorts of background information and fine details for your readers to ensure they aren't scratching their heads by your second paragraph. But you also have to be constantly vigilant about keeping them on the right track from sentence to sentence. As many of us learned from a hoary definition of *sentence*, each sentence is a "complete thought." The problem with churning out a series of complete thoughts is that sentences become little isolated units of meaning. The challenge is that you must make these little islands of thought seem to fit together, ideally, tightly and logically, which is perhaps the single most difficult thing to manage in your writing.

The good news: continuity is far easier to achieve and requires a whole lot less behavior modification than clarity. The bad news:

if your sentences don't fit together tightly, your reader is going to feel your document is badly written or confusing, no matter how many pains you've taken over getting the clarity straight.

While continuity contains five different principles that enable you to link your sentences together, you don't have to use all the principles at the same time. Unlike clarity principles, continuity rests in your using only two or three principles at any time to tie any sentences together. You always have to observe Continuity Principle #1, which appears immediately in the pages that follow. But you can use a mixture of Principles 2–5 to achieve continuity in any paragraph. So you can tether your sentences together by relying on either transitions or sequencing or common grammatical subjects, or even a mixture of these principles, if you feel your sentences are so complex that your readers need extra guidance to get through a particular paragraph.

Why is continuity so important?

Continuity is, arguably, the single most important aspect of your writing. Periods at the ends of sentences can turn them into archipelagos of meaning, isolated from the adjoining sentences by both white space and either gaps in logic or shifts in topic. When you leave these gaps between sentences, you require readers to cross open water to journey from one sentence to another. Actually, however, you should be building bridges or at least providing regular ferry services between sentences to prevent your readers from ever having to swim from one islet to another. Why? Remember, reading is a difficult, demanding task, even when you're not terribly aware of all the machinations you're going through as you read. Your readers are busily assigning meanings to words, recalling what you've already said, guessing about what you're going to say next, holding sentences in short-term memory to comprehend their meaning, then filing information away where it can be retrieved easily.[1] As a result, your readers are grappling with a serious amount of what psychologists call *cognitive load*.

When you require readers to build bridges between sentences, you're asking them to do one thing too many. When you send your readers into what psychologists dub *cognitive overload*,[2] not surprisingly, they are likely to get lost. Worse, readers can make the wrong assumptions and string your sentences together by making the wrong connections, which usually means your reader might seriously mistake your meaning – or just think you have strange ideas.

In any case, if you fail to build bridges between your sentences, you're almost certain to lose readers – and to seem like a lousy writer. But the act of reading relies on a mechanism that makes continuity still more crucial to good writing: prediction. In studies in the 1970s and 1980s, researchers discovered that readers are constantly and unconsciously making predictions every instant they read. In fact, cognitive psychologists agree, to understand the world around us we must constantly categorize everything we perceive, an act that requires us to predict the significance of what we're seeing or hearing at any given moment.

Understanding and perception

In the 1970s, cognitive psychologists argued for the importance of frameworks to our perceptions by pointing out that even ordering a meal in a restaurant involves a rather complex set of expectations.[3] For example, you have to understand the purpose of those rectangles of cardboard someone usually hands you when you sit down. You also have to grasp that the items printed on that menu refer to things you can order, eat, and pay for. And you have to realize that the person standing over your table is waiting to take your order, not to recommend treatment for that persistent headache you get when you've had too much caffeine.

Moreover, different types of restaurants require different categories of understanding. If you waltz into a Mickey D's and expect to be waited on, you could wait until you're past child-bearing age before anyone strolls over to your table. But you'd also be confused if you walked unsuspectingly into an *antipasti* restaurant in Italy and waited for a menu to arrive. *Antipasti* restaurants avoid menus. Instead, diners or waiters pass platters around, and you help yourself to whatever you fancy, then own up to what you've eaten at the end of the meal. (Antipasti restaurants also have their distinct benefits. Occasionally, the waiter toting up your bill will give you a break by refusing to believe you've had six glasses of the house white and three desserts.) To understand the meaning of what happens to us moment by moment in any situation, we have both to understand the entire context and be able to predict what's coming next.

Prediction is essential to understanding

Let's say you decide to go to the movies with some friends and end up watching a romantic comedy featuring Julia Roberts. If, halfway through the film, another character were to put a gun to her head and blow her brains out, you'd most likely be floored and wonder what sort of film you'd been watching after all. This reaction is due entirely to our brains' relying on established frameworks for organizing the world. When you believe you're watching a romantic comedy, you unconsciously expect two characters to be involved in a *Two Weeks Notice* sort of push–pull of attraction and bristling character differences. So, when she ventures into a dark alley or a particularly nasty-looking basement, you don't start looking for a serial killer lurking in the shadows. Romantic comedies mean characters fall in love, come together, pull apart, and, eventually, come together before the close. If, however, a film billed as a romantic comedy involves one or both of the main characters being murdered, you'd have great difficulty figuring out exactly what's going on from scene to scene. Similarly, a horror film without anyone being killed, in danger of being killed, or caught in a basement in the dark with (a) a confirmed serial killer, (b) the latest incarnation of Jason, or (c) ghosts, dead bodies, mummified mothers, or alien life forms would probably have you clamoring for your money back from the box office. Solid, conventional frameworks that organize stories, books, and papers help us to make firm predictions about the significance of our perceptions, which, in turn, help us to interpret moment-by-moment details. When you spot a knife lying around in a teenager slasher flick, you can bet someone's going to use it – sooner rather than later.

Reading and prediction

As a result, reading inevitably involves prediction. As your eyes scoot across a page, your brain is busily predicting the outcome of the document you're reading, as well as the content for the paragraph – even the ending to the sentence.[4] This mechanism, central to our ability to understand what we read, has two important implications for writers who want to create continuity between their sentences – perhaps the most essential component to good writing. First, you must recognize which parts of sentences, paragraphs, and entire documents receive the greatest amount of emphasis in your readers' minds. And, second, the more information you give readers at the beginnings of sentences, the better their predictions and their ability to process information.[5]

We'll call this concept *emphasis*, since studies have established that readers remember items that appear in emphasis positions better and longer than they do items that appear in non-emphasis positions. And we'll use the familiar term *transitions* to focus on how you can help readers to make better predictions about the sentences they're about to read – even as they begin reading them.

TERMS TO REMEMBER

Emphasis – The position in a sentence, paragraph, or document that readers recall best and longest. The ends of sentences, paragraphs, and documents always receive the greatest amount of emphasis.

Transitions – Words or phrases that tell your readers how to interpret the sentences they're about to read relative to what they've just read. Transitions include clauses and phrases, as well as words like *also*, *too*, *and*, *but*, *since*, *although*, *however*, *consequently*, and *because*.

Continuity Principle #1:
Place the most important information at the ends of things – sentences, paragraphs, and entire papers

When given a list of items to memorize, readers always recall the last items best, with the fewest errors and greatest number of items recalled from the last 25–30 percent of the list. Readers mostly remember items at the beginnings of things second best and items in the middles of things – lists, paragraphs, papers – the least well. In fact, if you have to give your readers bad news or disclose a weakness in your own argument, you should sandwich these revelations between positive items.[6]

How do you manage emphasis?

You should always make use of the emphasis position at the ends of sentences to put new or important information in the last quarter to one-third of the sentence. All too often, however, writers tend to allow sentences to limp to a conclusion, like this one:

> *My manager tore my proposal to shreds, told me I was a waste of space, then demanded I pack up my desk and get the hell out of the office during last week.*

Look carefully at this sentence. What's in the end of the sentence?

> *My manager tore my proposal to shreds, told me I was a waste of space, then demanded I pack up my desk and get the hell <u>out of the office during last week</u>.*

The end of this sentence contains the last seven words, which, if you know your grammar, consist of two lowly prepositional phrases. Even if you don't know anything about grammar, however, you can see that the least important items in the sentence are the indications of where and when the incident took place. Obviously, my audience cares more about your getting fired than when and where you got fired. Unless, of course, you get canned every few weeks, which could put a serious dent in your career.

To maximize the emphasis position, the sentence should read something like this:

> *Last week, my manager tore my proposal to shreds, told me I was a waste of space, then demanded <u>I pack up my desk and leave</u>.*

As you read, pay attention to the content of the last quarter to third of each sentence. Is the writer placing the most important information in the emphasis positions? As you write and revise your writing, make sure that you're doing the same. If you find a sentence ends in a whimper rather than a bang, like the first example above, rewrite it.

EXPERT TIP: Limit the number of items in lists

You can count on the beginnings and endings of lists to nudge your readers' recall – but only so far. Early studies of the number of items recalled from the beginnings of lists ran to three or four items, while the ends of lists benefited from a still-greater bump due to the recency effect. In studies dating back to the 1960s, readers accurately recalled as many as eight items from the ends of lists.[7] However, this recall is higher than either you or most psychologists should expect, especially given the broad durability of George Miller's "seven-plus-or-minus-two" estimate of the number of items an average person can hold in working memory.[8] As a result, try to limit items in lists to seven or fewer for bulleted lists, where items will stand out separately from the sentence that contains them. For items inside a sentence, try keeping to Miller's lower threshold of five items, as readers tend to skim or even skip dense lists contained within sentences.

If you're a typical human, you doubtless remember all those times you guiltily skimmed, scanned, or even skipped content in reading, from the dreadfully dense descriptions in those novels you had to read for AP English in high school to the financial prospectuses for funds in your 403(b). From a writer's perspective, as well as an editor's or teacher's, you might hope researchers have been busily scrutinizing the point at which your average reader bails on close reading and launches into skimming mode. But, surprisingly, few researchers have focused on how attentively your everyday native speaker of English reads dense paragraphs or lengthy lists. Eye-tracking software long ago easily established the number and length of eye movements readers use on lines and even individual words. However, since research tends to silo investigation into tidy categories, researchers have looked at what eye-tracking tells us about reading and comprehension, inexpert versus expert readers, rapid readers versus slow readers, and, most recently, how readers handle multimedia inputs. To date, no researchers have thought to investigate the relationship between paragraph or list density, independent of the syntactic complexity of the sentences and items, and readers' shifting from close reading into skimming. One study, however, found even the most expert readers had a reading span that encompassed only five items, meaning that writers should think carefully about putting more than five items in any list.[9]

This principle applies even to bulleted items in a list. Writers sometimes think dumping information in a list represents the most efficient way to get it to readers. But, since readers may recall, at best, five items in any list, you're virtually guaranteeing that they won't remember most of the contents in long lists.

Why are long sentences so difficult to read?

Wolfe certainly invokes the key figures – William James, Ralph Waldo Emerson, and Charles Sanders Peirce (rather sheepishly) – but he also draws upon Immanuel Kant, Jean-Paul Sartre, René Descartes, as well as more current figures such as Chantal Mouffe, Ernesto Laclau, and Cornel West, if only to remind us that pragmatism, especially Rorty's strain, may want to express an alterity, an outside of "theory," but it is very much a part of the system.

Cover the sentence above with your hand and try to recall as much of its specifics as you can. Now lift your hand and see how much you actually managed to remember. If you read the sentence and know something about philosophy, you might have noticed that this sentence is dedicated to covering key theorists relevant to the writer's study. Not surprisingly, most of the details in the sentence probably escaped you, especially the names of the key theorists. Why?

For starters, the entire example is a single sentence. Long sentences have three things going against them. First, they contain few cues informing readers which information in the sentence is particularly important – and that readers should remember. Second, long sentences also have the same amount of emphasis as any other sentence: the contents in the last quarter to one-third of the sentence. As a result, readers will tend to forget virtually everything else in the sentence. Worse, readers are likely to lose track of relationships between elements in particularly complex, lengthy sentences. In addition, readers may also forget the subject of the sentence by the time they reach the end, where contents are likeliest to lodge in their memories. And, third, long sentences place higher demands on working memory, making them difficult to read.[10]

Note, incidentally, how weak the writer's use of the stress position in the example above seems. Both *it* and *system* are ambiguous terms, particularly since the readers have to track backward through a lengthy sentence to try to identify the referents. Both factors ensure that your readers will have difficulty in figuring out how the sentence they've just finished reading connects with the one they're about to read. And this fact brings us to our next principle: using transitions.

Continuity Principle #2:
Use transitions to tie sentences together

Readers understand what they read by projecting forward, roughly anticipating the content of the next sentence. Your reader might struggle to pin down the meaning of the word *remit* to establish whether the word is a verb or a noun, strain to spot the verb in the major clause, or make sense of two apparently unrelated sentences. If you were paying attention in Chapters 2 and 3, you'd identify lexical, syntactic, and inferential processing in the string of readerly actions in the preceding sentence. At every stage, prediction is the engine driving comprehension in reading. However, because every sentence can theoretically be an island of meaning, readers stumble, pause, and reread when they read a sentence about pizza followed by one dedicated to bubonic plague.[11] Unless you're a card-carrying hypochondriac or an unmedicated obsessive-compulsive fretting about rat fleas in the kitchen of your local pizza joint, you're unlikely to see anything connecting the two sentences.

Transitions easily build minute bridges from sentence to sentence, bolstering your readers' ability to comprehend relationships between sentences. Essentially, you're telling your audience how to interpret the sentence they're about to read relative to what they've already read. When you use *and, also,* or *too* toward the beginning of a sentence, you're telling your readers that the next sentence is adding to the information they've just encountered in the preceding sentence. But when you use *but, however, conversely, on the other hand,* or *yet* as transitions, you're announcing to your audience that the content of the next sentence is going to contrast with what they've just read – the direction of the topic is about to perform an about-face.

Without these transitions, your readers will be left wondering how sentences are related. Occasionally, your readers may even have to backtrack and reread sentences when they discover that they haven't correctly guessed relationships between sentences.[12] And, as we've already discussed in Chapter 2, any time your readers have to backtrack and reread a sentence or several lines, you've fallen down on your job as a writer. Remember, transitions give you the most bang for your buck in cementing your sentences together, since transitions are generally both short and easy for readers to process.

EXPERT TIP: The power of causal transitions

Transitions like *as a result*, *therefore*, *because*, and *consequently* tell readers that the sentence they've just read caused the outcome in the sentence lying just ahead. Never underestimate the power of causal transitions, especially if you're a lawyer, an employee arguing for a merit pay increase, or anyone crafting a contentious bit of argument. Studies of causal transitions established that they significantly increase reading speeds.[13] In addition, given the central role causation plays in our perception generally, you're also encouraging readers to follow your line of thinking, rather than pausing to argue with your connecting pizza and bubonic plague.

Transitions toolkit

Transitions can be as brief as a single word or as long as a clause. Most transitions, however, are short and fall into ten categories:

Continuity: *also, and, besides, further, furthermore, in addition to, likewise, similarly, too, not only . . . but also, too.*

Contrast or exception: *although, but, conversely, despite, however, in contrast, instead, nevertheless, nonetheless, on the other hand, otherwise, still, though, yet.*

Conditions: *if, if...then, whenever.*

Frequency or time: *after, afterward, at the same time, before, before then, during, earlier, eventually, later, meanwhile, now, once, once again, sometimes.*

Order: *first, second, third, last, primarily, ultimately, finally, more importantly, most importantly, in closing, in conclusion.*

Example: *for example, for instance, specifically, particularly.*

Amplification: *apparently, actually, especially, in fact, in particular, indeed, of course.*

Cause: *as, as a result, because, for, for this reason, since, therefore.*

Result: *accordingly, as a result, consequently, hence, therefore, then, thus, so.*

Conclusion: *then, finally, generally, in conclusion, in the end, in short, ultimately.*

Studies of the power of transitions have also focused on the strength of transitions signaling shifts in time, particularly in narratives, which crop up in news stories as well as in those guilty-pleasure novels one tends to find in airport news agents.[14]

Conjunction junction

Remember: to be effective, transitions have to appear toward the beginning of any sentence. You must place a transition either before the grammatical subject or before the verb for the transition to function effectively. Once readers hit the verb in any sentence, their most substantial work in interpreting the sentence is over.[15] When writers whack a transition in at the close of a sentence, however, they've completely erased any benefits the transition might have given their readers. Compare:

Example A:
Rogers, Sanborn & Son had left the project and the site in limbo for several years. The team discussed the liabilities of building on the site, the difficulties in minimizing the environmental impacts, and the necessity of driving foundations on piles, then Sanders & Co. decided to give up on the project, too.

Example B:

Rogers, Sanborn & Son left the project and the site in limbo for over five years. Similarly, Sanders & Co. also decided to give up on the project after the team discussed the project's numerous challenges. These challenges include (1) the liabilities of building on the site, (2) difficulties in minimizing environmental impacts, and (3) the necessity of driving foundations on piles.

In Example A your readers might be prepared for the second sentence to also involve Rogers, Sanborn & Son, since the first sentence focuses on this company. But the second sentence switches the focus to Sanders & Co., which disorients readers who only encounter the change of company at the end of the sentence. And readers are likely to miss the continuity between the two companies giving up on projects on the same proposed site if they only stumble across the transition that links them, *also* or *too*, at the very end of the sentence in the first example. In contrast, Example B shifts the change of companies to the beginning of the sentence but also highlights the continuity between the companies that have both found the site equally difficult to work with. Note that Example B also breaks into two sentences the skinny on why Sanders & Co. decided to also abandon the project and helpfully numbers the three most important items, creating a list that helps readers retain the contents. The bottom line: if you're inserting a transition after the verb, forget it. You've just done the equivalent of offering a climber a hand-up *after* she's already scaled the entire bloody cliff.

Can you have too many transitions? Not really!

Typically, in American journalism courses, fledgling journalists are cudgeled into beginning every sentence with a transition. (Full disclosure: in one of my former incarnations, I performed a fair bit of cudgeling myself when I taught journalism and advised journalists on two student-run publications.) Journalists lean heavily on transitions, and American newspapers rely on the bracing brevity of single-sentence paragraphs for a good reason. Newspapers have pegged the average American reader's skill at a dismal fifth-grade level. When you grasp that unpalatable fact, you begin to see the sense of those single-sentence paragraphs, mostly containing sentences of twenty-odd words or fewer, all beginning with transitions that connect them snugly to the preceding sentences. However, transitions in journalism are not a sop to distracted readers who mouth words as they read silently. Transitions also work equally well in writing for audiences with longer attention spans and a bit more education by mortaring sentences together, supporting readers' subconscious predictions of inferences across sentences. With a single word as unobtrusive as *also*, slipped quietly between your subject and verb, you seamlessly link two thoughts that would otherwise seem isolated or require a bit of guesswork to forge connections.

While no one is going to breathe down your neck, insisting on a transition in every sentence, you should be using transitions approximately every two to three sentences. And, unlike so many other things in life, you can never use too many. Transitions also offer your sentences an additional benefit: they vary the rhythm of your writing. If you begin every sentence directly with a grammatical subject (or article and grammatical subject), the rhythm of your sentences will seem to be monotonous: *dum-dum-dum-dum*. But when you place transitions at the beginnings of your sentences, you end up varying this rhythm, even when you use transitions in two or three consecutive sentences.

Unlike music, a pleasing rhythm in writing involves variety, not similarity, a concept we'll explore in greater detail in Chapter 7. By varying the structure of your sentences somewhat, as well as their length, you'll establish the pleasing rhythm that is the hallmark of truly accomplished writers who are fully in control of their work. And remember, readers always subconsciously register the rhythm of their sentences, even when they're reading swiftly and silently.

Writing myths you'll wish you never learned:
Never begin a sentence with and *or* but

This edict, which teachers may have handed down to you in middle or high school, is simply *wrong*. Like the proclamations of the grammar mavens hung up on split infinitives – a rule derived from Latin to confer *gravitas* on the mongrel that is English – the ban on beginning sentences with conjunctions has two probable sources. First, coordinating conjunctions like *and, or, but* generally connect two major clauses. However, you won't flummox readers encountering *but* at the beginning of a sentence that clearly inverts or hedges on the suppositions of the preceding sentence for the simple reason that the full stop or period preceding *but* tells readers the conjunction here isn't connecting two major clauses. Instead, the conjunction merely functions as an additive or contrasting transition. (See the Supplement, page 164, for the role of punctuation as a means of avoiding garden-path stumbles by disambiguating the function of words.) Second, the rule also stems from what we might think of as the *training wheels effect*, where well-intentioned teachers lay down principles as immutable as the Ten Commandments for seven- and eight-year-olds, then neglect to tell them that these rules were merely supposed to curb wayward behavior, like writing sentence fragments, rather than serve as guidelines for a lifetime of practice.

In fact, you can begin any sentence with a conjunction. When you begin sentences with *and* or *but*, you cement your sentences firmly together. If, however, you feel a bit squeamish about beginning a sentence with *and*, or your readers may well have been born in the first half of the last century (and thus labor under the old canards about conjunctions beginning sentences), you might instead want to use *also* or *too* and sandwich these transitions between your subject and verb.

Rest assured that you can easily silence grammar mavens by noting that the injunction against split infinitives, which would've deprived *Star Trek* of its immortal opening phrase...*to boldly go* . . . was tacked onto English to provide this Johnny-come-lately of a language with at least one ancient rule derived expressly from Latin. The problem, of course, is that no one on the planet could split an infinitive in Latin or, indeed, in any Romance language. The reason? In Latin and all Romance languages, infinitives are single words, incapable of being split unless you're aiming to create a slang even more flummoxing than the Cockney rhyming slang that counsels you to answer the dog because *dog and bone* rhymes with *phone*.

Continuity Principle #3:
Sequence information in sentences in a
familiar–unfamiliar, familiar–unfamiliar pattern

The question of how to transmit what one speaker or writer knows to another, from brain to brain, has first transfixed philosophers, then linguists, and, finally, psychologists. Like the Artificial Intelligence fad, this question – linguistic and psychological – has driven research that would be a boon to writers everywhere, if only they were willing to troll through archival issues of journals with titles like *Language and Consciousness* and *Memory & Cognition*. Instead, most beleaguered writers just want to know how the hell you tie together two ideas, coupling them so tightly that even skeptical readers would have difficulty inserting a knife-blade of resistance between them. Enter sequencing. More difficult to describe than to actually employ, sequencing is your best means of binding sentences together when you're describing material that is highly technical, difficult to comprehend, or potentially contentious to your readers.

To sequence information, you follow Continuity Principle #1 and place new and important information at the end of your sentence. But you also introduce familiar information, continuous from an earlier sentence, into the beginning of the sentence, easing your readers into the unfamiliar material. Sequencing plays off three things driving the reading brain: assumptions about relevance, inference processing, and the priming effects of words in preceding sentences. First, in studies beginning in the 1970s, researchers realized that readers process material already familiar to them first, prior to tackling new information.[16] In addition, researchers also discovered that humans automatically see relevance in statements in the world around them, in speech and writing alike. We assume relevance between sentences, maximizing our comprehension with minimal cognitive effort. Sequencing explicitly takes advantage of this tendency to see relevance by establishing an explicit link between new information at the outset of each sentence and already familiar information introduced at the close of the preceding sentence.[17] Second, readers rely on relevance in the inference stage of processing, focusing on the immediately available content in the preceding sentence to make sense of the sentence awaiting them.[18] And, third, readers will also see as intrinsically related sentences connected by similar words, tied together by what researchers term *referential continuity*, where one sentence refers implicitly or explicitly to the content of the preceding sentence. In studies that deliberately scrambled or disrupted referential continuity, readers demonstrated significantly stronger recall of sentences that relied on referential continuity than they did sentences with no apparent connection.[19]

Put simply, readers interpret material most easily when they're able to position what they're about to read relative to what they've just read. As a result, sequencing is as effective as transitions, if not more so. Furthermore, when you use sequencing, you ease your reader into information by creating an unobtrusive chain of references that seem to be continuous, even if you're introducing new information at the end of every sentence.

Consider, for example, the following groups of sentences:

Example A:
Banks within a particular market tried to shore up their particular market share, a practice that left them exposed to a buyout. Other banking institutions were expanding outside their current markets. The federal government could force an institution to sell itself to a buyer that the federal government had already chosen. The buyer normally bought the bank being sold because the bank's sale price had fallen beneath its market value.

Example B:
Banks within a particular market tried to shore up their respective market share, <u>a practice that left banks exposed to a buyout. This practice</u> allowed for other banking institutions <u>to expand outside their current markets. In some cases</u> the federal government could force the entity to sell itself <u>to a buyer that the federal government had already chosen. When given this option, the buyer</u> normally bought the bank being sold because the bank's sale price had fallen beneath its market value.

If you leave Example A feeling confused about exactly what the hell happened, you're not alone. In this version, every sentence is isolated from the sentences before and after it by an absence of transitions. But these sentences also lack continuous content and any trace of referential continuity – shared words common to two or more sentences.

Now look at Example B where the sequenced material is underlined. Note how using sequencing requires you to refer to the same concepts, using some of the same terms to name them. You don't have to use the *exact same* words from sentence to sentence, although readers will recognize immediately that you're referring to the same things you've mentioned in the preceding sentence. However, to make this principle work, you need to introduce the familiar words and concepts toward the *beginning* of any sentence, immediately following their appearance at the end of the preceding sentence.

Continuity Principle #4:
Try to keep grammatical subjects consistent
from sentence to sentence

You can also build rickety bridges between those little atolls of meaning, less durable than the concrete causeways of sequencing that have your readers gliding from *terra firma* to *terra firma* without ever realizing they've just crossed a scrap of open water. In eye-tracking studies, readers typically lingered longer, not only at sentence boundaries, but also at sentences with evident shifts in topic from the preceding sentence.[20] When writers carelessly reference material they introduced as many as six or seven sentences earlier, even the *good* readers strain to integrate the sentence they're struggling to comprehend with content that cropped up much earlier in the same paragraph.[21]

Unlike transitions – the remedy for continuity that no writer can overuse – too much sequencing can make your reader feel as though you've dragged her through your document with a pair of pliers applied to her nostrils. Or he can feel as though you've lumbered him with a sort of *See Spot run. Run, Spot, run* elementary simplicity that comes across as a bit insulting for any reader north of second grade. While sequencing has limited applications, common grammatical subjects are instruments of continuity on which no writer can OD.

Grammatical subjects unobtrusively ease your readers from sentence to sentence by using a priming effect. Studied for decades, priming effects involve exposing readers to something as unremarkable and thoroughly unmemorable as a list of unrelated words, pairs, phrases, or sentences.[22] Readers shown a list of words like

elephant
rubber ball
bus
brochure

have accurate recall of the list, even a day or days later, when they see it again.[23] The impact on recall seems due to priming as a form of implicit learning that, remarkably, works as effectively with amnesiacs as with skilled readers.[24] The repetition of key concepts via the same word, used as a grammatical subject, has two effects. First, the priming effect subconsciously nudges your readers to identify the repeated grammatical subjects as important. Second, this same priming effect also enables readers to recognize the topic of the paragraph, aiding them considerably in inference building and intuiting what researchers have called the *macrostructure* of the paragraph.[25]

As off-putting as the term might sound, the concept of macrostructure is useful for writers to bear in mind as they craft paragraphs – as we'll see in Chapter 5. Put simply, the macrostructure is the organizing principle behind the paragraph, a central series of points or events that rely on readers' accessing a schema for understanding what's going on, that good old inference-building stage of comprehension. If I'm reading a paragraph that contains a screed on the fate of the apostrophe in the Internet era, I can move easily from a sentence on its disappearance from possessive plurals, as in *Two Days Notice*, to the unfortunate appearance of an apostrophe wherever plurals crop up, as in *Flea control for cat's and dog's only*. In other words, the macrostructure or schema of the paragraph is about the abuse of apostrophes in modern English. When you use the word *apostrophe* itself as a grammatical subject, you prime readers to expect the paragraph to bang on about apostrophes.

Moreover, since the beginnings of sentences receive second-ary stress, readers recall words from the beginnings of sentences fairly clearly. In addition, grammatical subjects represent the core of every sentence – or should, if you're not relying on lame words like *this* and *it*. Unfortunately, this linkage is seldom as sturdy as sequencing. As a result, you should use some transitions between sentences that you've connected only through same grammatical subjects. Also, once again, as with sequencing, you can use simi-lar terms to maintain continuity, rather than identical subjects in every sentence.

Compare the following two examples:

Example A:
The services proposed have clear advantage over the present services available, primarily due to the proposed low cost and high quality initiatives. Captive technologies will dissuade mimicry by new entrants through introduction of Mr. Hutton's "electronic notebook" training tools. Essential skills, captive to the organization, are adequate to the services offered with a high degree of flexibility due to the owner being the chief employee. The intended clients are both numerous and in need of the services offered, as expressed in the disclosed research.

Example B:
ITS' business plan offers clear advantages over its potential competitors, primarily due to the company offering low cost and high quality training. Moreover, the business will discourage competitors from entering the field via Mr. Hutton's "electronic notebook" training tools. Furthermore, ITS enjoys the advantage of its owner also acting as the company's chief employee, bringing valuable expertise to clients. Finally, ITS targets a potentially large client base who need its services, a claim the plan backs with market research.

As you can see from looking at the underlined words in Example B above, the grammatical subjects are different. Instead, in each sentence the grammatical subjects only refer to a common set of topics: the business, known as ITS, and its business plan. Notice, however, that transitions also help tie these sentences together. Remember, common subjects alone will not tie sentences together as tightly as sequencing or transitions will.

Writing myths you'll wish you never learned:
Vary your word choice

Primary and secondary school teachers have ensured that this particular myth thrives, mostly because they wanted to justify giving you all those horrible vocabulary spelling and definition tests every week. In this instance, the training wheels effect also applies, as teachers tend to encourage word variation for its own sake, which should remind you of the peacock's tail. Those long, drooping, brilliantly iridescent feathers that handily attract the females also make the peacock vulnerable to predators who can clamp onto his tail and turn him into dinner. Get just a tad too creative with a thesaurus and fail to double-check word choices against a dictionary, and you can end up looking like an idiot. Or implying something queasily *sub rosa* in a job application cover letter.

When you use multiple terms to refer to the same thing, your readers might be so confused, they'll fail to realize that you're talking about the same thing with each change in word choice. Varying *company* and *corporation* won't derail any readers. But if you use *doctrine, edict, manifesto, declaration, statute,* and *charter* to refer to the same thing in a single document, you'll almost certainly confuse the pants off any reader.

EXPERT TIP: Use consistent wording

In addition to priming effects from using consistent grammatical subjects, you also leverage your readers' availability biases – their tendency to recall things they encounter frequently. This attribute of perception was first discovered by Amos Tversky and Daniel Kahneman, a pair of psychologists whose thinking has proven influential in economics but applies equally usefully to writing.[26] In fact, your readers will spend less time focusing on words you repeat frequently – a sign that their brains aren't generating a head of steam to make sense of what they're reading – in contrast to words mentioned only once or twice.[27] These three beneficial effects – priming, availability, and frequency – apply even when you use consistent word choices in nouns that crop up in the middles or ends of sentences, lending continuity to your paragraphs.

Continuity Principle #5:
Continuity is more important than clarity. If you can only maintain a strong sequence or a consistent subject by using passive construction, then use it

I'll remind you of Ralph Waldo Emerson's famous quotation – usually mangled when quoted – "[C]onsistency is the hobgoblin of little minds" – since you're likely to be pissed off that, after my banging on about the Importance of Clarity in Chapter 3, I'm about to tell you to chuck it. While clarity has its place in making reading less arduous than digging fence posts, you can make readers work overtime if you omit continuity between your sentences.

In the early 1980s, researchers pounced on eye-tracking devices to measure the movements of readers' eyes and made several startling discoveries. First, readers' eyes paused significantly on detail at the beginning of sentences, evidently straining to link it to the content of the preceding sentence. Second, readers' eyes stopped longer on sentences that had no attachment to the preceding sentences than they did on sentences that clearly referred to the preceding sentence. And, third and most significantly, readers focused on the common wording from sentence to sentence, relying on this boost in making inferences about meaning, even when the actual meaning of the sentences themselves depicted highly implausible conditions.[28] In other words, those sequences and common grammatical subjects bolster your readers' ability to make sense of what you're saying – even when you're not making a whole hell of a lot of sense. This research should console procrastinators everywhere when they're pulling an all-nighter as they scurry to make the deadline on a proposal or research project.

"Aha," you're probably thinking. "Screw clarity and just observe continuity." Not so fast, Spiderman (or superhero du jour).

In about 90 percent of sentences, you can accommodate clarity and continuity principles without compromising either. In some instances, however, the two sets of principles clash. For example, let's say that you're using consistent subjects or topics to keep your readers on track. In the following examples, sequencing or using consistent subjects or topics led to a sentence with passive construction. Eagle-eyed readers may already have spotted the passive construction lurking in one of the sentences in the following examples:

Example A:
Not surprisingly, the paragraphs that follow the document head make up the document body. The document body can be broken into many parts, but every paragraph you write in the document body must contain a paragraph head and body.

Example B:
When you use and, also, or too toward the beginning of a sentence, you tell readers that the next sentence adds to the information they've read in the preceding sentence. In contrast, when you use but, however, conversely, on the other hand, or yet as transitions, you announce to readers that the content of the next sentence will contrast with what they've just read. In other words, the upcoming sentence will hedge on or even overturn the claim from the preceding sentence. Fail to use transitions, and your readers may wonder how one sentence relates to the other.

In Example A, both sentences are tied together through sequencing *the document body*, which appears in the stress of the first sentence and in the grammatical subject of the second – a good example of strong sequencing. This same sequencing, however, means that the second sentence uses passive construction *can be broken*. Nonetheless, in this instance the trade-off between continuity and clarity works well, since the sequencing binds these two sentences together tightly.

Now, in Example B, note that the consistent wording here falls at the beginning of sentences but is not part of the grammatical subject in any sentence. However, because this snippet of writing relies heavily on transitions, the sentences seem continuous.

As you might recall, readers struggle to forge links between sentences to grasp what you're writing about. As a result, when you occasionally must use passive construction to create a stronger sequence or more unified wording in your sentences, you're making the right decision. Just remember to try tweaking your sentence, attempting alternate phrasing or sequencing to see if you can maintain continuity *and* also use active construction at the same time. In most cases, you'll discover, both continuity and clarity function together seamlessly, without interfering with one another.

EXPERT TIP: Tying continuity together

Remember, you don't need to use *all* the continuity principles every time you write a sentence. While you need to always put important information in the emphasis position of every sentence, you can choose from the other principles to tie your sentences together tightly. If you use consistent grammatical subjects, you might not need to use a transition in every sentence, and you can probably skip sequencing for that sentence. Likewise, if you sequence tightly, you can skip transitions or consistent subjects for a set of sentences.

Takeaways for continuity: what you need to remember to write paragraphs that really hang together

- Continuity trumps clarity.
- Place important information in the ends of your sentences.
- Use one of three linking strategies to tie your sentences together:
  - transitions at the beginning of the sentences
  - sequencing of information in an familiar–unfamiliar, familiar–unfamiliar pattern
  - using consistent grammatical subjects or, at least, consistent wording to refer to common topics in some sentences.

CHAPTER 5

Organizing paragraphs and documents
The third C: Coherence

In this chapter you will

- master how to make documents seem tightly organized
- learn the best way to structure paragraphs
- understand when and how to break paragraphs
- discover how to recognize when a paragraph is too short or too long.

When you write a paragraph, do you

a. just start with the first item on your list of things to get through?

b. throw in a return and create a new paragraph, whenever the one you're working on begins to threaten to give *War and Peace* a run for its money?

c. observe the principles used by editors at newspapers like the *Times-Picayune* and *USA Today* and begin a new paragraph every sentence or two?

d. cop to being guilty of all of the above?

If you answered "yes" to any of these questions, consider yourself busted. And in bloody good company, since legions of other writers do exactly the same thing. However, avoid giving in to despair. Unlike the principles behind clarity and continuity, where nearly everything you learned was wrong-headed (if haplessly well intentioned), you'll discover you have a nodding acquaintance with the principles behind coherence. Provided you managed to stay awake during English in secondary school, you've already had some exposure to the fundamental principles underlying coherence. Your teachers were actually within shouting distance of practices psychologists and neuroscientists agree promote rapid comprehension and good recall of content.

Context is everything

In writing, as in life, where you say what and to whom is vital to whether you observe some of the coherence principles. For example, readers of email invariably expect messages to be dynamic, brief, and easily skimmed.[1] When writing an email, keep your message and paragraphs alike short – unless you're writing a chatty update to an old friend who's happy reading the kind of missive Henry James might have sent. To stay on the right track when writing an email or web page text, picture your readers stumbling through a Mato Grosso of sentences and know that, unlike doughty Portuguese explorers, your readers are liable to quit reading at the sight of a paragraph that crawls over three pages.

In an email as with most online text, readers tend to scan paragraphs quickly, focusing on the first few lines of the first paragraph and, if they find the content relevant, the next few lines of the second paragraph. After that point, readers generally bail on that email you spent so much time lovingly crafting as if your mother would read every word. While your mother might, however, your online readers won't, as revealed by eye-tracking studies of several hundred users reading online text.[2] In contrast, in a proposal for the US National Institutes of Health, a three-line paragraph would seem a bit flyweight, unless you were introducing your study's Specific Aims, usually broken down into sub-aims in detail that would be eye-glazing for everyone except (1) the study's authors, who are True Believers, (2) employees of the National Institutes of Health, or (3) eagle-eyed Subject Matter Experts, who can spot the questionable use of a particular assay at a glance.

And so endeth the good news about coherence. Now, brace yourself for what Orwell's Party Members in Newspeak would call the double-un-good news. Coherence trumps not only clarity but also continuity.

In fact, coherence is even more important to readers than continuity or clarity. If you've ever needed to reread a paragraph, you've likely blamed yourself. "I try to get at least four hours in bed," you think, or "Why am I attempting to read a manuscript on neurosurgery before I go under the knife, anyway?" However, as a reader, you're rarely at fault, especially not after you've launched yourself into higher education or the worlds of business and industry, all of which require us to read reasonably expertly. Instead, the likeliest culprit is the structure of the paragraph itself. If you're reading a paragraph that dives straight into the topic at hand *in medias res*, as a reader, you're left in the position of someone watching a film without knowing its genre. If you don't know whether you're watching a romantic comedy or a slasher flick, you can't determine whether you should go warm all over at the prospect of romance lurking in the basement or whether your sphincter should tighten before the heroine reaches the bottom of the stairs. Without knowing what we're reading about, we're left scrambling to figure out the plain sense of what we're reading.

Drunk, sober, and savvy cinema-goers: three models of comprehension

We might think of readers as being like a pair of drunks who wander into a cinema, purchasing tickets purely to escape the Arctic blast of winter air outside. Our drunks weave their way into one of the shoe-box cinemas inside a multiplex without the foggiest notion of what's playing onscreen. As they stare at the flickering images – provided they're not so soused they simply doze off or would fall over during a sobriety test – they use what happens during each scene to piece together what they're watching. If a meat axe appears onscreen, they'll expect great lashings of gore to follow. In contrast, the watchers around them have forked over cash to watch a thriller, so they realize the appearance of the meat axe merely augurs a bit of heart-pounding excitement as the heroine dashes through a crowd to evade villains.

Without quite realizing it, our audience of drunk and sober cinema-goers represent one of the models researchers have constructed to account for the way readers comprehend written texts. The drunks rely on bottom-up processing, piecing together cues from moment-by-moment occurrences, seeking the schema that will impose sense on the bloody thing. In the same way, readers accumulate tidbits from words and sentences to work out a paragraph's main point.[3] As we've already seen in our scrutiny of continuity, readers fall back on this bottom-up approach when they fail to make sense of the sentence they're reading.

In contrast, the sober souls sitting alongside our boozy pair know they signed up for a thriller, giving them a ready-made schema to impose order on the events they see unspooling onscreen. The seduction scene between our hero and heroine isn't a step toward the film's end-game of happy romantic union, despite the attraction of opposites or improbable odds that are the hallmark of a romantic comedy. Instead, that make-out scene is just a scrap of local color, the modern-day equivalent of Shakespeare throwing a bit of banter between grave-diggers in between scenes in a tragedy to give audiences a breather from so much strong emotion awash onstage. Whether you're watching *Three Days of the Condor* or *The Bourne Legacy*, you're not suddenly bewildered by this swerve into romantic territory. You know the kissing and sex are just a quick detour before the ducking and shooting recur. In this way, you're functioning exactly as most expert readers do when they're reading anything half-decently written. As researchers discovered, readers rely on knowledge of schemas gleaned from tens of thousands of documents to enable them to immediately grasp the meaning of paragraphs and entire documents. This top-down strategy lets readers identify helpful cues like headings and topic sentences that, in turn, speed reading and comprehension further.[4]

Now imagine yourself in the cinema, watching *Psycho* on the night the film debuted in cinemas. You haven't heard from your mother that she hasn't been able to step into a shower since the first time she saw the film in 1960. In fact, based on the early scenes, you believe the entire film is going to be about an adulterous couple embezzling wads of cash. And, when Janet Leigh climbs into the shower, you no more believe anything is going to happen to her than you grasp that Martin Balsam is going to inexplicably take a knife through the forehead (a kitchen knife pitted against a skull is a no-brainer of a non-contest), just when he seems poised to put an end to whatever the hell is going on in the spooky house behind the Bates Motel. Why? Janet Leigh has top billing. Headliners never get knocked off midway through a film. And the trail of embezzled cash we thought we were following disappears when the car carrying it sinks, the money unseen in its trunk. To make sense of this film on a first viewing, you either needed to be (a) born well after 1960, (b) the second person you knew to see it and given the skinny on what to expect before the opening titles rolled, or (c) able to understand the way director Alfred Hitchcock toyed with his audiences by making the object you think matters turn out to be so trivial, the MacGuffin that vanishes or is forgotten mid-film. But, if you were among those first audiences to see *Psycho* and not make for the exits after the shower scene, you would've used the third strategy readers rely on for comprehending texts: a combination of both bottom-up and top-down processing. With this strategy, readers use local detail to fine-tune their sense of the big picture, then leverage the big picture's schema to make comprehensible the local details.[5]

We can take away one striking detail from this dust-up among researchers who advocate for each of the three different models of comprehension. Regardless of whether they subscribe to the bottom-up, top-down, or interactive processing – a combination of top-down and bottom-up processing – researchers agree on the centrality of having a sense of a robust schema to make sense of what we read. Even if we can tease out the meaning of individual sentences, if they fail to add up to a coherent paragraph, we're bound to either reread the paragraph or throw up our hands in bewilderment. (Rather like the early audiences who made it to *Psycho* during the film's opening week, before the spoilers got out.) We understand what we read only because we can make sense of the Big Idea governing the local content.[6] So, after listening to me harping on about the importance of clarity and continuity, you now have to constantly remind yourself that coherence is more important than either of the first two Cs. At least I have some consolation for you in this third C. The coherence principles you're about to learn function independently of both clarity and continuity. In other words, you'll never have to choose between observing clarity and continuity on one hand and sacrificing coherence on the other to preserve the first two Cs.

Remember, the primary reading mechanism – prediction – applies to coherence in spades.[7] When you focus on coherence, you're providing readers with the all-important context they need to help them understand what they're reading and what's coming next. And strong coherence also helps your readers to slot what they've just read into what they already know – the familiar–new strategy. In short, if your documents lack coherence, your bosses or editors are likely to return them to you so covered in red that, even with Track Changes on a digital page, you might wonder who's had the serious nosebleed.

How do you write for distracted readers?

Journalists write under what most of us would like to see as a mercifully unique set of conditions. They end up writing for people with wandering attention, who are giving cursory once-overs to news stories while also paying attention to a host of other things, including traffic and maybe the location of the commuter bus they're riding on, not to mention droning colleagues, the blast of music from someone's ringtone, Facebook updates, and Twitter feeds bristling with hashtags. While your readers may grapple with the same distractions, when you sit down to write a proposal or a legal memo, you probably still naively picture your intended audience studying your writing attentively like a student memorizing material for a test. Fat chance. Instead, try picturing your audience sitting elbow-deep in a stack of papers – or, worse, a queue of virtual papers that could fill a modest-sized library – in an office where the phone rings incessantly, reading snippets of your *magnum opus* while fielding requests for signatures on incomprehensible documents and emails from a department head enquiring into their last six expense reports. Unlike a swotting student, your typical readers are unlikely to hang on your every turn of phrase as though they're reading *Ulysses* for their doctoral oral exams.

Journalists compete with all this noise from the outside world by breaking paragraphs frequently to hold readers' attention – an approach that similarly can help most of us hold our audience's attention. But these relatively brief paragraphs also ensure that readers can easily keep track of ideas and relationships between ideas, events, and characters. These relationships are easiest to track when paragraphs each contain only a single focus, topic, or angle on a topic. Conversely, when you pack lots of content into a lengthy paragraph that runs on for several pages, you're practically guaranteeing that your readers will emerge from that paragraph with only the vaguest notion of what you've been writing about. And your readers will probably feel close to punch-drunk, to boot.

Why is brief usually better?

Cast your mind back to Chapter 4, where we focused on why long sentences were so horribly difficult to read and recall. Remember? Long sentences have few opportunities to flag important items for readers, since a long sentence contains the same number of opportunities to emphasize information as a short sentence – one. Furthermore, in long sentences, readers will only recall material in the emphasis position at the end. And, if you're lucky, your readers will recall details from the beginnings of sentences, while their grasp of the relationships between items is likely to be tenuous, at best. If you find yourself unable to recall the continuity principles about emphasis and using more short than long sentences, page back through Chapter 4 and reread them. We'll still be here.

These coherence principles also apply to your readers' abilities to recall content in paragraphs. Coherence principles don't necessarily require you to start fresh paragraphs every three sentences or to ensure that you tackle only simple, easily developed ideas in your paragraphs, things you can safely cover in a handful of sentences. On the other hand, in breaking your paragraphs, you should be attentive to even minute shifts in focus on a topic. For example, while this paragraph still deals with the topic of paragraph length, I've used a new paragraph to accommodate a shift in focus from the preceding paragraph, which dealt with the reasons why long paragraphs are difficult for readers to understand. Both paragraphs still technically cover the same topic – paragraph length – but each paragraph offers a different focus on paragraph length. By using a series of relatively brief paragraphs to chart shifts in focus, as well as shifts in topic, you will help your readers organize the information they're absorbing.

Your readers can perceive your paragraphs as resembling either a stand of woods or a wilderness. Even if you've used continuity principles to mark out a series of clear paths for them, your readers will generally be happier making their way through a small wood instead of a vast, seemingly unbroken wilderness. Shorter paragraphs – like small stands of trees – mean less cognitive overhead for your readers. And frequent changes in focus will also help maintain your readers' interest – no small thing in the age of 140-character microblogging and 3-second sound bites.

Coherence Principle #1:
Begin each paragraph with a set of comprehensive overview sentences, a *paragraph head*

If you suffered through band in middle or high school, you probably know what an overture is – a piece of music that contains snatches of musical themes that are expressed more fully later in an opera or symphony. Think of the paragraph head as your overture, the sentence or series of sentences where you provide your audience with an overview of what you'll cover in detail in the paragraph. An overture helps situate your readers, previewing for them the claims or topic you're about to address. This preview also provides them with a detailed set of expectations, giving your readers the best possible set of blueprints to guide them through even pernickety details, twists of logic, or barrages of statistics that may turn up in the rest of the paragraph. Put simply: your paragraph head promises; your paragraph body delivers – an analogy that functions a bit like the way a successful proposition in a club might.

> **Writing myths you'll wish you never learned:**
> Begin every paragraph with a topic sentence
>
> I once had a graduate student who referred to topic sentences – then required of high-school students on the New York State Regents exam – as the "spawn of hell." She loathed having to teach topic sentences to her students. But she couldn't avoid them because her

students had to write paragraphs using topic sentences to pass their Regents exams and get out of high school. However, she hated them for the same reasons we all have loathed them. Topic sentences are nearly impossible to write.

Why? For starters, unless your paragraph is very brief or barely has two ideas to rub together, you'll need more than a single sentence to provide a comprehensive overview. You'll experience pure torture when you try to shoehorn an introduction to a new topic, as well as an overview of your central ideas or claims, into a single sentence. This feat is also next to impossible. So avoid busting a gut to cram everything into a single sentence, unless you're dealing with a short paragraph on a relatively uncomplicated topic.

The good news about writing a paragraph head rather than a topic sentence: you can stretch your legs a bit. Think blogging rather than tweeting. If you need more than a single sentence to provide a comprehensive overview of your paragraph's content, write two or three. Just ensure you begin each paragraph with the head, where readers expect to see an overview of the paragraph's central point.[8]

Paragraph heads focus readers' attention and help them to track and even recall content effectively for three reasons: (1) by priming readers, (2) by giving them linguistic cues about content that enable readers to generate inferences to make sense of what they're about to read, and (3) by providing explicit indications about the relevant content to follow. Priming, as we saw in spades in Chapter 4, nudges readers to recall content on a second encounter with it. And, as we saw in Chapter 2, readers engage in inference processing to make sense of content. When I. A. Richards deprived his undergraduates of the titles and authors of poems, they foundered, waffled, and generally waxed uncomprehending about what the hell the poem was about. Fancy reading the following scrap of text without knowing its author or the poem's title.

> *Thou still unravish'd bride of quietness,*
> *Thou foster-child of silence and slow time,*
> *Sylvan historian, who canst thus express*
> *A flowery tale more sweetly than our rhyme:*

> *What leaf-fring'd legend haunts about thy shape*
> *Of deities or mortals, or of both,*
>   *In Tempe or the dales of Arcady?*

Who, in God's name, is this *thou*, which the seven lines of description that follow this segment make more, rather than less, puzzling? Think back to reading's three-step dance. We can make sense of the words – sort of. But still *unravish'd bride of quietness* immediately throws down a gauntlet. Is the poet punning with *still* and *quietness* or is *still* telling us that the bride is a *virgo intacta*, *still* hanging onto her hymen? Since we know from the arrangement of the stanzas that we're reading poetry, we're willing to hang fire to some extent on the role each word plays syntactically. But, as the problem with how to interpret *still* reveals, recognizing what role a word plays in a sentence grammatically and what the word means are as inextricably bound together as a virgin is to her hymen.

Even readers who manage to stumble through to the last stanza end up remaining mostly in the dark about the subject the poet addresses, despite these last lines laying things out a bit more concretely than the waves of metaphor that wash over us in the opening stanza:

> *O Attic shape! Fair attitude! with brede*
> *Of marble men and maidens overwrought,*
> *With forest branches and the trodden weed;*
> *Thou, silent form, dost tease us out of thought*
> *As doth eternity: Cold Pastoral!*

The capitalization of *Attic* helps a bit, if we know the adjective refers to something that harkens back to the Athens populated by the likes of Socrates, rather than the box-cluttered space at the top of your house. Yet, even a gifted reader – or one of Richards' undergraduates studying English literature at Cambridge, no less – ends up drowning, not waving, if you were to thrash out the poem's meaning sans title or author. But tell us that we're reading Keats' "Ode on a Grecian Urn," and we read the stanzas as descriptions of a scene arrested for millennia on the side of a Greek vase without feeling as though our brains had just completed an Ironman competition.

While poetry represents challenging territory for interpretation, you can nevertheless see why page editors of the likes of *Vanity Fair* as well as the *Washington Post* have long held dear the importance of a good headline – juicy or not. Consider the quandary of your average reader of the *New York Post*, the newspaper even New Yorkers love to scorn. The paper will, of course, convey details of everything from the latest grisly crime committed in the city's five boroughs to a heart-warming feature on cops in Chinatown receiving sensitivity training, to the triumphs of a pint-sized chess champion. Readers need to determine which stories they read closely, which, they skim, which, they will skip without more than a glance. In these millisecond-long bouts of decision-making, headlines equip them with vital cues about the potential value each column contains. Moreover, the pages themselves strategically segregate stories: big stories on the front page, local news tucked inside, features relegated to pages in the center of the paper. Your digital edition of the typical newspaper appears, at a glance, infinitely more democratic. Rather than relegating local features to the unread ghetto of pages buried far inside, the digital edition, instead, can put an abbreviated table of contents for the entire paper on a single page. But even this democratized, flatter playing field privileges only the stories editors judge likeliest to gain a wide readership. Buried, mostly unread, beneath those leading stories lie the stories that formerly languished mostly unread in the paper edition.

Furthermore, the vast quantity of news contained in national newspapers sprawls across areas of interest, as well as nomenclatures specific to politics, real estate, finance, and the arts. Here, too, headlines provide invaluable guides through what would otherwise seem a wilderness of sometimes enigmatic details. If the average newsreader were to consume the entirety of the behemoth that is the *New York Times* Sunday edition, a paper a British friend once mistook for an old-fashioned phone book, he or she would encounter everything from quantitative analyses of market fluctuations on Wall Street to speculation on how a Roseate Spoonbill turned up in Staten Island. A headline tells readers at a glance (a) whether they even want to read the story beneath it and (b) what to expect from the story. The headline performs some of the heavy lifting of inference building. At the same time, headlines clearly delineate the scope of the story to follow, particularly headlines for what journalists refer to as *hard* news stories, pieces that convey developments to the audience in terms of proximity, personal relevance, and the importance of the characters involved.[9] In fact, news stories have three components that give readers a leg-up in inference building: a headline, a lead, and what journalist call the *nut graph*. The lead, or *lede* as the *New York Times* likes to spell it, is the short, ostensibly compelling hook that snags readers' interest. In contrast, the nut graph is a telegraphic, one- or two-sentence representation of the story's gist, the journalist's equivalent of a thesis sentence. Together, the headline, lead, and nut graph summarize the content of the text and provide readers with a sense of its scope.[10]

Can skimming be smart reading?

Despite everything your teachers told you, sometimes faster *is* better. In one study, readers skimmed a text at 500–700 words per minute, compared to the less brisk pace of close reading at approximately 225 words per minute. Although this study emphasized longer texts of 3000 words, making recall more challenging, subjects who skimmed the sample answered general questions as accurately as readers who read every word. In addition, eye-tracking devices established that skimmers spent longer periods – albeit milliseconds – looking at sentences and lines containing important information, skipping some words and phrases entirely. Skimmers used early lines in paragraphs and texts to grasp the structure of what they were about to read, enabling them to read more efficiently, including skipping entire lines.[11]

Can you use more than one sentence in a paragraph head?

Depending on the complexity of your paragraph, you can use one, two, or three sentences in your paragraph head. Just remember to keep your paragraph head to less than a third of your paragraph's length. In that study you just read, above, about skimming readers, researchers discovered that skimmers (in the reading, not hand-in-the-till sense) distributed their focus more intensively on the beginnings of paragraphs. This fleeting bit of scrutiny might stem from our conventional expectations that the openings of paragraphs tell us to expect a paragraph on skyrocketing property values will focus on prices per square foot and increased market demand, rather than, say, the grazing habits of gnus.

In studies of readers in both primary and higher education, readers expertly identified anomalous sentences quickly and accurately when paragraphs began with one or more overview sentences.[12] In most paragraphs, your paragraph head will occupy from one to three sentences. As long as these sentences appear at the outset of the paragraph, readers will have no difficulty in identifying more than one sentence as the paragraph overview.[13] Generally, you'll need a sentence to introduce your readers to your topic or shift in focus. Then you might need a second sentence to sketch out your claims. If your paragraph is complicated and long, you might even need a third sentence to lay out your claims and their limitations. In studies examining the effects of topic sentences, researchers identified the opening sentence of paragraphs as holding a privileged position for readers, indicated by the speed with which they used the opening sentence to identify the paragraph's topic. The takeaway from the opening sentence as the paragraph's most memorable: the farther your paragraph head stretches from the outset of the paragraph, the less likely your readers' recognition of the subsequent sentences as announcing the paragraph's topic.[14] As a result, your head should occupy only a third of the total length of your paragraph.

Studies, using eye-tracking devices, of readers' focus on the introductory snippets of web pages discovered similar eye fixations on the opening sentences of web pages. However, with a single overview sentence, readers performed far better than they did with multiple overview sentences. The greater the number of overview sentences – paragraph head sentences, for our purposes – the more time readers' eyes lingered over them, and the poorer their recall.[15]

As you read the following paragraphs, one written by a graduate student, pay attention to how long you keep reading before you latch onto its central point:

Example A:

For the large competitors such as PricewaterhouseCoopers, Deloitte, and the others, their biggest strength is their name and the resources available to them. These companies are able to enter almost any market and to provide employees with a particular expertise in the client's subject matter. The major weakness, however, exists in these companies' overhead and the lack of specialization in a particular area. With resources spread all over the country and world these companies can find costly and time-consuming the effort of bringing the right employees together. This location issue and high overhead costs translate into high billing rates. These high billing rates of the "Big Four" consulting firms are heavily watched by the senior executives in our client's firm. As a result, we find it often difficult, even impossible, to sign long-term contracts with our clients because we are one of the "Big Four" and such an engagement would set off red flags with the senior executives. Our smaller competitors have realized these weaknesses and have designed business models to get around many of the issues faced by the largest competitors in the industry.

Example B:

The size and reputation of the "Big Four" accounting agencies can actually work against them where clients are concerned. With resources scattered nation- and world-wide, Big Four agencies often expend substantial costs merely bringing the right employees together. Unfortunately, these location and overhead costs translate into high billing rates. As a result of these costly rates, many clients seek out smaller firms, since senior executives would view contracting with PricewaterhouseCoopers, Deloitte, and others as needlessly costly. On the other hand, our smaller competitors have realized these weaknesses and designed business models to take advantage of them.

Note Example A's problem with coherence. By the time readers have ventured as far as the third sentence, they're through with lifting vines and checking their compasses to determine the direction of the trail through the jungle ahead. Readers expect that you've set them on a fairly straight path through the territory ahead. Instead, in Example A, the writer probably uses the first two lengthy sentences to segue from the preceding paragraph and only introduces the actual focus of the paragraph in the third sentence. By this point, even the most stalwart of readers will have abandoned all searches for the paragraph's topic and will stagger forward, armed with a thoroughly lousy map of a paragraph that dwells on the strengths of large US-based accounting consultancies. Unfortunately, the paragraph actually focuses on the potential liabilities of these behemoth consultancies. Net result: your reader trudges back through this paragraph, but likely only if he or she is the writer's workplace inferior. If the writer is a bottom-feeder in her organization's food-chain, she would likely have ended up looking for another job after cranking out forty or fifty paragraphs like these. In contrast, in Example B, the paragraph head primes readers to batten onto the paradoxical proposition that bigger is not invariably better – a paradox that might have been slightly modified by the 2008 "Too Big to Fail" US financial debacle. By the end of that single sentence, readers will identify every sentence that follows it, on locations, on overhead, and on the resulting competitiveness of smaller firms, as clearly supporting that paragraph head.

The upshot: if your paragraph head is longer than a third of your paragraph's length, your readers might be confused about where your paragraph head ends and its body begins. Readers tend to recall content at the beginnings of things relatively well. As a result, front-loading your information ensures your readers will actually recall your paragraph head even once they're hip-deep in statistics or examples. But when you make your head longer than several sentences, you almost inevitably end up placing your most important sentence – the one that lays out your important claims – in the middle of the paragraph. And the middles of anything are veritable Dead Zones in terms of your readers' ability to recall content. These Dead Zones include sentences, paragraphs, and entire documents, as you'll recall from Chapter 4.

In most cases, you can preview for your readers the contents of even fairly lengthy, complex paragraphs in only a sentence or two. As with paragraph length, remember that shorter is better. If you end up sketching out a paragraph head that seems even to you to be horribly complex and hopelessly lengthy, try dividing the paragraph into two, separating the contents according to slight shifts in focus or topic. Your readers will unconsciously thank you for it. Or at least they'll emerge from reading your documents without feeling as if they need a whacking good dose of Ritalin and a couple of hours of rereading to grasp what you were probably saying.

Spot the difference

Still skeptical about the utility of a paragraph head (or, if you're stubbornly Old School, the topic sentence)? Compare the ease with which you read the following two paragraphs. Example A comes from the first paragraph of an undergraduate's research paper on Irish emigration. Specifically, his manuscript focused on the role played by Irish emigrants who departed for Europe, aiming to enlist assistance in freeing Ireland from English rule – and on their descendants' political influence and widespread cultural legacy throughout Europe. Example B represents part of a graduate student's feasibility analysis of a business plan, written for an audience of potential investors who are mulling over the prospects of a small company that proposes to offer training to company employees on common software applications.

Example A:

<u>Throughout Irish history, countless generations of exiles have cast off from the shores of Ireland in search of sanctuary, adventure and alliances. After the signing of the Treaty of Limerick in 1691, the "Flight of the Wild Geese" marked the watershed moment of Irish migration to the European Continent.</u> Nineteen thousand Catholic Irishmen and their families sailed to France in the hope of one day returning to free Ireland from English tyranny. For the next hundred years ships arriving on the west coast of Ireland would depart with Irish recruits listed in ships' manifests as "Wild Geese" for the armies of Europe. Using this label to escape detection by English authorities, these Wild Geese would serve in armies across the Continent, including Napoleon's. Ultimately, these Irish soldiers and their descendants would fan out across Europe and eventually influence power, politics, and business throughout the Continent well into the twentieth century.

Example B:

The "hands-on" approach with personal instruction certainly appeals to the typical student. Although labeled as innovative, the approach outlined by Mr. Hutton details no new techniques for training that differentiate ITS from competitors. With 15 students anticipated per class, Mr. Hutton's ability to provide individual attention to a particular student will be constrained. Also, the business plan fails to make clear the range of services ITS will provide. Furthermore, small businesses may be unwilling to invest in training for standard software applications, like the programs in Microsoft Office, since most entry-level jobs now require these skills of would-be employees.

In Example A, the underlined paragraph head announces the paragraph's main topic. The paragraph head, with its focus on Irish emigration, swiftly zeroes in on a particular wave of emigrants, listed as "Wild Geese" on ship manifests. The paragraph body then delivers on only the promise of the head sentences, fleshing out the roles, destinations, and influence of the Wild Geese. Note, also, that the paragraph culminates in a sentence that serves as the paragraph's conclusion and also serves as the thesis sentence for his entire manuscript – both features explored later in this chapter. In this paragraph, the writer has expertly escorted readers through material that supports a nuanced and relatively complex point, rather than leaving readers the difficult task of determining what on earth the paragraph is about and how its content contributes to the writer's overall argument.

In contrast, however, Example B has no unifying statement in the paragraph head. Instead, the opening sentence simply represents a place to begin the paragraph. As a result, the paragraph covers five different points:

1. the business has an innovative, personal approach to delivering instruction on computer applications to students;
2. the approach is not as innovative as its instructors would like investors to believe;
3. the instructor-owner will have only a limited ability to provide hands-on, one-on-one training to classes of fifteen students or more;

4. the business plan omits any mention of precisely what kind of training ITS will cover;

5. many businesses require employees to have basic knowledge of common applications, potentially nixing ITS' attractiveness to employers.

EXPERT TIP: Organized paragraphs

Fortunately, we have an easy solution to avoiding sounding like the writer in Example B. You can address this difficulty of both marshaling your main points and writing them down in an order that makes sense to your readers by using four strategies.

1. Try sketching out your points for your paragraphs on a scrap of paper before you begin writing each one.
2. Write a brief sentence or two that cover the contents of those points.
3. Work on your paragraph heads in even informal modes of writing, like email.
4. Focus on identifying paragraph heads whenever you read any form of published writing.

These strategies will also help you write tightly constructed, well-organized paragraphs, no matter how difficult your topic or complicated your points.

Creating a good paragraph head

If you write, think eternally of the mantra, "Prediction is the engine that enables comprehension." Just as we saw the power of prediction in all matters concerning clarity and continuity, prediction is likewise a heavy-hitter in coherence. The more specific the details you give readers in your paragraph head, the faster their reading and better their recall of the details to follow.[16] So you should avoid saying *This business plan has particular promise, if the management team addresses several issues concerning its target market*. Instead, specify the number of reasons why the business plan might not be the equivalent of playing slot machines in Vegas: *This business plan has particular promise, if the management team addresses four issues concerning its target market*. Your readers can now track the issues, via helpful transitions like *First...Second...Third...Finally*.

Caveat: avoid looking ahead to future paragraphs

A good paragraph head, like a soundly constructed paragraph, focuses on a single topic and only on the content of the immediate paragraph. Why? Your readers' working memory is less like a bottomless pit than it is a shoe-box – our working memories can only hold a limited number of propositions at one time. Stuff more than a single pair of shoes into any shoe-box, and the lid comes off, then the shoes tumble out, a reasonably apt analogy for your readers' brains when you introduce three propositions crammed into a single paragraph.[17] In addition, remember that your paragraph head primes readers for the content to follow and also provides a structure for your readers to hang their inferences on as they work out your paragraph's meaning. If you mention content that crops up in another paragraph, readers may believe they've missed something in the paragraph body.[18] As a result, they'll reread the paragraph head and puzzle anew over the paragraph content. Researchers performed this particular trick in experiments on hapless undergraduates, in which researchers deliberately mismatched introductory sentences and the content that followed them. As a result, students' reading times increased significantly.[19]

In short, think of writing a paragraph head as akin to driving. You're forever looking approximately one to three cars ahead of you, not constructing models of what the traffic and road will look like in a half-mile. At least not if you want to avoid mowing down a few pedestrians and skateboarders in your immediate vicinity.

Coherence Principle #2:
Support each paragraph's head with a body

As in anatomy, the body supports the head – and also occupies a lot more space than the head. Your paragraph body should be about three times the length of its head and flesh out the concepts or claims introduced in the head sentences. Your paragraph body should also use examples, well-established facts, analogies, statistics, quotations, and other forms of evidence to make credible the statements you've trotted out in your paragraph head.

Again, remember, you're not writing for the harried readers of *USA Today* who prefer their paragraphs bite-sized and flattened to a single concept. Even if you're writing a blog post, your readers need a bit of detail to believe the claim you've just made in the paragraph head. The paragraph body not only substantiates the claim rolled out in the head, the body also lends you a bit of credibility by providing a sense that you've done your homework and can shore up your main contention with evidence.

For all the wealth of research on priming and primacy effects from paragraph heads, research on the body itself is surprisingly thin. In addition, researchers have traditionally focused more on the ways arguments unfold within paragraphs, specific to different kinds of arguments, rather than on the number of sentences necessary to redress readers' ignorance or skepticism about the content in the paragraph head.[20] Nevertheless, researchers have determined that, as readers work their way through paragraphs, their speed increases when the sentences fulfill expectations established in the paragraph's opening sentences.[21]

Writing myths you'll wish you never learned:
Point-last paragraphs

If you never learned this particular approach to turning out paragraphs, feel free to skip ahead. However, stop right here if you read Joseph Williams' mostly useful *Style: Toward Clarity and Grace.* Williams was a pioneer in exploring the components of clear writing and in debunking myths about grammar and usage. But he also provided his readers with some terrible advice on what he called "point-last" structure in paragraph bodies or "discussions" to use Williams' parlance.[22] In point-last paragraphs, writers put readers through a Lewis-and-Clark sort of expedition into the meaning of the paragraph, so that we discover the paragraph's topic the way the explorers stumbled across the Continental Divide, except your readers lack the assistance of Sacagawea as a trusty guide. Unfortunately, when you oblige readers to replicate your own process of thinking about the topic, you cast them completely adrift, without the cues that enable them to build sturdy inferences.[23]

Remember, most of us write to facilitate rapid and easy understanding of complex topics, not to earn a Nobel in literature, a Pulitzer on feature writing, or an award for arty non-fiction. A paragraph trots out a claim, then shores it up. You're also not writing an episode of *Murder, She Wrote*, where, by telling your readers up front what to expect, you completely kill both the suspense and one's reason for watching the bloody episode. Writing for entertainment: suspense, good. Writing a murder mystery: suspense, absolutely *de rigueur*. Writing a prospectus, a cover letter for a new job, or a letter of resignation: suspense, positively bloody deadly.

Now, imagine the poor sods struggling through a paragraph in the *London Review of Books* in October 2001, in a short commentary by one of the myriad of commentators writing on the events of September 11th:

> *Historical events, however, are not punctual, but extend in a before and after of time which only gradually reveal themselves. It has, to be sure, been pointed out that the Americans created bin Laden during the Cold War … and that this is therefore a textbook example of dialectical reversal. But the seeds of the event are buried deeper than that. They are to be found in the wholesale massacres of the Left systematically encouraged and directed by the Americans in an even earlier period. The physical extermination of the Iraqi and the Indonesian Communist Parties … were crimes as abominable as any contemporary genocide. It is, however, only now that the results are working their way out into actuality, for the resultant absence of any Left alternative means that popular revolt and resistance in the Third World have nowhere to go but into religious and "fundamentalist" forms.*[24]

Floundering a bit, after reading that paragraph? Or, if you're honest, at what point did you bail on the paragraph entirely? Or, for the more anally retentive among us, how many times did you reread the sample? If you fall into the last category, you only stuck with the paragraph out of diligence, masochistic tendencies, or willingness to believe that the paragraph will eventually make sense if you only keep on reading. Nevertheless, the likelihood is close to nil that you got much sense from the paragraph, which unfortunately is no easier to read if you got the whole shebang. All four paragraphs of it.

What's wrong with this paragraph, aside from every sentence violating nearly all the clarity principles we've already explored? First, the paragraph head contains a *however* that immediately cues readers that the content to follow is about to refute the content of the preceding paragraph. But the preceding paragraph (not excerpted here) mentions neither history, nor historical events. Instead, the earlier paragraph focuses on media reports of American flag-flying in the days following the terrorist attacks in New York and Washington, DC on September 11, 2001. In addition, the likeliest culprit for the paragraph's actual topic is buried in mid-paragraph:

> *But the seeds of the event are buried deeper than that.*
> *They are to be found in the wholesale massacres of the Left*
> *systematically encouraged and directed by the Americans in*
> *an even earlier period.*

The paragraph has three problems tied directly to this paragraph head. First, the topic of the paragraph, the one that should have cued readers about the content at the outset, occurs several sentences after readers traditionally expect the writer to have clearly stated the paragraph's topic. Second, the paragraph shifts its head from the beginning to the dead zone that falls between primacy and recency effects and thus tends to have the weakest recall by readers.[25] In fact, priming effects apply even to novel material, rather than the already familiar material used in the design of many experiments on memory and recall.[26] If you're an attorney, you should thank the human brain for having a dead zone that enables you to bury in the middle of a lengthy set of conditions a particularly nasty disclosure guaranteed to freak your readers out – like the fact that a passenger runs a slender risk of being decapitated while on a world cruise for which they've forked out over tens of thousands of dollars. But the rest of us should view that paragraph's dead zone as strictly the spot to shore up the propositions in the paragraph head. Third and finally, the sheer number of propositions crammed into the excerpted sentence can make the reader feel punch-drunk, especially without the handy continuity devices we explored in Chapter 4 that keep each sentence tightly bound to both the preceding one and to the paragraph's overall theme. With each shift in topic, readers struggle increasingly hard to keep track of the paragraph's trajectory[27] at the same time the shifts in topic run bang up against the limits of even skilled readers' working memories.[28]

Writing myths you'll wish you never learned:
Keep it short

Remember: you need at least one sentence in your paragraph head to introduce your readers to your new topic and to trot out your main claims. But, since your paragraph body needs to support its head, your paragraph body should be at least two to three times the length of the head. To shore up claims made broadly in your paragraph head, you need to introduce examples, analogies, statistics, quotations, and other forms of evidence. In studies of readers, researchers identified readers' expectations that paragraph bodies provide generalizations or support for the paragraph head.[29] At the barest minimum, that requirement means that you need at least a one-sentence head and two sentences in the body for even the briefest paragraph. Anything shorter than two sentences – in any form of non-fiction writing outside journalism – is more an amputated piece of a paragraph than a full-fledged version.

One final caveat on paragraph bodies

Never introduce a topic in your paragraph body that you haven't mentioned or covered in your paragraph head. The shift in topic – even just a shift in focus on a topic – can confuse the hell out of your readers, who will absorb information most easily if they have a clear set of expectations for the paragraph. The paragraph's opening sentence or sentences provide readers with a schema for understanding the paragraph. As a consequence, if you miscue readers about content, their reading speed declines and their recall of content gets fuzzy. One particular study about prediction and reading makes me long for the 1960s, when employees chain-smoked in their offices and drank Scotch midday. In that memorable study, Bell Labs paid secretaries who knew nothing about chess to read about the game and earn the princely sum of $7.50 if they correctly recalled the moves associated with each chess piece. In 1969, that $7.50 would've probably bought the secretaries – then predictably a veritable redoubt of estrogen – at least a tank of gas. When the paragraphs used the opening sentences to cue readers about the characteristics of each chess piece, the secretaries displayed significantly better recall about bishops and knights. In contrast, when the paragraphs contained no paragraph head to prime readers about the content to follow, secretaries' recall was poorer. And, when a single paragraph contained sentences that jumped from details about pawns to knights to bishops, secretaries performed still more poorly in recalling the characteristics and moves for each chess piece. We can guess this last group of secretaries failed to take home an extra $7.50 that week.[30]

If you have reread one of your own paragraphs and discover that even you find its information difficult to absorb, carefully check the contents of the paragraph body. You've probably introduced a shift in topic or a change in focus that ranges outside the scope of your paragraph head. If you can locate a place where you can easily spot the shift in focus, break the paragraph at that sentence. And, if necessary, craft a new paragraph head to clearly anticipate the full scope of the new paragraph. Just remember not to cut the paragraph off at the knees – or the paragraph head, a bad practice with people, equally deadly for paragraphs.

Coherence Principle #3:
Documents need heads and bodies. Apply paragraph head and body organization to your entire document

You should organize any document the way you would handle a paragraph. Like paragraphs, documents need heads and bodies to aid readers in inference building. Without a suggestion of the main point(s) your document makes, readers spend more time straining to figure out the macrostructure or overall argument contained in the document. At a result, readers fail to grasp what they're reading, because their brains are busily shunting cognitive resources to figuring out what they're reading.[31]

For your entire document, document heads are introductions to the overall content. These document heads may occupy one or more paragraphs. Exactly as with paragraph heads, document head paragraphs front-load your important information, informing readers what they can expect in the paragraphs to follow. In addition, these front-loading paragraphs also provide your readers with a blueprint that helps them in making predictions as they read. And the better informed your readers' predictions, the easier the reading process and the better your readers' grasp and recall of your content in your text.

Unlike an abstract, a document head simply cues your audience of the overall scope of your proposal, article, or report. For example, the document head for a research article tells readers why the topic is important and worthy of research, prevailing wisdom on the topic, and how your research will redress gaps in prior research. In contrast, a document head for a feasibility analysis of a business plan introduces would-be investors to the business' product or service, its target market, potential competitors, and how the business will (or won't) prove profitable. In a second or third paragraph of a feasibility report, writers should explicitly tell readers whether they recommend funding the business or whether investors should steer clear. Remember, your would-be investor is hardly expecting *Murder, She Wrote* and thinking your recommendation will be a lovely surprise…at the end of the analysis. Instead, investors want to know soon after discovering the basics about the business whether you recommend funding it or not. When readers lack cues about the central hypothesis or conclusion of your document, they also lack the knowledge of which details they should recall or even how to interpret the content they're about to read.

Like your paragraph head, your document head should occupy several paragraphs for longer documents, perhaps only a single paragraph for shorter texts under three pages. Longer documents like proposals or research papers might have document head paragraphs that occupy as many as three pages. However, unlike the paragraph head, the length of your document head doesn't have to take up about a third of the document's total length. Instead, you should focus most intently on covering the full scope of the content of your document in the document head paragraphs.

Document heads should have three components. First, use a series of sentences introducing your readers to your topic, employing the same wording you'll rely on in the document overall. Second, your document head should contain specifics about what your document will cover: the most central points you make in the paragraphs to follow. And, third, contrary to everything you've heard about not repeating yourself when you write, repetition actually *benefits* your reader. When we encounter familiar words, particularly ones we've recently encountered in the same document, we read more rapidly. In addition, during reading, we also dedicate most of our working memory for recalling the concepts we've just read.[32]

Avoid Big Bang Beginnings

Like many writers, you're probably tempted to begin with the history of what you're writing about, an extensive rationale for the action you're advocating, or a narrative of how you got where you are. However, as far as your readers are concerned, you're beginning with the Big Bang, crawling through the Cambrian through the Pleistocene and gradually working your way to the beginning of human history, before *finally* getting to your topic. The entire time they're reading, your readers are either thinking "For God's sake, get on with it" or "What on earth am I reading?" And these scenarios are the positive ones. In the worst-case scenario, your readers simply bail, your document going almost entirely unread.

The takeaway: skip the backstory. Your readers seldom want to hear a history, rationale, or narrative until they already know the scope and purpose of your document.

Coherence Principle #4:
Place your thesis at the end of the head paragraph(s)

At last! You probably thought you'd never reach a familiar term, something you could recognize from earlier writing instruction. In this particular instance, your secondary school teachers who once ranted about the importance of a thesis were absolutely on the money. Your thesis *is* the single most important sentence in your entire document.

Here, again, you don't need to take either my word or that of the martinet who gave gimlet-eyed scrutiny to your papers, bent mostly on pinpointing your thesis (or lack thereof). A thesis exerts a strong priming effect, just like paragraph heads. Moreover, any piece of writing with an identifiable thesis also speeds reading times and results in better recall than documents that contain none. In one study, readers confronting a news story – which always contains a thesis via its nut graph – read more rapidly and constructed better representations of the story's overall structure than did readers of a literary story, which inevitably omits anything resembling a thesis.[33] We can think of a thesis as a schematic cue that prevents us from glomming onto trivial details and also ensures we don't make wrong inferences about what we're reading.[34] Just as our understanding of a taxi schema stops us from asking the driver to tote our groceries indoors and unpack them, the thesis tells your readers what they can reasonably expect to encounter in a single text. For example, imagine you're reading an article that begins

On a Friday morning in April, I strapped on a headset, leaned into a microphone, and experienced what had been described to me as a type of time travel to the future of higher education. I was on the ninth floor of a building in downtown San Francisco, in a neighborhood whose streets are heavily populated with winos and vagrants, and whose buildings host hip new businesses, many of them tech start-ups. In a small room, I was flanked by a publicist and a tech manager from an educational venture called the Minerva Project, whose founder and CEO, the 39-year-old entrepreneur Ben Nelson, aims to replace (or, when he is feeling less aggressive, "reform") the modern liberal-arts college.[35]

One paragraph into an article with an inviting beginning (*On a Friday morning in April…*), and we already know the article's central focus: a tech company focused on delivering education entirely online. As we read on, we're not looking for an AA meeting in a church basement that will wean winos off the sauce or a journalist's foray into virtual reality via a headset and microphone. Instead, the last sentence cues us to the entire article's focus, directing our attention and memories to the Minerva Project's aim to put higher education entirely online.

Note how the placement of the thesis in the final sentence of the opening paragraph enables us to easily and quickly identify it, even a thesis as colorful and descriptive as the one in this *Atlantic* article. In studies spread across a variety of disciplines, from linguistics to educational psychology, researchers have linked the strategic placement of a topic overview sentence to rapid reading, better recall, and a distinct sense of a document being well organized. In one study, native speakers of English markedly preferred texts with an easily identifiable thesis statement early in the content.[36] Still other studies document the impact of a thesis sentence in helping readers to identify and recall relevant material, boosting reading speed.[37] Most strikingly, in one study of nearly 1000 student essays, two judges scoring for overall discourse coherence had a mind-blowing 100 percent agreement in identifying each essay's thesis and impact on the essay's coherence.[38] If the words *mind-blowing* and *student essays* don't seem remotely related, consider the infamous 1961 study involving 300 papers and fifty-three readers, drawn from six different fields. When the furious scribbling of scores ceased, 90 percent of the student papers received seven different scores on a mere nine-point scale. One shudders to think what scores the papers would have received had the scoring scale run to even ten, let alone 100, points.[39] With its long and vexed history, the issue of scoring student essays and what researchers call inter-rater reliability has few instances of 100 percent agreement on anything, including probably the color of the walls of the rooms in which the readers scrawled their scores or the direction in which the sun rises. The agreement on the location and centrality of a thesis to an essay's coherence is, as I said, either mind-blowing or a testament to the power of thesis sentences to prime and frame reader expectations – or both.

Now, why place the thesis sentence at the end of the document head paragraph or paragraphs? Admittedly, reader expectations on what they'll find and where they'll find it play a role in the utility of thesis sentences.[40] However, the end of any paragraph also receives a bump in recall from the recency effect. The recency effect extends over the ends of lists, sentences, and, most importantly for our concerns here, paragraphs and documents.[41] By putting your thesis sentence at the end of a series of introductory paragraphs, you ensure the thesis receives greater memorability than the sentences around it, making it stand out and also act as your readers' guide to the thickets of details that lie ahead.

The skinny on thesis sentences

For those of you skimming this chapter for the meaty bits of advice you can use on that proposal you've put off writing until the night before it's due, look no further. Your thesis is a one-sentence summary of what your document covers. If your document is a proposal, your thesis should summarize what you aim to do and what benefits your readers might enjoy if they green-light your proposal. If your document is a report or an analysis, your thesis should state your chief findings or your recommendations for action. If your document is an argument, your thesis should state your anticipated conclusion. (Incidentally, if you are uncertain about your conclusion when you start writing your thesis, you're in big troubs and should go back to brainstorming and outlining your ideas before you proceed.)

Make your thesis your clearest sentence

Your thesis must be your clearest sentence. If your readers misread or misunderstand your thesis sentence, you've set them up for difficulties in understanding the contents of the paragraphs to follow. The weight of your entire document rests on your thesis, so take time writing and rewriting it.

EXPERT TIP: Use a preliminary thesis

Face it, your readers aren't seven-year-olds stumbling through *See Ginger claw. Claw, Ginger, claw.* sentences. You might be writing about monoclonal antibodies or antitrust law for people who've never been within shouting distance of a science laboratory or college of law. But you're still writing for people who're bloody good at reading. Consequently, you're addressing readers who expect to learn something from what you've created and are as expert at extracting information from your paragraphs as seasoned miners working a seam underground. Your readers rely on signals they expect to see in the text. The more signals you provide, the faster and more efficient their reading.[42]

So what happens when you need to introduce something complex and to also engage in all sorts of hand-waving about the importance of your topic? In the sciences, law, and finance, writers need to elbow their intended audience in the ribs: "Pay attention!" This nudge about the growing number of people with diabetes worldwide or the compatibility of doing good and making money can run to several paragraphs. Meanwhile, your readers' brains are busily scanning for the important stuff, while they might consciously think "Where's the bloody point?" If we think back to the top-down and interactive models of reading, your readers might well fail to register all your points about the importance of what you're about to tell them. To stave off this possibility, you need to get to the point before you get to the point, in a manner of speaking. In other words, we need a ballpark sense of where you're going to take us before you get to the thesis three paragraphs into the thing. And the title of your article or proposal or manuscript ain't going to cut it. For starters, titles of things tend to be relatively brief and most likely strike at the central ground between your overall focus and the specific point you're going to make.

Instead, in these situations, you should create a *preliminary thesis*, a sentence that informs readers of the main topic of your document. The preliminary thesis belongs in the last sentence of the first paragraph of your document head paragraph, where it receives emphasis from the recency effect, contributing to its memorability and the attention readers will give it.[43] When you use a preliminary thesis sentence, you're preventing your readers from scratching their heads, wondering what your article or proposal is about as they try to take in the details you're giving. Your preliminary thesis provides readers with a temporary bit of scaffolding they can use for handling information and storing it in working memory before they reach the thesis sentence.

Coherence Principle #5:
End complex paragraphs with a conclusion sentence.
And end complex documents with a conclusion paragraph

Ideally, you want readers to perceive your writing as tightly organized – the equivalent of those Inca-built stone walls so well put together that, even today, no one can slide a knife-blade between the massive stones. To achieve this effect, you might want to introduce conclusion sentences to some of your more complex paragraphs. Your conclusion sentence serves as the foot to your paragraph's head and body. Conclusion sentences tell your readers exactly what they should take away from the paragraph they've just read.

In a paragraph conclusion sentence, recency can even trump primacy or help readers sift through complex details to arrive at a conclusion, as researchers discovered when they sought merely to assess the influence of descriptions of a character's behavior on students' perceptions of character. Readers who encountered an assessment about a fictitious man, Jim, and his personality traits after they read about his behavior, made more accurate predictions about Jim's behavior than readers who encountered an assessment of Jim's character first, then his specific behavior later. Contrary to what we might think about the potency of primacy effects, recency can trump primacy, particularly when a thesis or conclusion is involved. Occasionally, even when researchers are looking at social behavior, they're telling us something valuable about reading – with distinctly useful applications for writing.[44]

Think of conclusion or paragraph conclusion sentences as providing readers with an explicit, one-sentence summary of your paragraph's takeaways. In addition, because conclusion sentences occupy the emphasis positions of paragraphs, your readers will remember them longer and better than they do other sentences from the same paragraph. Moreover, conclusion sentences can help your readers transition from one paragraph to another seamlessly.

Like conclusion sentences, document conclusion paragraphs help readers by doing a bit of their work for them. Document conclusion paragraphs flag important findings and conclusions from your document, singling out the central details you want your readers to recall. In addition, by conforming to readers' expectations about document structure, these conclusion paragraphs help readers group the important information you've provided in a single or series of coherent chunks they can easily recall.[45] And, because the conclusion paragraphs are the very last things anyone reads in your text, your readers will remember them better than any other paragraphs in your document, courtesy of the recency effect on memorability.

> ### Writing myths you'll wish you'd never learned:
> #### Repetition is always a bad thing
>
> I can hear you thinking "But isn't this head–body–conclusion structure committing that fatal sin of repetition my teachers always warned me about?" Actually, repeating yourself has its moments, in spite of everything you've heard. When students confronted complex explanations or presentations in one experiment, researchers discovered students demonstrated more accurate recall of information when they encountered it more than once.[46] This recall was especially strong when readers encountered data represented graphically that reinforced information presented in a text, potentially due to our brains having separate systems for perceiving and comprehending visual and verbal information.[47]

EXPERT TIP: Headings and subheadings are your readers' life rafts
Remember, your readers aren't poring over your document for pleasure. Nor are they reading every word in the way they might study for a test. Instead, they're looking to extract information as efficiently as possible.[48] Expert readers, as we've seen earlier in this chapter, rely on markers that enable them to understand both the gist of the text and the information they seek. Imagine your readers stumbling around in your document as haplessly as I. A. Richards' undergraduates floundered when the authors' names and titles were ripped from their poetry. Then help them out with headings and subheadings that cue them to content they're about to read. Headings and subheadings prime and fine-tune our expectations about what lies ahead, resulting in better comprehension.[49]

Takeaways for coherence: what you need to remember to make your paragraphs and documents tightly organized

- Check that your paragraph heads provide a comprehensive overview of the paragraph body.
- Make sure your paragraph heads occupy only a third of the length of the paragraph.
- Ensure your paragraph bodies only contain information referred to in the paragraph head.
- Use document head paragraphs to introduce readers to your topic, its significance, and relevance for your readers.
- Place your thesis sentence in the last sentence of the last paragraph of your document head.
- If your paper has multiple head paragraphs, insert a preliminary thesis at the end of the first paragraph.
- End complex paragraphs with a conclusion sentence that summarizes the paragraph's highlights or importance.
- End complex documents with a conclusion paragraph that stresses your paper's conclusions, as well as their significance or relevance to your readers.

Maximizing efficiency
The fourth C: Concision

> PRESIDENT: Well, you had quite a day, today, didn't you? You got, uh, Watergate, uh on the way, huh?
>
> HALDEMAN: How did it all end up?
>
> DEAN: Uh, I think we can say "Well" at this point. The, uh, the press is playing it just as we expect.
>
> HALDEMAN: Whitewash?
>
> DEAN: No, not yet; the, the story right now –
>
> PRESIDENT: It's a big story.
>
> DEAN: Yeah.
>
> PRESIDENT: (Unintelligible)
>
> HALDEMAN: Five indicted,
>
> DEAN: Plus,
>
> HALDEMAN: Just so they have the fact that one of –
>
> DEAN: plus two White House aides.
>
> HALDEMAN: Plus, plus the White House former guy and all that. That's good. That, that takes the edge off whitewash, really – which – which was the thing Mitchell kept saying that...
>
> PRESIDENT: Yeah.[1]

In 1974, the *Chicago Tribune* published a forty-four-page excerpt of taped Oval Office conversations, unedited and never intended for public consumption. The meeting, held September 15, 1972, followed on the heels of the press airing a link between the Nixon Administration and five men arrested during a break-in at Democratic Party headquarters, which they clearly intended to bug.[2] At the time, the American public found Nixon's vocabulary shockingly rich in the four-letter words some media outlets still touchingly bleep out as if protecting our tender ears from corruption. But this snippet of business-as-usual conversation in the White House might also seem remarkable for the lack of real information traded between an American president, his Chief of Staff, and the White House Counsel.

However, if you think Nixon and his two aides have banality cornered, you might want to turn a microphone on your own conversation and assess how much information and how much noise get exchanged. Answer: you might sound more like Nixon than like Lincoln on the stump or Churchill addressing the House of Commons in the thick of the Battle of Britain. Verbal conversations tend to rely heavily on shared understandings and on the presence of someone who can grunt in acknowledgment, nod, wince, smile, or ask us what we're talking about. Speech can be vague, elliptical, and maddeningly redundant. No matter how badly you might yearn to fast-forward through your colleague's soliloquy on his plague of in-laws – that five-minute number on endless repeat where you can just hear the semicolons slotting into place – you can't. Still, even the party bore's endless nattering has some tenuous relationship with meaning. When we converse, we assume the words we exchange are informative, relevant, succinct, and also avoid conveying more information than we need to hear.[3]

In contrast, writing lies there on the page, extending your voice beyond your physical reach, beyond the confines of space, even beyond the reach of time. We can read Plato no matter how long he's been dead. And, if we fail to understand exactly what's got him so exercised in *Phaedrus*, we can reread his words until we're satisfied we've made sense of them. We can skim ahead or prospect. More important, we can look back or retrospect, especially when we discover we were wrong in our predictions about where a paragraph was headed.[4] Writing, as Plato had Socrates complain in *Phaedrus*, just keeps saying the same thing, no matter how frequently you return to it.[5] Modern-day jeremiads about how our intelligence or memories are all going straight to hell, courtesy of our ability to look up what's-his-face on imdb.com, should consider the dual ironies of Plato's own miniature jeremiad against the written word. Plato simulated a conversation in *Phaedrus*, as he did in his other dialogues, using the written word to fix his own convictions about the evils of the written word. As the French would say with a Gallic shrug, *La plus ça change...*

Unlike the first three Cs, the fourth C, concision, involves leaving aside neuroscience and psychology in favor of examining the origins of our linguistic hangers-on, those unnecessary words Strunk and White so helpfully tell us to omit without specifying exactly what sorts of words we should be looking to cut. We're taking a detour through linguistics, where hard-headed data from labs meet the study of why people say the things they do, with a side helping of the history and development of English.

If you skipped "An extremely short history of English" on pages 31–32, you might want to read that now. Why? The history of English has implications for practically every sin against efficiency committed in English, the topic that brings us to the heart of concision.

Think you already avoid "unnecessary words"? Think again

Imagine you're an employee of county government, somewhere in the United States in a county I daren't name. Now imagine a two-page, single-spaced memo lands on your desk, one of two dozen memos you have to read every morning. Moreover, the memo begins:

> *During our staff meeting of November 11, I had an opportunity to discuss my personal and professional feelings and thoughts regarding recent events that surround our government. More specifically, the unpleasant experiences we have had as of late with continuing revelations of mismanagement, political patronage and, worse yet, corruption in significant parts of our organization. In the past few weeks, subsequent to*

*extensive media coverage on the pavement/repair contracts
at the Water and Sewer Department, I have been approached
by our Mayor and Commissioners, members of the media
and residents of this community expressing their outrage and
dismay at County government. All, without exception, told me
(as I expressed to you during this meeting) that they are fed
up with the ongoing reports on corruption. Frankly speaking, I
too am fed up not only with these revelations but more so with
our "business as usual" attitude, our perceived inability to
act and the lack of professional and personal concern shown
throughout the years for these issues.*

Chances are, if you didn't reread that first paragraph outright, you'll start skimming the rest of the memo at warp speed. Unfortunately, the rest of the memo reads like the first paragraph, since the memo was written by a writer who should be called the Double Man.

The Double Man seldom says anything in a single word if he can use two – or even, on occasion, three. He also specializes in throat-clearing, sentences that sound as if they're communicating something but instead simply showcase the debris knocking around the writer's head while he figures out what on earth he's going to say. The Double Man is the equivalent of the party bore who bends your ear for hours with the juicy details of his last four meals at McDonald's, the contents of this year's 1040 tax return, and the kind of really great beer he once drank at a restaurant whose name he now can't quite recollect. Like the party bore, the Double Man seldom gets to his point, or, if he reaches it, you can't spot it amid all the debris. The Double Man can also sometimes display a weakness for Big Bang Beginnings. And the Double Man will fit beautifully into most law firms and some of the civil service, where he will spend a career writing sentences so complex, lengthy, and riddled with jargon that you'll have to hire a lawyer yourself to ensure the contract you're about to sign won't end up bankrupting you.

What's double about the Double Man's writing?

Enough about the Double Man. Let's look at what earned him this title:

> _During our staff meeting of November 11, I had an opportunity_
> _to discuss_ my _personal and professional feelings and thoughts_
> regarding recent events _that surround our government._

Every underlined word in the sentence above is unnecessary. For instance, the audience for this memo only recently attended the meeting, so the date is unnecessary. Presumably, since the people receiving the memo were also at the meeting, they also can skip the reprise of the last meeting, especially since the Double Man seems like the kind of guy who would have held forth for a hefty chunk of the meeting, making a reminder of what he said also superfluous.

Furthermore, while the Double Man had the opportunity to do something, readers only care about what he did, not whether he had an opportunity to do something. Think of telling your readers about having an opportunity as the equivalent of the old saw about a tree falling in the forest with no one to hear it. If you did something fairly routine – as with the Double Man holding forth at a meeting – then the opportunity is the equivalent of the tree falling with no one to hear the crash of its contact with the forest floor. Ditto, if you had the opportunity and failed to do anything with it. You should report an opportunity only if you were denied one and pulled off a coup against all odds, capitalized on an extraordinary opportunity, or are in the throes of some scandal and are avidly denying accusations. So a writer should scratch _I had the opportunity to discuss_.

Finally, _that surround our government_ is also superfluous, as well as a bit Big Bangish, since Water and Sewer employees are unlikely to care about what their fellow civil servants are doing over in, say, Tax Collection or Waste Management. If the details involve their department, the Double Man should tell them so. If the details don't, the Double Man should refrain from sending the Water and Sewer employees a memo about the other divisions, period.

In every instance, the Double Man is sinning against written English by producing a memo that might bring to mind a two-pound textbook on legal writing. In addition, he's violating the basic rules for conversation identified by one of the godfathers of the study of speech and communication, Paul Grice. Like the pro that he is, the Double Man trips right over Grice's first two rules on the quantity of communication required to grease the wheels that spin during our conversations:

1. Make your contribution as informative as required to keep the conversation going.
2. Avoiding packing your contribution with more information than is necessary.[6]

Remember, everyone reading the memo was present at the staff meeting the Double Man recounts in the exhaustive detail common to doting parents' descriptions of their kid's Little League game. Everything in those opening lines is a review of an experience for an audience who were at the same meeting. If the Double Man were speaking to you in the flesh, you could at least cut him off for violating Rule #2 and usher him to his point – whatever the hell his point is. But we're reading and miles away from the Double Man. Worse, we're reading a memo with more than a passing resemblance to *Bleak House* without the good prose. Furthermore, the memo lacks paragraph heads or anything with remote kinship to a thesis. In other words, the Double Man has produced a memo that frustrates our every attempt to skim it, at the same time he's produced a masterpiece illustrating every sin against concision. The Double Man is the Hieronymus Bosch of business, painting ''The Seven Deadly Sins'' that handily illustrates every deadly sin against concision in action, as his memo proceeds to its second through fourth paragraphs of a seven-paragraph, two-page memo:

While it is evidently clear that events at this department are not the makings of present management as some would like us to believe, it is also evident that those who throughout the years had oversight responsibilities for these areas failed to act. They are now shedding their responsibility by indulging in hollow rhetoric or pointing the finger in an opposite direction. Let's not fall in this trap. Our job as professional public administrators is to stay above this fray and stay the course by continuing to work through these difficult times in a professional manner.

That is what our community and our elected officials expect of us. That is what we must expect of ourselves and what I expect of you. We must say "enough." As

we discussed, we are all on notice. I expect each of you
(and your department management teams) to have a
"zero tolerance" attitude towards any factual revelation
of mismanagement, malfeasances, misfeasances and
public corruption. I will hold departmental management
accountable for these instances. In return, you must
hold your managers and employees accountable as well.
Furthermore, you have my strongest support when taking
appropriate actions.

I want to take this opportunity and clarify a major
misconception some of us have. We must be cognizant that
when it anywhere [sic] in County management it is not
their problem, but ours. All of us are touched and stained
by these unacceptable actions. As I stated, most of the
cases I know may not directly be our doing, but we are
here now; and it is up to us to make it right, and make
it right immediately. At the same time we must not act
hastily and capriciously for political expediency; we must
be thorough, fair and deliberate in our actions irrespective
of the unwarranted criticism to be expected from those with
different agendas.

Are you referring to a feeling or a thought?

Now look at *personal and professional* and *feelings and thoughts*.
Again, the Double Man's audience really cares only about the professional, not the personal. In any case, you can bet that the other
civil servants in the Water and Sewer Department are not going to
lounge around the local bar, wagering about whether the Double
Man's feelings are *personal* or *professional*. Better yet, the Double Man should just axe the adjectives *personal* and *professional*
altogether, since his audience already knows the context is professional. Similarly, his readers are unlikely to care whether the
Double Man is airing a feeling or a thought. He should just stick
with one, probably thoughts, as most employees in business really tend not to care about feelings – or at least not about feelings
other than their own. Talk about violating Grice's second principle about quantity in conversation. Moreover, offenses against

quantity in conversation are merely an obnoxious waste of time. In contrast, excessive details, especially narrated detail already familiar to readers, fly in the face of the *raison d'être* for writing. Writing ensures we can abandon the redundancy inherent in speech,[7] unless we're emphasizing a point we particularly need readers to remember, the good-repetition phenomenon that makes a paragraph conclusion helpful, rather than a waste of time.

The Double Man reminds us why researchers assessing student and professional writing inevitably include concision as a category in their evaluation criteria, irrespective of whether they're assessing legal briefs or engineering student projects. Most of us sense vaguely that we're thrashing around in swampy prose with masses of passively constructed sentences. Or that we can't pick out the important ideas in paragraphs that run to several pages, studded with sentences peppered with semicolons and bristling with clauses. In contrast to clarity, continuity, and coherence, we can spot a lack of concision easily and put a name to that particular affliction on the page before us. Most reviewers and researchers easily identify redundancy, the reason why the experts from so many fields agree on whether a writer can write concisely – or is doing an uncanny impression of the Double Man.[8]

In any case, the Double Man's memo is the perfect specimen of anti-concision. Writing concisely entails saying what you need to say in the fewest words possible. The Double Man, in contrast, seems to have written the equivalent of *A Tale of Two Cities* into his memo. His employees get every nugget of what's happened since November 11, except for the one all-important piece of information they're looking for: what they're supposed to do after receiving the memo. In fact, if you were to analyze the Double Man's full memo – which I've mercifully avoided reproducing here in its full glory – you'd discover that he never really gets to his point in the memo, let alone calls for any action from his audience. But, nevertheless, we should be grateful to the Double Man for providing us with a sterling example of all the ways in which the English language can conspire to pad out your sentences, waste your readers' time, and generally make your message as confusing and inefficient as possible.

Concision is also precision

Concision is what Strunk and White are after when they instruct you to "Omit needless words." Concision is what your high-school English teachers meant when they scrawled "wordy" in your margins. But, to eliminate these evils, you first must learn how to recognize the ways in which English nearly automatically lends itself to repetition – and how to guard against this purposeless kind of redundancy in your own writing.

English: the doubled language

English is a mongrel language, a hybrid of several languages that developed after the Normans, formerly Norsemen, invaded what later became England. As a result, after 1066, residents of England spoke three languages: French, Latin, and English. French became the language of sophistication, a heritage that even today distinguishes English speakers who use words and phrases borrowed from French like *façade*, *charade*, and *tête-à-tête*. Latin, on the other hand, rapidly became the language of government, law, and religion. Even today, most legal terminology comes to us from outside English's Anglo-Saxon roots, evident in words like *felony, perjury, plaintiff,* and *attorney*.[9] English, however, survived because the Normans almost immediately began intermarrying with English speakers. As a result, speakers tended to pair words, using a term from Anglo-Saxon alongside a term from either French or Latin, to ensure they made themselves understood – or sounded appropriately learned – in this mixed linguistic environment. After the Norman Conquest, you could call the head of state a *king*, using the Old English standby, or be a bit flashier and plump for *sovereign* and *royal*, both shamelessly pilfered from French, or *regal*, which debuted the same year as *royal* but arrived courtesy of Latin.[10]

At first glance, this embarrassment of linguistic riches seems like a boon, one of the few spoils of the Norman Conquest left around to comfort the illiterate, conquered inhabitants of what later became England. But, instead, the westward drift of French and Latin across the English Channel merely continued what had been a long-held tradition in Old English: seizing whatever interesting linguistic tidbits washed ashore and using them alongside existing words. Hundreds of years before the Normans busied themselves turfing their illiterate English-speaking subjects from their lands, English speakers used Old Norse words alongside Germanic and Old English words. The Latin-scribbling Normans used written titles to lay claim to English lands, whereas the illiterate English speakers used objects, oaths, and seals – all infinitely more difficult to falsify than a single deed. However, 300 years later, the English still used both systems – objects and oaths alongside written deeds. Apparently, the English were as reluctant to surrender to a single system as they were to a single language.[11] As a consequence, today you can *rear* (English) or *raise* (Old Norse) a child,[12] or *ask* (Germanic), *question* (French), or *interrogate* (Latin)[13] the bartender over that monstrous bar tab you ran up while buying rounds for people you actually didn't know.

Today, these redundant pairs dog English, long after the reason for their pairing vanished, largely because English became a written language soon after speakers began using redundant pairs. And if writing freezes language, then the invention of Gutenberg's printing press ossified English, halting any dramatic developments in structure, usage, or grammar.[14] Ultimately, we can blame the written word and history for English's abundance of redundancies. But look on the bright side. Once you know how to spot English's infamous redundant pairs, you're well on your way to avoiding ever becoming the Double Man.

Concision Principle #1:
Avoid redundant pairs

Redundant pairs clutter up sentences, providing stumbling blocks for your readers or wearing out their patience as they plod through unnecessary pairs like *first and foremost* or *basic and fundamental*. Since each word in the redundant pair is similar or even identical to the other, you should only use one word. Any time you spot a redundant pair, drag your pen or mouse over the *and*, plus the offending first (or second) word, and delete two of the three. In retaining one of your pair of nouns or adjectives or verbs, go for the familiar and axe the arcane. Some of the words in these pairs are linguistic fossils, a word with a meaning that survives only inside a larger expression, as in *hale* within *hale and hearty*.[15] Try using *hale* next time as an adjective to describe someone and watch the befuddled response. Just be careful to try this fossil out only on your friends.

Snares to avoid: redundant pairs

Not all redundant pairs feature a word from French and a word from Old English. Some, as the list below reveals, borrow one word from French and the other from French, or a noun from Latin and a noun from French. Or one of the pair from Norse or Old High German or whatever language was available:

> *aid* (French) and *abet* (French)
> *any* (English) and *all* (Old Danish)
> *basic* (French) and *fundamental* (Latin)
> *breaking* (English) and *entering* (French)
> *cease* (French) and *desist* (French)
> *each* (English) and *every* (English)
> *first* (Old High German) and *foremost* (English)
> *final* (English) and *conclusive* (Latin)
> *fit* (English) and *proper* (French)
> *full* (English) and *complete* (Latin)
> *holy* (English) and *sacred* (French)
> *heirs* (French) and *assigns* (French)
> *new* (English) and *novel* (French)
> *null* (French) and *void* (French)
> *peace* (English) and *quiet* (Latin)
> *so on* (English) and *so forth* (English)
> *true* (English) and *accurate* (Latin)
> *various* (Latin) and *sundry* (English)

Writing myths you'll wish you never learned:
When in doubt, copy other writers

At some point, most of us find ourselves under tight deadlines or on uncertain footing with the subject we're writing on – the moment when we decide to just imitate what other writers have done.

After all, their work survived and made it into print or some kind of record, right? Actually, if only writers had ignored this timeless and wrong-headed bit of advice, writing everywhere would be far easier to read.

Even the non-legal minds among you will recognize the unusually high percentage of legal terms that seem eternally shackled to one another, despite each word meaning nearly or exactly the same thing as the other word. Education has a long and distinguished history of once-useful but now crappy advice, beginning in the Renaissance with Erasmus, who remained convinced that imitating other writers should continue being taught as a staple of rhetoric. But the first rhetoricians were gifted orators in an illiterate society with no means of circulating brilliant speeches, aside from memorization and imitation. Thousands of years later, Erasmus was either caving to the Renaissance tradition of ennobling all elements of the classical education or to the relative scarcity of books during the early Renaissance period.

The same principle trickled down into the nineteenth century, where clerks hunched over their desks learned how to write correspondence by copying already-existing letters, warts and all.[16] This practice of parroting and preserving in amber every dreadful verbal tic of our predecessors today survives most durably in legal writing, where legal drafters were once paid by the word, making wordiness a boon to the bottom line. Today, instead of slicing through the thickets of verbal tics and redundancy produced in earlier statutes and codes, legal drafters mostly bolt extra bits onto boilerplate text as new scenarios and technologies occur.[17]

Concision Principle #2:
Avoid redundant modifiers

Redundant modifiers represent a slightly different case from redundant pairs because one term in the duo only implies the other rather than repeats it. However, since one term implies the other, one of the words is unnecessary. In one study, researchers provided an explanation for how we almost immediately grasp the meaning of a paired modifier and noun or verb. Even when we're merely hearing, rather than reading words, we assign meanings to the blur of syllables, so we need to fix the words' grammatical function as well as the plausibility of the novel pair. But using that same mechanism for comprehending potential millions of novel combinations immediately, we also expect the second word to convey new information, providing a constraint that illuminates the use of the other word.[18] In redundant modifiers, however, the added word merely repeats the core word, both violating our expectations and eliminating the extra word's usefulness.

As a result, you should omit one of the pair, whenever you spot a set of redundant modifiers. Grammar mavens will notice, if they scan the list below, that redundant modifiers involve adverbs and verbs or adjectives and nouns, or, occasionally, a verb and preposition. While redundant pairs take different grammatical forms, the pairs are nevertheless a sign that you're writing at less than maximum efficiency.

Snares to avoid: redundant modifiers

basic (French) *fundamentals* (Latin)
completely (Latin) *finish* (French)
consensus (Latin) *of opinion* (English, French)
continue (French) *on* (Old English)
each (English) *individual* (Latin)
end (English) *result* (Latin)
evidently (Latin) *clear* (French)
final (French) *outcome* (English)
free (Old High German) *gift* (English)
future (French) *plans* (French)
important (French) *essentials* (Latin)
more (English) *specifically* (Latin)
past (French) *memories* (Latin)
personal (Latin) *beliefs* (English)
revolve (French) *around* (English)
split (Middle Dutch) *apart* (French)

Not surprisingly, the Double Man proves as fond of redundant modifiers as he is of redundant pairs, chucking a perfect pair like *evidently clear* into his second paragraph. If things are evident, they are also, not terribly shockingly, clear. Likewise, most of us are unfamiliar with things like unimportant essentials or semifinal outcomes or impersonal beliefs or incompletely finished tasks for the simple reason that these things, if they exist, are a bit like Lewis Carroll's mome raths that do a bit of outgrabing in the poem "Jabberwocky." We can guess that they might exist, but don't ask us to describe them. Words like *evident* also imply that something is clear, just as to finish something means to complete it. Likewise, we expect essentials to be important, fundamentals to be basic, and outcomes to be final. On those rare instances, however, where the outcome is preliminary, rather than final, we expect a modifier like *preliminary* to inform us of the fact. Similarly, while plans can exist in the past, most plans apply to the future, so readers expect that *plans* describes a blueprint for a project or actions that have not yet taken place. If, on the other hand, the writer is referring to a blueprint for past actions that didn't quite pan out, readers expect this sort of plan to be modified by the word *past*, satisfying our notion that the added word is actually informative. Likewise, *each* refers to a single individual, while most gifts tend to be free – unless someone in retail or travel is offering one to us, in which case *free gift* is usually an oxymoron, or anything but free.

Yet another holdover from Ye Olde Englande

Intrigued by the mystery of precisely why English has such a superfluity of extra words knocking around? Consider the early English tendency to refuse to surrender anything that washed ashore: traditions, Latin, French, stray words from invaders and trading partners alike. If we examine the etymology of the most common redundant modifiers, we discover the same pattern we found in redundant pairs. One word stems from English or French, the other from French or Latin, or whatever other language happened to land on the western side of the Channel.

In a few instances, pairs like *future* and *plans* could have ended up paired for hundreds of years because English was still tottering from its collision with two distinctive types of French – that spoken by the Parisians and the dialect used by the Normans who marched over England after the Conquest, their French tinged (tainted, the Parisians would've said, tartly) with shards of their

Norse forebears. This persistence of French doublets accounts today for the ever-so-British *gaol* (Norman) and the more common *jail* (Parisian). But the borrowing from two rather different sorts of French also gave us *warden* (Norman) and *guardian* (Parisian), as well as *warrant* (Norman) and *guarantee* (Parisian).[19] We might wonder what we can learn about English speakers by their excessive preoccupation with all matters legal... right down to the niceties of the penal system.

Concision Principle #3:
Avoid negatives

When my brother once exhibited some squeamishness about his qualifications for a job in Hollywood, a friend stuck his face close to my brother's and advised, "Don't tell nobody nothin'." I puzzled over that bit of advice for at least a few hours, struggling to determine whether that meant he should tell everybody everything – or nobody something. Check out some of the US Internal Revenue Service publications online or practically any legal document, and you'll also discover convoluted thickets of negatives, the sort that prompt you to wonder if you should apply the old rules you learned in elementary school math and make a positive of two negatives.

Don't use no negatives
Actually, negatives are just plain difficult for readers to process, period, a discovery researchers made when they tested the cortical activity and slowed-down speed of readers struggling through both passively constructed and negative sentences.[20] Any negative in a sentence implies *what is* to readers by telling them *what isn't*. Put simply, your readers have to perform the mental equivalent of the old game Twister to figure out what on earth any sentence containing negatives means. So when a boss writes a memo stating, *Anyone found violating company policy may be subject to a range of disciplinary actions, up to and not excluding termination*, his employees are nearly standing on their heads in the mailroom, trying to determine whether he means *including termination* or *not including termination*. The difference for

some of us is the distance between a paycheck and the dole queue. That old rule about double negatives, hanging over from math, also tends to mess with your head. Does *not entirely unpleasant* mean *unpleasant*, *mildly unpleasant*, or *so dreadful I can't tell you about it without resorting to four-letter words beginning with f*?

Simply put, avoid negatives whenever you can. Instead, state things positively. Substitute *young* for *not old enough*, and *different* for *not alike*, or *lacks* for *does not have*. Once you sensitize yourself to negatives, you'll start seeing how easily you can avoid them. Moreover, writers avoid negatives fairly naturally when they start making their grammatical subjects and verbs actively do stuff. Seriously. Try it in your next email.

Swaps for concision: replacing negatives

not the same – different
not many – few
did not – failed to
does not have – lacks
did not stay – left
did not accept – rejected
did not remember – forgot
did not consider – ignored
not necessary – unnecessary
not possible – impossible
not certain – uncertain

Concision Principle #4:
Avoid narrating or hedging

In other words, just bloody get to your point, or, as Joe Friday in *Dragnet* would've said, "Just the facts, ma'am." I love the *ma'am* bit, suggesting that women always need to be steered away from imminent hysteria or great swaths of irrelevance and kept on the straight and narrow path to Fact-dom.

Joseph Williams had a name for about 90 percent of the content in the Double Man's memo – *metadiscourse*. By metadiscourse,

Williams meant writing about the act of writing, as in the *You're-probably-wondering-why-I've-asked-you-all-here* moment in the library in so many cozy mysteries that involve murders in vicarages. Nevertheless, Williams could be downright beady about what counted as metadiscourse, including helpful transitions like *In conclusion*, which signals to our working memories that they can take a breather after the next sentence.[21] Williams broke metadiscourse into three broad categories: *hedges and emphatics, sequencers and topicalizers,* and *attributors and narrators.* In Williams' examples, metadiscourse besmirches any prose it lays its greasy little mitts on – and even mostly useful transitions receive an indictment. In contrast, Ken Hyland of the University of London broadened Williams' skimpy taxonomy into categories that suggest entire families and species of metadiscourse, some of which serve useful purposes when writers are mindful of why they use them. Hyland and his colleagues identified two basic types of metadiscourse, *interactive* and *interactional.* Then Hyland broke each type into categories, giving us eight specific types of metadiscourse, sorted according to the purpose each serves on the page.

Can metadiscourse ever serve a purpose?

Rather than contenting himself with exorcizing metadiscourse wherever he discovered it bedeviling a perfectly innocent piece of prose, Hyland instead set about investigating why writers used it. Some types of metadiscourse were *interactive,* anticipating readers' responses to the words on the page, including *transitions, frame markers* to indicate shifts in topic, and *evidentials* or external sources, all of which you've already met in these chapters in spades. (For examples of each type of metadiscourse, see "A shortcut to understanding metadiscourse," below.) In contrast, *interactional* metadiscourse preserved Williams' *hedges* but replaced *emphatics* with *boosters,* then added *engagement markers* that explicitly anticipated readers' responses, *attitude markers* that draw the author's emotions and opinions directly onto the page, and *self-mentions,* which explicitly put the writer in the material as either a narrator or commentator.[22] For example, *You'll note that this paragraph contains an engagement marker* contains an interactive bit of metadiscourse. In addition, Concision Principle #3's explanation contained a scrap of self-reference: *I puzzled over that bit of advice for at least a few hours…*

A short-cut to understanding metadiscourse

Type	Category	Examples
Interactive	Transitions	*but, however, in addition, first, last, for example*
Interactive	Frame Markers	*this study proposes to, we intend to, in conclusion*
Interactive	Evidentials	*according to a White House source, Douglas et al. state*
Interactional	Hedges	*virtually, probably, in all likelihood, most likely*
Interactional	Boosters	*indeed, clearly, evidently, of course*
Interactional	Engagement Markers	*<u>This attitude contrasts strikingly with our expectations</u> for the way readers' brains process metadiscourse; This methodology relies on retrospective data analysis, <u>lending itself to biased interpretations of data</u>*
Interactional	Attitude Markers	*<u>We were surprised</u> to discover; <u>I can only imagine</u> your distress at this development*
Interactional	Self-mentions	*<u>I</u> find this researcher's explanation to be clever but also slick and insufficiently explanatory for why our brains respond to art; <u>I</u> can recall sharing our community's outrage during that media event; <u>I</u> am convinced <u>I'm</u> the perfect candidate for this research fellowship.*

In other words, certain types of metadiscourse have their uses and are even obligatory in certain scenarios. Most works of non-fiction, including articles in the *Daily Telegraph* or *Chicago*

Sun-Times contain evidentials in the form of attributions for quotes and statistics, without which the article's credibility heads straight down the bog. Similarly, advertisers in the United States lean heavily on weasel words like *virtually, may,* and *might* to keep them from being fined by the Federal Trade Commission for faulty advertising.[23] Moreover, researchers routinely rely on hedges to ensure their peer reviewers don't rip them into bite-sized bloody chunks and fry them up as a starter. As Hyland and other researchers have discovered, hedges including *likely, probably, usually*, and that hybrid, the hedging self-mention, *we speculate* or *we suggest* or *we expect*, all crop up depressingly frequently in academic writing. Hedges and self-mentions figure heavily in graduate student dissertations and even in well-regarded medical journals including the *BMJ* and *Lancet*, normally redoubts of good writing. Unsurprisingly, qualitative research in the social sciences, seen as squishy and relatively unrigorous, features significantly more hedges than the biological sciences, perceived as quantitative and robustly data-driven, which has fewer.[24] Hedges let us assert something without losing sleep over whether we're going to be sued into penury, particularly in America, where many elementary schoolers master the immortal phrase, "My daddy will sue you."

But stay clear of most metadiscourse

Stop before you begin your next email with *The reason I'm emailing you* or worse, in cold-call emails, *My name is Gustavo Skuratowicz* – a surreal bit of overkill, given the hefty signature block at the bottom of the email and the emailer's own name, helpfully staring at us from the first line. In addition to some form of metadiscourse turning up on the shit-list of most guides to writing, metadiscourse also gets short shrift for, among other things, authors relying on it to self-promote their own work.[25]

Nevertheless, researchers have studied the usefulness of metadiscourse for one of the primary reasons researchers scrutinize the usefulness of any phenomenon...because they're astonished to discover something so universally reviled actually has its occasional uses. In some studies, a writer's use of metadiscourse enabled researchers to determine whether blind reviews of manuscripts enabled subject-matter experts to determine a writer's levels of expertise (graduate students or professionals), familiarity with discipline-specific conventions, and even gender. The reviewers responded strongly to the anonymous author's use of frame, attitude, and engagement markers in creating a sense of the author as a male graduate student, writing for a seminar. In reality, the author was a male graduate student whose manuscript – the one the reviewers both rejected – had recently been accepted for publication by a major journal in his field.[26]

Think of metadiscourse as the linguistic equivalent of bug spray, marvelous in small quantities at steering away from our whereabouts all the pests that bite or sting or spread germs, but toxic in large quantities. From the studies on metadiscourse, we can extrapolate five basic principles:

1. Use frame markers only in the form of transitions or when you can incorporate the shift in topic centrally in the sentence.

   Metadiscourse Frame Marker: *This study aims to establish the potential for Ehlers–Danlos Syndrome Hypermobility subtype to prevent adverse cardiovascular events.*

   Textual Frame Marker [no explicit metadiscourse]: *Ehlers–Danlos Hypermobility subtype can potentially prevent adverse cardiovascular events.*

2. Unless you're a journalist, incorporate evidentials into the central sentence structure.

   Metadiscourse Evidential: *In a 2012 study, Douglas et al. found that minocycline had anti-inflammatory effects…*

   Textual Evidential [no explicit metadiscourse]: *Douglas et al. (2012) noted minocycline's anti-inflammatory effects…*

3. Use engagement and attitude markers, as well as self-mentions, only to establish a conversational tone or direct rapport with an audience.

   Attitude Marker: *Unfortunately, our calculations for profitability in Q4 failed to take into account declining demand for new construction.*

Engagement Marker: *We appreciate* your input on our new employee engagement survey.

Self-mention: *I* apologize for the delay in your shipment of pelleted goat feed.

4. Avoid all other metadiscourse like the bloody plague, especially emphatics and boosters.

5. Avoid considering transitions as forms of metadiscourse – as Joseph Williams did in his *Style* series – as transitions boost readers' speed and ease of comprehension in reading. Williams included transitions like *first … second … finally* in his list of forms of metadiscourse, a misleading classification, as transitions perform uniformly useful functions in sentences, whereas metadiscourse plays a meaningful role in only the handful of exceptions in item 3, above.

Concision Principle #5:
Avoid throat-clearing

Throat-clearing, like its name suggests, rarely conveys any meaning whatsoever. Like pesky burrs, these verbal tics have stuck to our everyday prose, with the chief offenders including *for all intents and purposes* and *in order [infinitive]*. While no audience cares particularly if a speaker clears his or her throat periodically during a lengthy speech, even an audience of Mother Theresas would probably exhibit visible signs of intense suffering through a talk where the speaker *ahem*ed, *ummm*ed, and *aahhh*ed in every sentence – the fate of readers encountering persistent throat-clearing.

To all intents and purposes debuts, predictably, in legal language, that first and last refuge of all things redundant. In 1546, Henry VIII's Act 37 includes *to all intents, constructions, and purposes*, which, by 1709, has morphed into the more abbreviated *to all intents and purposes*.[27] While not quite a linguistic fossil, the expression no longer means anything wherever it appears – even in legal documents. Try covering it up, rereading any sentence in which the expression appears, and seeing if the meaning changes one whit. You needn't fret, even you lawyers. *To all intents and purposes* fails to tells readers what intents or purposes are involved, even in legal writing. If you want to specify intents or purposes, go ahead and be specific about them. If you're not, forget the expression exists.

And, finally, the most ubiquitous and utterly meaningless example of throat-clearing is *in order to*, which never contributes so much as a smidgen of meaning to any sentence. If you simply delete *in order* and leave the infinitive *to* _____, the meaning of your sentence will never change. But, given how the expression *in order to* crops up in sentences everywhere and how little it contributes to any sentence, we might wonder just what bog hatched this particular bit of throat-clearing. In the early decades of the twentieth century, a crusty old school master, H. W. Fowler, published what became the Bible of English usage, *Modern English Usage*. Fowler's edicts in that little tome saddled writers for decades with an imperative to begin restrictive adjective clauses with *that* and the fluffier, non-restrictive clauses with *which*. If you've ever suffered under this rule during a Microsoft Word spell-check – invented because Fowler thought the unregulated use of *that* and *which* seemed shamefully sloppy – you can curse Fowler. On the other hand, the school master also had little patience for that bugbear, *in order to*. According to Fowler, the expression once represented a means of flagging an analogy.[28]

In order to _____ could, however, also just as easily have come to us courtesy of the Norman Conquest and the French *en train de [faire]*, which translates as *to be in the process of [doing something]*.[29] Tellingly, the *Oxford English Dictionary* records *in order to* first popping up in the Douay Bible in 1609. The Douay (or Douai) Bible represents the first translation of the Bible into English, the product of untold toil by the University of Douai in the service of the Catholic Church.[30] Douai is in France, and the Bible's translators both lived in France and worked during an era when English was still shamelessly borrowing words from Latin and French, as if conscious of its mongrel origins. We probably use *in order to* _____ because French scholars who spoke Latin relied on *en train de [faire]* over 400 years ago. News: we can stop now.

Whatever its origins, *in order* is white noise in any sentence. Run the same acid test on the meaning of *in order to* _____ by covering *in order* wherever you find it and reading the sentence without it. You'll discover *in order* contributes absolutely bloody zero to any sentence's meaning. To weed the expression out completely, run a Find and Replace search on your entire document for *in order* and systematically delete it. You'll need to use tools like Find and Replace because *in order to* _____ is so ubiquitous that spotting it is rather like seeing air. You know air is around you. You just need help in seeing it.

EXPERT TIP: Prefer short and simple to lengthy and complex

For clarity, choose short and simple words – the ones preferred by George Orwell in "Politics and the English Language" over those invasive, Frenchified species. Short, simple words give sentences concreteness and also invite readers to see cause and effect. For concision, short and simple words have an extra benefit. We read simple, easy-to-pronounce words more rapidly and recall them far more clearly than we do more complex terms, a good reason for preferring *use* to *utilization*.

Once he discovered that shorter words led to sharper recall, Alan Baddeley and colleagues aimed to isolate the reason behind the improved recall. Hypothesizing that readers needed to *subvocalize* longer words (that thing you do as you move your lips when you first encounter, say, *defenestration*), Baddeley prevented readers from rehearsing any of the words. Rehearsing longer words, Baddeley and his collaborators supposed, together with the words' greater complexity, overloaded some part of the brain's speech systems, which could account for the fall-off in recall of these more complex words compared to simpler ones. In addition, Baddeley's study also controlled for the complexity and potential unfamiliarity of words on readers' ability to recall them. To do so, he and his colleagues generated two sets of words with the same numbers of syllables, letters, and phonemes. But, in their study, one list had words that readers would have needed more time to articulate, had they spoken them aloud. Even after discounting for these alternative effects, the study revealed something startlingly simple. Words that needed to be spoken slowly were harder to remember.[31] Orwell was, in a way, right after all. Most words with their roots in Old English tend to be simple and more memorable than their Latin or Frenchified counterparts.

Takeaways for concision: what you need to remember to make your writing efficient

- Eliminate redundant modifiers and pairs.
- Prefer positives to negatives whenever possible.
- Avoid hedging, amplifiers.
- Use frame markers and evidentials in the main parts of your sentences, not as extra phrases.
- Only use self-mentions or attitude and engagement markers to create a conversational tone or rapport with readers.
- Weed out throat-clearing.
- Prefer short, familiar words to longer, less common words.

CHAPTER 7

Making music with words
The fifth C: Cadence

In this chapter you will
- learn how our brains recognize the rhythm of sentences even when we read silently
- know how to handle items in a list or series
- discover how to create a sophisticated cadence to your sentences by varying their length and structure.

In our clumsy and unscientific way of assessing writing that works – or spectacularly fails to – we resort to using vague terms to diagnose issues that neuroscience, psychology, and linguistics can help us pinpoint. When, for example, readers fuzzily describe a paragraph as just not *flowing*, as we saw in Chapter 4, they're identifying discontinuities between sentences. But they're also straining to put a finger on something harder to pin down, the thing that most books on writing are content to breezily label *style*. Unfortunately, most of us aren't aiming for the next Nobel in literature (or even favorable critical reviews savoring our prose), so glowing explanations of how writers avoid clichés, use bracingly fresh analogies, or powerful rhetorical devices like antitheses are noticeably less helpful in getting our proposals or memoranda out the door than great lashings of caffeine. At 3 am, you don't give a shit whether you sound like Richard Dawkins at his most sparkling and original. You just want to avoid sounding like an illiterate, sleep-deprived, nine-year-old chucking together a report hours before your deadline.

Follow the four Cs and you'll end up sounding as though you've at least had the benefit of an education, in addition to ensuring your writing project will receive generous amounts of time, thorough attention, and thoughtful consideration. Notice if I'd said… *in addition to giving your writing project generous amounts of thorough attention, thoughtful consideration about the mating habits of wombats, and time*, you'll tilt toward the illiterate, sleep-deprived and time-pressed nine-year-old end of the spectrum, rather than away from it. Why? Our notions of *flow* and *style* alike have one thing in common that few of us (aside from rhetoricians) consider – cadence.

Open any book on writing or even scrutinize studies of reading or writing, and you'll be hard-pressed to find any references to cadence, outside of three areas: studies of rhetorical devices, certain categories of stroke, and of how beginning readers in their native or second language tackle unfamiliar words. Cadence is currently the province of rhetoricians, neurologists, and linguists obsessed with phonology, all of whom spend their lives immersed in issues that concern cadence or the rhythms of our speech. Notice, for starters, that the key word here is *speech*. In contrast, in writing, cadence mostly resembles death – the thing we all know exists but seldom witness and lack a vocabulary to discuss without resorting to weird approximations and euphemisms. Just as we use *passed* or *gone* to describe death, as though your dead grandfather merely ducked into the john and will be back momentarily, we use words like *choppy* or *awkward* to clumsily identify problems tied strictly to cadence.

And yet cadence is central to our sense that something is particularly well written, beyond clarity, continuity, coherence, and concision. Even if you observe nearly all the principles tied to these first four Cs, if you write in nothing but short, simple sentences, you can still come off like that mostly illiterate nine-year-old.

Cadence Principle #1:
Vary the structure of your sentences

Sentences sound monotonous when you begin every one with either your grammatical subject or words like *the* or *this*. Begin some sentences with a transition or a brief phrase, or, occasionally, an introductory clause. Compare the following two examples:

Example A:

Your sentences seem to lack syntactic complexity. Your reader can feel jack-hammered by your sentence structure. Your reader might guess that you stopped reading even cereal boxes long ago. Your sentences all observe clarity and continuity principles. And yet something feels wrong. Something is wrong. Your sentences are all the same type – simple. Your sentences all begin the same way. Your readers perceive your writing as the equivalent of "Twinkle, Twinkle, Little Star" rather than something by Rachmaninoff. You're not out to win the Van Cliburn International Piano Competition. You just aim to sound authoritative, not amateurish or idiotic.

Example B:

When you ignore cadence, your sentences will seem to lack syntactic complexity. Your readers can feel jack-hammered by your sentence structure, and they might guess that you stopped reading even cereal boxes long ago. Note that all these sentences observe clarity and continuity principles – yet something feels wrong. In fact, something is wrong. Your sentences are all the same type – simple. (If you're flummoxed by the difference between simple, compound, and compound-complex sentences, see the Supplement, page 164). For starters, your sentences all begin the same way, with not only the same words but also the same sentence structure: Subject–verb. Subject–verb. Subject–verb. Moreover, with your over-reliance on one kind of sentence structure and length, your readers can perceive your writing as the equivalent of "Twinkle, Twinkle, Little Star" rather than something by Rachmaninoff. While you're not out to win the Van Cliburn International Piano Competition, you do, however, aim to sound authoritative – not amateurish or idiotic.

Aside from the bit of parenthetical advice on the definition of *simple sentence* and the introductory adverb clause in the first sentence, *When you ignore cadence*, all other changes between Examples A and B are trivial in terms of meaning. Example B only offers several transitions, a few bits of jazzy punctuation, and changes in sentence structure, complexity, and length. However, try reading the two examples aloud, preferably to someone who hasn't read this book.

If you feel a bit like you've been sledge-hammered by the rhythm of Example A, you're not alone. Nearly every sentence in the first example begins with the grammatical subject and – worse – with the same word, *You*, varied only by the delightfully unpredictable insertion of *Your* and the shocking novelty of *Something* beginning one sentence. But no matter how you size these sentences up, they have the same, relentless structure, as though pounded out on a die: *Subject–verb. Subject–verb. Subject–verb. Subject–verb.* In addition, every sentence in Example A is a simple sentence, confined to just a major clause. Both the rhythm and similarity of the sentence type and beginning have more than a little of the elementary school *My Dog Spike*-sound to them. Generally, this sort of monotony is the hallmark of a careless or inexperienced writer – or of someone pounding away at the keyboard with a scant three hours remaining to a thesis' drop-dead due date.

In contrast, Example B begins with a complex sentence (a minor coupled with a major clause), followed by a compound-complex sentence (two major clauses joined by a coordinating conjunction with a minor clause embedded in the second major clause). The passage rolls on with variations of complex, compound-complex, and even a simple sentence in the mix. In addition, the opening clauses of the compound-complex sentences, as well as an ample use of transitions, ease readers into the sentences from both cognitive and rhythmic perspectives. Moreover, this variation in sentence structure is one of the features that distinguishes polished writing by a writer in control of his game from writing by someone who sounds as if he might belong back in the *My Dog Spike* leagues.

EXPERT TIP: Just use transitions, period

Observing Continuity Principle #2 will also even out the cadence of your sentences, eliminating the risk of your writing sounding monotonous, choppy or, worst of all, as though a sleep-deprived and not particularly well-read nine-year-old produced it.

Cadence is always with us

While the authors of books on writing wax endlessly lyrical about matters of style, which seems bound up nebulously with fresh phrasings, adroit metaphors, and sentences that gracefully unfurl, no one tells us why in god's name we would *hear* something we read silently. Both scholarly and popular titles on style remain silent on how and why we hear cadence in signs on a page, all read without speaking. And the silence is widespread for a bloody good reason. To explain cadence scientifically is extraordinarily complicated and involves delving into the history of the written word and the specific areas of the brain that work to produce and comprehend spoken and written language alike. In other words, you need more than an appreciation of Shakespeare's use of iambic pentameter or the artful way F. Scott Fitzgerald's *The Great Gatsby* genuflects linguistically to Joseph Conrad's *Heart of Darkness*. You need to understand at least a scrap of neuroanatomy and possess a willingness to engage with neurologists' debates about the parts of the brain that may be involved every time we drag our eyes across a line of text.

For all our silent reading and zapping emails in the throes of some effortful standing on the elliptical at the gym, we hear what we read – one reason why *c u l8or* remains comprehensible rather than reading like a rune. As early as 1512, Renaissance scholar Erasmus, writing in Latin, advised writers to focus on variation in their sentences, counseling writers to take a group of their sentences and phrase them in as many variations as possible.[1] By 1926, H. W. Fowler was nothing short of rabid on the subject of rhythm. *Modern English Usage* is straightforward and bracingly opinionated on issues like the use of the word *queer* ("It has become dangerous to apply this apparently innocent adjective to a person…"). But when Fowler gets to the topic of rhythm, his entry reads the way the Nile floods its banks, spreading a bounty of edicts and exhortations over pages in columns of mouse type that bring to mind the King James Bible:

> [L]ive speech, said or written, is rhythmic, and rhythmless speech is at the best dead…So it is that the best prose writer's guide to rhythm is not his own experiments…but an instinct…cultivate[d] on one condition only – that [he]

will make a practice of reading aloud … [R]eading aloud
need not be taken so literally; there is an art of tacit reading
aloud … reading with the eye and not the mouth, that is, but
being as fully aware of the unuttered sound as of the sense.[2]

And that's the Morse Code version of the entry. Fowler's strident
insistence on rhythm seems peculiar to Americans, who seldom
read aloud after their earliest years in school. His insistence on the
virtues of reading aloud might seem potentially a bit much even
to Brits made to suffer untold humiliations at the hands of their
teachers for stumbling over bits of Gerard Manley Hopkins as they
read aloud at school. However, his advice has surprising scientific
weight behind it, much of it undreamt of by Fowler, for all his
volubility on the subject.

We "hear" the words on the page for three reasons. First, we
rely on sounding out words or phonological processing during
the lexical or word-identifying stage of reading. This phonological
phase sticks with us beyond our earliest stumbles in learning to
read, surfacing whenever we encounter new or unfamiliar words
or tackle a new language. Second, during the long history of the
written word, reading was far from silent. Reading was public, vo-
cal, and voluble. And, third, our brains use overlapping auditory
and visual processing in the act of reading, particularly during our
early attempts at learning to read. Our brains "hear" prose when
we encounter too many short, simple sentences or strings of
lengthy, complex sentences – the outliers that violate our sense of
cadence. To learn just how profoundly our brains "hear" language,
we only need to consider the brains of readers of sign language
and braille, as well as the brains of stroke patients with neural
deficits that impair one of three primary areas implicated in using
and reading language.

Before reading was silent

When he read, his eyes scanned the page and his heart
sought out the meaning, but his voice was silent and his
tongue was still. Anyone could approach him freely and
guests were not commonly announced so that often, when

we came to visit him, we found him reading like this in silence, for he never read aloud.[3]

The man who would later become St. Augustine thought the sight of the future St. Ambrose reading silently so remarkable that the thirty-year-old St. Augustine recorded this soundless reading in his *Confessions*. In AD 383, silent reading was so rare that St. Ambrose represented St. Augustine's first encounter with it. Moreover, in the West, silent reading would not become commonplace until the tenth century.[4]

However, reading aloud lived on far beyond that century in universities where, until considerably after Gutenberg overhauled an old wine press to print Bibles, books remained scarce. Students' encounters with books came from that now-familiar staple of education, the lecture. In fact, the very word comes to us courtesy of Latin, *lectio*, where the word actually means *reading*. Teachers passed on the wisdom of others by reading aloud to students from books still expensively created by hand in medieval scriptoria. In other classrooms, students attended dictation sessions to make up for the paucity of texts.[5] The act of reading aloud for centuries was impelled not by any impulse toward being sociable – after all, when you slept, screwed, and chewed within earshot of your family, sociability wasn't exactly thin on the ground – but by economics. Books were pricey and scarce, lumbering students with the need to learn the wisdom of theologians and philosophers through a lecturer's droning reading aloud.[6]

Why do we "hear" written language? Three neural explanations

Our ancestors depended on reading aloud for their education and for learning about the world outside their village. Or, in the case of my illiterate great-grandfather, outside the Glasgow docks. But as early readers, we also replicate this reliance on the relationship between hearing speech and reading. In addition, we rely on what we've heard spoken conversationally around us to begin deciphering what we see on the page. Of all our adaptations as a species, the widespread use of reading and writing is perhaps our most breathtaking – and not for our having produced *King Lear* or *Middlemarch* or *Moby-Dick*. After all, the same system of alphabetic script also gives rise to *The National Enquirer,* hardly material you'd want to hurl into the galaxy aboard a capsule as representative of humankind's greatest achievements. Instead, reading and writing require a complex ballet within our brains. That first step in the three-step dance of reading, the lexical or word-identifying phase, requires our brain's visual areas to break down words into letters and *graphemes*. Graphemes are the smallest components of words that include roots of words, prefixes, and suffixes, all useful in figuring out what the hell *defenestration* means the first time we come across it.

Think back to the last time you came across an unfamiliar word. Can't remember? Try this one, then: *glomerulonephritis*, a word I can never come across in the classroom without my lips moving to sound it out. Every time I do it, I'm doing that ontogeny-recapitulates-phylogeny shuffle because I'm reliving the birth of reading in phonological processing or translating the graphemes, bits of words, into sounds or *phonemes*. We first do this phonological, lips-moving, muttering translation of marks on the pages into bits of sound with lowly words like *place* during our earliest attempts at reading. And, if you're an intellectual carpetbagger, you can manage to stay mired in this phase into your dotage by coming across words like *glomerulonephritis*. For *place* or even the perversely spelled *poignant*, hearing the word aloud is sufficient for us to grasp what it means because we've heard others use the same word in speech. For *glomerulonephritis*, however, that translation of graphemes into phonemes helps us break the word down into its meaning, as if we're breaking a suspect under interrogation. Stare at the guy sweating under the bright light, and, eventually, something's gonna give. Here *-itis* tells us we're dealing with an inflammatory disease, *-nephr-* tells us kidneys are involved, and the really tricky bit, *glomerulo-*, with the aid of a dictionary, resolves into a problem with the minuscule, looping blood vessels within the kidney.

Every time you struggle to learn to read in a new language or encounter a novel word, you engage a route to reading you otherwise abandoned once you stopped reading while moving your lips. You use the brain's visual areas to break marks on a page into letters, then units of words, and, finally, words. But you do so expertly and silently. However, to understand how these letters and bits of words work together, your brain must also rely on areas of the brain reserved for both speech and hearing.[7] This concerted coordination of visual, auditory, and speaking areas of the brain in the act of reading is what makes widespread reading and writing one of the more marvelous inventions of our species. Despite our being non-nephrologists or even non-scientists, we can decipher and make sense of even a sentence dense with unfamiliar terminology:

> *Glomerulonephritis is an inflammation of the kidney characterized by proteinuria, impaired filtration, and the accumulation of extracellular matrix within the damaged glomeruli.*

When we emerge at the end with more than a glimmer of comprehension – at least, the non-biomedical types among us – we engage in an activity that repurposes parts of our brains never designed to read the *Daily Mail*, let alone *Nature* or an explanation of how credit default swaps work (or mostly don't). Unfortunately, to explain how reading and writing harness and, depending on your view, repurpose or even rewire our brains, we need to examine three hypotheses of how the reading brain perceives speech that's frozen and silent on the page.

Explanation 1: Speech, auditory, and visual systems work together in reading or *this is your brain saying* **glomerulonephritis**

In 1993, researchers used positron emission tomography – known to the rest of us as PET scans involving significant amounts of radioactive material – to measure cerebral blood flow during silent reading. Even though the experimental subjects never spoke a word, PET scans revealed increased blood flow to areas previously believed to be dedicated solely to the physical or motor side of speaking: the supplementary motor area (known as the SMA) and cerebellum. Researchers expected to see increased blood flow, indicating specific areas of the brain were at work, in the left lingual gyrus, a part of the brain that, when damaged by a stroke, prevents right-handed patients from being able to recognize words, let alone read. This area researchers had suspected must be associated with some visual processing of letters. However, they were floored to find blood flow also increased to Broca's area, a part of the brain hitherto believed to be responsible only for understanding and forming spoken words.[8] Even during silent reading by expert readers of familiar words and phrases in a noiseless environment, their brains apparently relied on the sounds of words. Together, the involvement of Broca's area, the left lingual gyrus, SMA, and cerebellum all signify an overlap with our auditory and visual systems, as well as the motor and comprehension systems for speech. Even seasoned readers who consume the *New York Times* with breakfast apparently rely on a loop for articulating and hearing speech during silent reading. This mechanism preserves the order of words, phrases, and clauses, at the same time that the speech–auditory–visual loop helps us detect errors and wend our way through particularly challenging bits of prose – like an explanation of how credit default swaps work.

An extraordinarily brief tour of the reading/speaking brain

Talk about reading and speaking with any neurologist, and you'll mainly hear about two areas of the brain: Broca's and Wernicke's areas. Broca's area, once thought to deal mainly with our ability to speak, takes its name from Pierre Paul Broca, who identified an area in the brain's frontal lobe as responsible for robbing two patients of their speech after injury to the posterior inferior frontal gyrus. While some people with damage to Broca's area can speak, they speak in telegraphic shorthand, packed with nouns but mostly devoid of function words like *of* and *from* and, rather more important for communication, also lacking in syntax. On the other hand, Wernicke guessed at a link between the area of the temporal lobes named for him and another type of aphasia, this one involving the ability to comprehend speech or to produce speech that conveys meaning. Someone with Broca's aphasia battling a severe sinus infection might say, helpfully, "Nose," as her entire explanation to her doctor. In contrast, a patient with Wernicke's aphasia would produce strings of functional words and lovely syntax, all sound and fury signifying nothing that her doctor or any of us can make sense of. "Well, there's smelling, a lack sensate, only a mucus and tile then tonations and inability to trinagulate the cogulatory."[9] If you think I'm exaggerating, try reading transcripts of what actual Wernicke's patients say, and, by comparison, my attempt will seem as comprehensible as an entry in the *Oxford English Dictionary*.

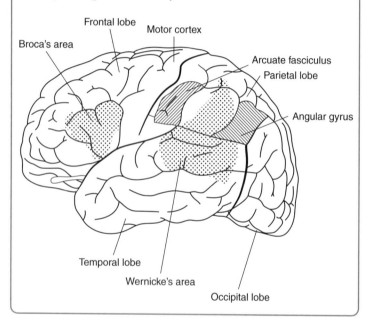

Explanation 2: Your visual, speech, and auditory centers are hard-wired together

Viewed in terms of evolutionary time, humans have been reading for a mere sliver of our species' history. And we also spend so little of our days reading – some of us, at least – that our brains are unlikely to have formed a neural circuit dedicated solely to making sense of, say, instructions for operating a Taser. Instead, reading seems to have become possible from connections among the areas of the brain enabling us to translate visual marks into speech, areas enabling us to speak, and areas that convert torrents of sound into sentences with syntax. Broca's area (think: rhythm, affect, and syntax) in the frontal lobe and Wernicke's area (think: words and meaning) in the temporal lobes are linked by a band of fibers called the arcuate fasciculus. Moreover, the other part of the brain central to language, the angular gyrus, is helpfully positioned at the bottom of the parietal lobe at a point where the occipital (visual functions) and temporal (auditory functions) lobes intersect. In fact, our brains recruit more blood to the angular gyrus in both the temporal and occipital lobes when we read relatively unfamiliar words like *exsanguinate* or *epistemology*. But, surprisingly, introduce a pseudo-word, resembling the kind produced by someone with Wernicke's aphasia – say, *cogulatory* – and the brain sends more blood to both Wernicke's and Broca's areas. Because we fall back on trying to sound out unfamiliar words to make sense of them, we recruit speech, hearing, and visual areas. Except, in this hypothesis, borne out by PET scans of brains of subjects reading single words and lone pseudo-words, this circuit exists because these areas are interconnected by proximity and the arcuate fasciculus.[10] You can read this sentence, according to this view, because the visual and speech processing areas of the brain have both a junction box in the form of the angular gyrus and hard-wiring via the arcuate fasciculus.

The angular gyrus uses visual associations that enable us to work out the meanings of words by separating the *in-* and *un-* and *de-* beginnings of a word from its root and *-ation* ending, acting as a visual dictionary that matches the words on a page with our knowledge of what they mean. In right-handed readers, we rely on the left angular gyrus when we read familiar words. But we also use Broca's and Wernicke's areas when we encounter words like those in Lewis Carroll's "Jabberwocky" that includes pseudo-words which native speakers of English recognize as unlikely to be actual words: *brillig* and *toves* because we see letters clustered together in formations unlikely to exist in real English words. The *-ig* in *brillig* fails to crop up in words we know, just as the *tov* in *toves* fails to conjure up any word root in English. In one study of skilled and dyslexic readers, pseudo-words cause us to fall back on our earlier sounding-out strategies in reading because the angular gyrus fails to identify the word on the page with our visual dictionary of words and their meanings.[11]

Explanation 3: Neuroplasticity – reading and writing wired your visual, speech, and auditory centers together

We've all heard two old saws, or, at least, the undeniable geeks among us have. First, neurons that fire together, wire together. And, second, that, when we lose one sense, our other senses mysteriously become sharper. We now know that neuroplasticity exists in the language areas of the brain, courtesy of some striking studies of parts of our brains becoming repurposed for other functions. If you were born without sight, when you read braille, your visual reading areas light up – even though you're relying solely on your sense of touch to read.[12] Similarly, if you're congenitally deaf, the supratemporal gyri, normally reserved for processing sound, instead get hijacked for understanding sign language. But, if you lose your hearing after learning how to talk, sign language engages only the visual processing areas of your brain. Our brains may well have recruited areas for speech and hearing to enable us to understand written language, following the evidence of our brains' neuroplasticity in the experiences of braille and sign users who rely solely on touch or sight in understanding communication.[13]

No matter how you look at it, reading is a multi-input process

If you survived these for-geeks-only explanations, you might have spotted that none of the three explanations rules out the validity of the other two. In other words, we can read because we can sometimes fall back on the old phonological–lexical loop in reading unfamiliar words, just as we did in elementary school when we learned how to read – especially if you're reading new terminology that you'll have to use later in discussions with experts. And we can read because the parts of our brain that now turn "Whoops! I did it again!" into sound and sense are interconnected. And we can also read due to our brains' ability to adapt to the demands placed on it, even within a single lifetime or relatively brief span of years.

If you're still wondering what the hell this detour into neuro-anatomy has to do with cadence, the answer is *everything*. Even when you're one of those showy sods who can consume an entire issue of *The American Scholar* during the über-predictable flight-safety information preceding take-off, you're still hearing the sound of words on the page. If you're reading the *New York Review of Books*, the non-uniform lengths of sentences – those bracing simple sentences, bracketed by compound and compound-complex sentences that go on a fair old bit – will telegraph to your reading brain a pleasing cadence, one caused by a lack of monotony in sentence length. If you're reading a legal statute or doctoral dissertation in the humanities, the pages whisper to your auditory and speech processing centers of the droning monotony of apparently endless sentences, heaving with semicolons, colons, commas, and parentheses. Or, if you're reading anything by Hemingway or Twitter feed, you "hear" staccato, almost entirely simple sentences of similar lengths, as in this example from one of Hemingway's *The Nick Adams Stories*:

> "Oh, well. He's pretty small," his father said.
> "That's no reason to bring him into the woods with us."
> "I know he's an awful coward," his father said, "but we're all yellow at that age."
> "I can't stand him," George said. "He's such an awful liar."
> "Oh, well, forget it. You'll get plenty of fishing anyway."[14]

Cadence Principle #2:
Vary the lengths of your sentences

Even if you use transitions, you still might not be safely out of the "What I Did on My Summer Vacation" stakes if you fail to vary the lengths of your sentences. Sentences of roughly the same length can put your readers to sleep or make your sentences seem choppy. Exceptions here include novelists or professionals straining to imitate Hemingway and perfectly happy to face the prospect of the dole queue after a pitch fails to charm clients the way *The Sun Also Rises* has generations of American writers. For instance, compare the following examples:

Example A:

People enjoy corporate-owned coffee joints. Even people who don't enjoy drinking coffee enjoy corporate coffee joints. They love this magical land where the word "tall" equals small. People love using words in Italian and not knowing what they mean. They like how every store has the same atmosphere. There's a certain comfort to be found in familiarity.

Example B:

People enjoy corporate-owned coffee joints. Even people who don't enjoy drinking coffee enjoy corporate coffee joints. They love this magical land where the word "tall" equals small, where they get to use words in Italian and not know what they mean. They like how every store has the same atmosphere and find a certain comfort in familiarity.

If you're not reading attentively, these two paragraphs might seem like the old "Spot the Difference" games you played when you were a kid, intently scanning two drawings that looked, at first glance, nearly the same. But, if you're reading reasonably carefully, you'll notice that the third sentence in Example B is nearly two lines long – about twice the length of every other sentence in this little paragraph – and the final sentence combines what were two short sentences in Example A. In contrast, Example A's sentences are all nearly the same length – a little under a line. The result: in Example B, the student writer's short, snappy sentences seem as if she crafted them for deliberate effect, their rhythm balanced by the longer and more complex third sentence. In Example A, however, readers could get the impression that the writer lacks the ability to write a fluid, reasonably complex sentence. The choppy sentences seem a tad on the simplistic side – and their rhythm is monotonous. One reason why Hemingway took the literary world by storm was his journalistic prose, a dramatic and telegraphic break from the you-need-eight-breaths-to-read-this-sucker sentences penned by the likes of Henry James, who was still alive when Hemingway was a reporter for *The Kansas City Star.*

Cadence matters even in fiction – perhaps most of all in fiction

We can amuse ourselves, after stalwartly bearing up under so much neuroscience, with a brief comparison of the thing Hemingway might have been rebelling against in that excerpt from *The Nick Adams Stories*, quoted above. To avoid inflicting undue pain and suffering on writers who remember Henry James only as the guy who wrote that spooky story that inspired a few films called *The Turn of the Screw*, we'll consider one of James' more palatable works. James wrote *The Aspern Papers* during an era when he wasn't busily embedding clauses within clauses within phrases and joining apparently endless sentences with colons and semicolons. In other words, he hadn't yet got to the sort of writing you produce after you complete a PhD or DPhil:

> *Their name had been mixed up ages before with one of*
> *the greatest names of the century, and they lived now*
> *in Venice in obscurity, on very small means, unvisited,*
> *unapproachable, in a dilapidated old palace on an out-*
> *of-the-way canal: this was the substance of my friend's*
> *impression of them.*[15]

But, predictably, Hemingway summarizes the entirety of *The Aspern Papers* in considerably fewer words and sentences than James needs to preface the introduction of one of the novel's main characters:

> *Did you ever read Henry James? He was a great writer who*
> *came to Venice and looked out the window and smoked his*
> *cigar and thought.*

Tellingly, *The Kansas City Star*'s guide for reporters gave advice to its journalists that applies to everything Hemingway wrote after his stint there as a cub reporter: "Use short sentences. Use short first paragraphs. Use vigorous English. Be positive, not negative."[16] Note to anyone writing anything today: use this advice if you want to seem like an imbecile or a seven-year-old not terribly keen on this dreadful thing called *writing*. Even on Twitter.

To vary the lengths of your sentences, first assess the typical sort of sentence you tend to write. Most of us lean toward either relatively short sentences or sentences that stretch for lines, spilling into cascades of clauses and little puddling phrases. If you tend to write on the short side, try joining two shortish sentences together. Rather than simply using *and* to join your sentences, try tying sentences together via phrases or short, modifying clauses. The undergraduate who wrote Example B could have simply tied the sentences together by saying, *They love this magical land where the word "tall" equals small, and they love using words in Italian and not knowing what they mean.* Instead, she chose to unite the two ideas more subtly, tacking on another *where* clause to parallel the first one: *They love this magical land where the word "tall" equals small, where they get to use words in Italian and not know what they mean.* Her writing signals to her readers that they're in the hands of an accomplished writer who has a way with stringing sentences together.

Cadence in the brain is also real

Our ability to make sense of a stream of syllables is remarkable, as you discover quickly when you toddle into the beginning stages of learning a second language. You get along swimmingly in forming sentences like *Où est le petit coin?* which can give you the slangy sort of cachet you achieve as a non-native speaker of French the first time you ask for the john, rather than the toilet or that euphemistic American alternative, the rest room. Then you watch a Parisian police procedural, where every third word is verlan slang or listen to a French pop song and want to request the nearest *petit coin* – the slangy term for that little corner where the medieval peasants relieved themselves – so you can stick your head in the bog to drown your despair at ever making sense of French.

But, hell, you don't even need to venture into a second language to encounter the cognitive strains of comprehending speech gone terribly wrong. Witness the mishearing of "Hark, the herald angels sing," which a childhood friend insisted was "Dark the hair, old angels sing," an interpretation that makes rather more sense than the original lyrics when you think about it. Or the coda in Michael Jackson's "Wanna Be Startin' Somethin'," which includes the line "mamako, mamasa, maka makossa." Most of us probably equated those sounds with the Squeeze lyric in "If I Didn't Love You": "Cocoa mugs sit side by side." A friend sang that line as though Squeeze had written scat with only vague aspirations toward sensible English, which is how most listeners interpreted the coda to "Wanna Be Starting' Somethin'." In fact, Jackson's "mamako, mamasa, maka makossa" was Duala, not English at all, and handily borrowed from a 1970s Cameroonian dance hit. Predictably, because the borrowing involved an American with deep pockets, a lawsuit eventually ensued. But until 2009, few of us knew we were singing scraps of Duala.[17] With their blending of musical and speech cadences in lyrics, songs remain the testing ground where even native speakers can realize the limits of their abilities to disambiguate one word from another.

Music also gives us two further clues about how deeply entangled cadence is in our ability to understand speech, both spoken and written. Damage to Broca's and Wernicke's areas have two striking impacts on our perception and production of cadence. Someone who has Broca's aphasia speaks, if at all, with an absence of functional words or meaningful syntax.[18] Yet, startlingly, people with Broca's aphasia can sing with all the words correctly articulated if the stroke impacts the left hemisphere, where most of us (the right-handed among us, at any rate) process language after we learn to read.[19] Reverse the location of the stroke and impact the right hemisphere, and the aphasia leaves patients able to speak normally but unable to sing, chant, or recite even daily prayers familiar from childhood onward.[20] Furthermore, and perhaps more crucially for our perception of cadence and rhythm, Broca's and Wernicke's areas seem centrally involved in our ability to perceive tone and harmony in music. Patients with either Broca's or Wernicke's aphasia, depending on the hemisphere affected, have marked inabilities to perceive tones and harmonies in music easily perceived by others.[21]

> **The upshot: your reader will hear your writing. Always**
>
> Just practice the three cadence principles here, the fifth C, as religiously as you will the other four Cs. The same mechanisms that enable us to read, even silently and speedily, transmit the sounds from the page and into our heads.

Cadence Principle #3:
In a list, series of phrases, or entire sentence, place
the item with the least number of words and syntactic
complexity attached to it first, with the longest item, last

Ever feel like some sentences screech to a halt, like a beginning driver stomping on the brakes in Drivers' Education? Or can you recall some lists that seemed to stumble to a conclusion, rather than winding down gracefully? Both sentences and lists with these characteristics suffer from poor cadence. In this instance, however, the problem is more widespread than a jarring rhythm in a sentence we expect to roll out smoothly. When you place the most complex items at the beginning of a list, you knock your reader's sense of cadence off-kilter. Compare, for example:

Example A:
We ended the day with a recall of the week's events:
the days spent digging ditches, swatting at plane-sized
mosquitoes, squinting into driving rain, and work.

Example B:
We ended the day with a recall of the week's events: the
work, the days spent digging ditches, squinting into driving
rain, and swatting at plane-sized mosquitoes.

Example A's off-kilter list strikes us as awkward for two reasons – and these two reasons leave aside the entire issue of the list's disruptive, jarring cadence. First, the rhetoricians in ancient Greece were onto something when they insisted on using the principle of *klimax* or what Romans termed, less provocatively to our sensibility, *scala*. In a well-turned scala, items proceed in order of importance (least-to-most), size (smallest-to-largest), or syntactic complexity (simplest-to-most complex).[22] More important, when you shoehorn items into a series in any old order, you inflict significant cognitive burdens on your reader's brain. Remember, way back with the first C, clarity, how readers needed to hold items in working memory until they reached the verb and object? The more detail you embed early in a list, the harder your readers' brains must work to keep track of which word is playing which grammatical and syntactic roles.[23]

EXPERT TIP: If you don't regularly read something well written, start. Now

Studies have demonstrated that reading exerts a stronger influence on writing than writing does on reading.[24] Look carefully at the writing of your colleagues and superiors, and you can tell who's been reading PowerPoint decks on YouTube videos and who's been reading *The International Journal of Occupational and Environmental Health*. The lost soul who reads PowerPoint decks on YouTube for intellectual enrichment will avoid writing anything aside from emails and, when confronted with a writing task, will produce something that sounds wretchedly like the "My Dog Spike" essays school children labor over. In contrast, you can also easily spot the reader whose diet consists solely of academic journals – and nearly all of them read as woodenly as *The International Journal of Occupational and Environmental Health* and many, far less comprehensibly. He or she will produce those apparently endless sentences, as well as paragraphs that straddle three pages, all rife with passive construction and cluttered with jargon.

In writing, as in speaking, we tend to adopt the style, vocabulary, and rhythms, however non-existent they may seem, of the things we read.[25] On the other hand, readers tend to perceive our prose as more sophisticated when sentences contain rhythmic cadence and syntactic complexity, one hallmark of good writing on which most researchers agree.[26] If the last book you read was a textbook, subscribe to one of the two notably well-written magazines in English, including *The Economist*, *Atlantic Monthly*, *American Scholar*, *The New Yorker*, *The Times Literary Supplement*, *London Review of Books*, or *New York Review of Books* or dailies like the *Guardian*, *New York Times*, and *Wall Street Journal*. Get in the habit of at least reading the interesting bits over breakfast. And make a point of reading something well written before you write anything, where the *language style matching* James Pennebaker observed in conversations applies equally strongly with the word choices, sentence length and complexity, and overall cadence of our writing.[27]

We can even see the impact of mangled syntactic complexity in a sentence innocent of lists or anything faintly resembling a *klimax*. The original writer of Example A might have intended some snappy ending to a sentence after artfully creating tension via syntax, a sort of whodunit encapsulated in a sentence – even if the topic is genetic engineering described at its most prosaic level and not in a cloning-Dolly-the-Sheep sort of way.

Example A:
Of the many areas of science important to our future, few are more promising than a new way of manipulating the elemental structural units of life itself, which are the genes and chromosomes that tell our cells how to reproduce to become the parts that constitute our bodies, or genetic engineering.

Example B:
Of the many areas of science important to our future, few fields are more promising than genetic engineering, a new way of manipulating the elemental structural units of life, including the genes and chromosomes that both instruct our cells on reproduction and ultimately create our entire bodies.

Example A stumbles to its knees around the same time the reader's brain does, figuratively speaking. After we reach *few*, we feverishly root around for the noun to anchor the tsunami of appositive, gerundial phrases and adjective clauses that pile up, then teeter, precariously, atop the minute noun, *genetic engineering*, that, unlike Atlas, fails to hold up the miniature world stacked above it. When you place the least complicated item first, *genetic engineering*, your reader's brain no longer strains to hold the sentence open and keep syntactic complexity in place. In Example B, we can easily assign syntactic roles to the still-significant drifts of clauses and phrases after *genetic engineering* because we've already made sense of both the sentence's basic meaning and its sentence structure. We also have better recall of the modifiers that introduce us to the wonders of genetic engineering. And we're unlikely to need a second reading of Example B, in contrast to Example A. If the writer's lucky, a forgiving reader actually dives back into the pile to make sense of Example A. If she's unlucky, the reader decides the writing is unworthy of a close reading, skims the rest, or simply chucks the entire thing.

Takeaways for cadence: what you need to remember to make your writing rhythmic

- Vary your sentence structure.
- Use transitions at the beginnings of sentences to create variation in your sentence structure.
- Vary the lengths of your sentences.
- When introducing lists, put the simplest item first and the most complex item, last.

Remember, for all of us, rereading is a luxury and effort we spare only when stakes are high. We all face our queues of email waiting for replies and exponential increases in communication – spurred by how freely and quickly we can send out emails, entire books, proposals, pitches, memos, texts, and the ubiquitous social media updates. To hold our attention, you have to write well. The scarcity of both our time and attention demands nothing less.

Everything you ever wanted to know about grammar, punctuation, and usage – and never learned

This short guide serves as a single reference for all of you who were never taught grammar, punctuation rules, or usage by (a) ruler-wielding nuns, (b) Old School English teachers born prior to 1945, (c) parents who worked as high-school English teachers, or (d) the necessity of mastering at least the grammar of another language. Written after a lengthy search failed to turn up a single guide that was brief, readable, and not rife with errors, I posted this comprehensive guide online over fourteen years ago to serve merely as a reference for my students tormenting themselves over grammar and punctuation. Nearly a decade later, I received a query from IBM's head of in-house publications, requesting permission to use "Where do you put the ___? Punctuation made painless," a rump version of the guide I posted online, That guide, she explained, was superior to every other source they'd investigated as a guide for writers company-wide. Of course, IBM was only too glad when I idiotically made the entire guide available to them – gratis. In the same spirit, I'm now idiotically making the same easy-to-access reference available to you, to complement the writing skills you've just mastered in the preceding pages.

Note that I've tried to use plain, commonsense terms instead of the labels nuns and Old School types prefer. During the small hours, when you're fretting over the final draft of a proposal or manuscript, you'll be grateful for my using *subject pronoun*, rather than *nominative case*. Likewise, when you need only know whether a pronoun can act like a subject or an object and which one does what, I avoid delving into the differences between personal, demonstrative, and relative pronouns. Ultimately, you need to know how to use something correctly, rather than what the experts call it. Unless you're aiming to compete on a quiz show. Or put off someone you've met on a first date.

Grammar made (relatively) painless

Subjects

The subject is the main person, place, or thing in a clause or sentence, always paired with a verb. You must know how to locate the main subject of any sentence, as the dynamism and clarity of your sentences rely on your using an actor or a tangible object as your subjects in most sentences. To pinpoint the main subject of any sentence, *find the major clause in it*. You can recognize major clauses, as these clauses can stand on their own, without reading like either a sentence fragment or an unfinished sentence.

> **Example:**
> *Before he became the original James Bond, <u>Sean Connery had worked as both a bricklayer and a truck driver.</u>*

Note how the second clause can stand completely on its own, if you sever it from the rest of the sentence:

> *Sean Connery had worked as both a bricklayer and a truck driver.*

If you try the same tactic with the first clause, however, the result reads like a sentence fragment, a piece of a sentence that's clearly missing something:

> *Before he became the original James Bond.*

Now find the main actor or thing in the sentence's major clause – the noun or pronoun that refers to the main action or verb in the sentence.

Sean Connery is the main noun in the sentence, since that proper noun refers to the main verb. *He* in the first clause doesn't count, as the first clause is a minor clause. Incidentally, *Sean Connery* is a *proper noun*, since we're looking at the specific name of a person, place, company, product, or object. Proper nouns are *always* capitalized. In contrast, *common nouns*, which refer to general categories of objects, places, and things, are *never* capitalized.

COMMON PROBLEMS WITH SUBJECTS

Subject–verb agreement refers to how the subjects and verbs of sentences must be consistent in *both gender and number*. *Gender* refers to masculine or feminine; *number* refers to singular or plural. You can try saying, *Before she became the original James Bond, Sean Connery had worked as both a bricklayer and a truck driver.* However, you're giving Sean Connery a sex change, albeit purely a grammatical one. In the same way, you can try the American delicacy about gendered pronouns by using the genderless plural *their*, but you're violating subject–verb agreement. You can say *As every employee knows, they must squash their cigarettes at least fifty feet from the building.* But *employee* is singular, while *they* is always plural. You can exercise delicacy or American political correctness in avoiding assigning a universal *he* to nouns that refer to people by simply using the plural: *As all employees know, they must squash their cigarettes at least fifty feet from the building.*

1. When you have two nouns or pronouns as your subject linked by *and*, the verb should be plural, since the subject is multiple:

   The buoyant economy and astronomical growth of the Internet have contributed to the attractiveness of investing in high tech startups.

2. When you have two nouns or pronouns linked by *or* or *nor* (usually preceded by *either* or *neither*), the verb is singular:

   Neither Carlos nor Adele was able to accurately forecast the market trend.

3. Be wary of collective nouns, which include the names of companies and institutions, as well as groups. These usually refer to groups acting as a single unit:

   General Motors is holding its annual meeting in Dearborn.

> **Note:** For a nation of believers in rugged individualism, Americans have a peculiar habit of using the singular to refer to companies and organizations. In contrast, British speakers of English tend to refer to companies in the plural, presumably because they are made up of scores of people, not because Brits are a fractious lot who have difficulty working in groups:
>
> *Cunard are pleased to offer their passengers the first-ever cruising awards incentive programme.*

4. Be wary when using *their* to escape identifying a person or position with a gender when you've been using the singular. While we commonly use this dodge in spoken English, in standard written English pronouns and nouns must be consistent in number and gender:

   Wrong!
   The <u>employee</u> had left <u>their</u> files in an utter disarray.

   Correct versions:
   The employees had left their files in an utter disarray.
   The employee had left his files in an utter disarray.
   The employee had left her files in an utter disarray.
   The employee had left his/her files in an utter disarray.

5. Beware of seizing on the number or gender of the noun closest to the verb and allowing that to determine the number and gender of the verb:

   The <u>task</u>, with its complex details and hours of mind-numbing repetitions, <u>seem</u> endless. [The writer has relied on *repetitions* to determine the form of the verb, which should be *seems.*]

Pronouns
Pronouns replace nouns, relieving us of the need to repeat the same noun in a sentence or string of sentences.

COMMON PROBLEMS WITH PRONOUNS

1. Pronouns can make unclear what they refer to, especially if the pronoun refers to (a) a noun in an earlier sentence or, worse, (b) the content of an earlier sentence. Your readers will have to hunt through an entire preceding sentence or sentences, or, worse, may assume you're referring to a different noun entirely from the one you intended. As a result, ensure your pronouns refer clearly to only a single noun, preferably one reasonably close to the pronoun.

   Wrong!
   Guilt, bitterness, and cruelty can be emotionally destructive to you and your family. You must get rid of them.

   Correct versions:
   Guilt, bitterness, and cruelty can be emotionally destructive to you and your family. You must get rid of these emotions.

   Guilt, bitterness, and cruelty can be emotionally destructive to you and your family. You must get rid of these destructive feelings.

Unless, of course, you actually *mean* to get rid of your family.

2. Even if you use a string of pronouns, you can make their references clear by tying each pronoun to a single noun:

   The office manager bought cheap, knock-off <u>netbooks</u> for her <u>assistants</u>, but the <u>netbooks</u> fell apart quickly because <u>they</u> were not suited to heavy use. [Readers otherwise might think the *assistants* are unsuited to heavy use – not a particularly pretty image.]

3. Place pronouns as close to their referents as you can, since the more distance between the pronoun and the noun it refers to, the greater the likelihood your reader will get muddled:

   Wrong!
   The statement that the supervisor made and that she issued it as a formal policy inflamed the city council, who knew it would result in widespread anger.

Correct version:
*The supervisor made a statement and the mayor issued a
formal policy. This policy, however, inflamed the city
council, who knew the new policy would result in
widespread anger.*

4. Ensure that the pronouns *it, this, that,* and *which* refer to only
   one referent, since multiple pronouns can make sentences
   especially difficult to understand:

   Confusing!
   *According to some sources, the Federal Reserve ought to
   have interceded before Lehman Brothers crashed and
   burned, and the markets responded with panic. That
   contributed to the Dow Index losing more than 1,000
   points in a single day.*

   Clear version:
   *According to some sources, the Federal Reserve ought to
   have interceded before Lehman Brothers crashed and
   burned, and the markets responded with panic. That
   bankruptcy filing and subsequent market panic
   contributed to the Dow Index losing more than 1,000
   points in a single day.*

5. *Who* versus *that* or *which: Who* always refers to people or
   groups of people (even companies); *that* or *which* refers to
   animals and inanimate objects, as well as some groups.

6. Some grammarians and people of a certain age, as the French
   like to say, insist *that* should be used only for what we'll call
   defining adjective clauses, while *which* should be used solely
   for *non-defining* adjective clauses. In a *defining* clause, the
   clause identifies the object being modified absolutely, nailing
   its identity down to a single thing:

   The book that I had laid on the table has been stolen.

In a *non-defining* clause, the clause only provides more information about the object being modified:

> *The book, <u>which has grease spots on its dust cover,</u> is one I consult frequently.*

While the *Oxford English Dictionary* – the bible of modern English usage and grammar – no longer observes the rule governing when you use *that* and when you use *which*, some fogeys out there will swear by it. However, one rule still does legitimately refer to the difference between the two: **never place commas around a defining clause; always place commas around a non-non-defining clause**. You need the defining clause to identify a specific noun, hence the lack of commas around it. In contrast, you should bracket the non-defining clause with commas, as the clause merely tells readers more about the noun – rather than fixing the identity of the noun.

7. Pronouns fall into four cases that reflect whether they flag a subject, object, possession, or self-reference.

    a. Use *subject pronouns* when your pronoun is the subject of a sentence or a pronoun to which the subject refers. Subject pronouns include *I, you, he, she, it, we, they, who, whoever, this, that, which, these,* and *those.*

If you've actually read Chapter 3, you already know that using *this, that, these,* and *those* as grammatical subjects will kill the clarity of your sentences. However, you can use *this, that, these,* and *those* to modify nouns, which, for the record, turns them into adjectives. Confused? Just keep reading.

> *I know of no other person in the company who is as smarmy as <u>he</u>.* [Here, *he* refers to an implied *is* commonly left unstated after an *as* clause.]
>
> *Yes, this is <u>she</u>.* [*She* is a predicate pronoun, a pronoun that modifies the subject *this.*]
>
> *It is I.* [Sounds bizarre or the sort of thing reserved only for the pompous? Try saying "It's [your name]." Problem solved.]
>
> *It's me.* [In this sentence, you're identifying a hero or culprit or the person in charge, *not* your identity as, say, the person on the end of a phone call or at the door.]

b. Use *object pronouns* to refer to a pronoun or noun that receives action – or to pronouns that receive action or which flag relations in space and time in prepositional phrases. (Confused? See p. 178 for a discussion of prepositional phrases.) You can always tell a word receives action if you can insert *to* or *for* before it without changing the meaning. Object pronouns include: *me, you, him, her, it, us, them, whom, whomever*:

> *Whom can you send to help us?* [*Whom* receives the action from the verb *send*.]

> *The website gave my sister and me some interesting ideas.*

c. Use *possession pronouns* to indicate ownership or, at least, someone attached to something. Possession pronouns include *its, your, their, whose, hers, his, mine, my, yours, ours, whose, whosever*.

Note that *it's, you're, they're, and who's* are all contractions, that is, combinations of words where a missing letter is represented by an apostrophe.

Note: Possessive forms of pronouns are dicey only when they modify entire phrases, when most writers tend to mistakenly rely on the objective form:

Wrong!
We were miffed at <u>him</u> running out on us like that.

Correct version:
We were miffed at <u>his</u> running out on us like that.
[*His* modifies the entire phrase *running out on us like that,* which acts as a single part of this sentence.]

Also correct version:
We were miffed at <u>him</u>, running out on us like that.
[*Him* is the object of the preposition *at*.]

d. Use *self-reference* pronouns to intensify or to pinpoint an earlier pronoun:

I myself stopped believing my mother could blow on traffic lights to make them turn green after our car ran straight through a red light. [Intensify.]

I can see myself turning up for the first day of school in the seventies – sporting clothes Shirley Temple might have worn during the Depression. [Pinpoint.]

Verbs

Verbs are shape-shifters, conveying information through changes in their form.

Verbs can convey:

- Time – when action takes place: past, present, future.
- Person – who or what acts or experiences the action.
- Number – how many subjects act or receive action.
- Mood – the attitude expressed toward the action.
- Voice – whether the subject acts or is acted upon: active or passive voice.

In addition, verbs can be either active or passive: *Non-action* verbs express states of being: *is*, *appears*, *has*, *exists*, *seems*, *represents*, *has been*. *Action* verbs express concrete action.

COMMON PROBLEMS WITH VERBS
1. *Lie versus lay*
Lie means to repose. *Lay* means to put down:

> *To lie:* [Not in the sense of telling porkies.]
> Present tense: *I lie down all afternoon.*
> Past tense: *I lay down all afternoon.*
> Present perfect: *I have lain down all afternoon.*
> Future: tense: *I will lie down this afternoon.*
> *To lay*:
> Present tense: *I lay my iPhone on the desk.*
> Past tense: *I laid my iPhone on the desk.*
> Present perfect: *I have laid my iPhone on the desk.*
> Future: tense: *I will lay my iPhone on the desk.*

2. Moods

Ah, moods: verbs have three of them – unfortunately not as straightforward as good, bad, and indifferent. We most commonly use what we'll call the *default* mood to express action, since English's most common forms of verbs indicate statements and questions of fact.

We use the *imperative* mood to express commands and direct requests. In the imperative mood, the subject is almost always omitted and is always *you*. That is, the verb form always agrees with *you*:

[You] *Shut your mouth.*

[You] *Please, just stop talking.*

Speakers of French, Italian, and Spanish rely on the *subjunctive* mood more frequently than do speakers of English. The subjunctive expresses conditions, speculations, recommendations, wishes, and indirect requests – in other words, something that, while stated, hasn't yet come to pass. When you use the subjunctive mood, always use *be* for the future tense and *were* for the present, with no fiddly guessing about whether to use singular or plural forms of the verb:

Whether it be now or later, we must eventually face the truth.

If he were going to remain my manager, I might be inclined to stay.

3. Passive versus active construction

Passive construction is wordier and more difficult for readers to follow than active construction. If you've blithely skipped Chapter 3, you might want to skip this brief section, and, instead, read the chapter's description of the mostly negative effects of using passive construction.

Verbs fall into passive construction when the action is performed *upon* the subject, rather than *by* the subject:

A mistake has been made.

You should prefer the passive over the active whenever you're wriggling out of assigning blame:

McMurty was passed over for promotion for the nineteenth time.

You should also prefer passive over active only when emphasizing someone's status as victim or focusing more on the effects of an action than on its actors:

> *My ideas were thoroughly shredded by everyone at that bloody conference.*

Or when you cannot identify who performed the action:

> *The fateful phone call was made at 6 am, but we're still investigating who made it.*

> **Note:** *Cannot* is one word, not two. Just one of those lovely irregularities of English.

Adjectives and adverbs

Since both adjectives and adverbs are *modifiers* – or words that describe other words – telling one from another can be tricky.

Adjectives, however, describe a noun or pronoun, while adverbs describe a verb, adjective, or another adverb.

In most cases, you can't use them interchangeably. *Good* is an adjective that should modify a noun or pronoun. *Well* is an adverb that should modify a verb or adjective. One reason why *You done good* sounds awful is that, while you can do good work, you can only do work well. In addition, think about the standard American greeting which actually is anything but an enquiry after your current state of mind or health: *How's it going?* or *How're you doing?* If you're bursting to be grammatically correct, the answer is *[I'm] good* if your life is going swimmingly. However, if you're describing the state of your health, the answer is *[I'm] well*.

Whatever you do, just don't tell an American you had a root canal or that your cat has feline leukemia. By the time you finish your sentence, the American, who seemed so solicitous with that greeting, has disappeared down the hall.

COMMON PROBLEMS WITH ADJECTIVES AND ADVERBS

1. Use the *comparative form* (the *-er* or *more* form) to explicitly compare two things – which must be in the same sentence:

Donald Trump is <u>more successful</u> than Don Ameche or Don Ho. [adverb]

Your memory is <u>better</u> than mine. [adjective]

2. Use the *superlative form* to compare three or more things; the items to which the noun or pronoun is being compared don't need to appear in the same sentence:

That meeting was the <u>worst</u> one in our company's history. [adjective]

He finished the exam <u>quickest</u> of all. [adverb]

3. Don't be tempted into overkill and use both *-er* and *more* or *-est* and *most* at the same time, or you'll end up with *the most heaviest sentence of all.*

4. While you *can* get away with using *less* and *fewer* interchangeably in many instances, if you have a bona fide grammarian as a superior or you're in the military, chances are someone will point out to you that *less* refers to *amounts that you can't count (as with volumes)* while *fewer* refers to *items that you can count.*

I'm drinking less milk these days than I did when I was still growing up.

This milk has fewer calories than what I used to drink.

Common disasters: or, what the hell's a split infinitive, anyway?

BEFORE WE BEGIN...WHAT'S THE DIFFERENCE BETWEEN A CLAUSE AND A PHRASE?

A *clause* always contains a subject and a verb. If the string of words excludes a verb, you're looking at a phrase, not a clause. In addition, clauses either play *major* or *minor* roles in a sentence. If the clause plays a *major* role, the clause can stand alone, severed from the other clause, without seeming like a rump of a sentence. *Major clauses* (dubbed *independent clauses* by grammarians) may have other clauses alongside them in a sentence or may occupy the entire sentence. In contrast, *minor* (also called *dependent* or *subordinate* by grammar grouches) *clauses* accompany *major clauses*. In addition, *minor clauses* prove useful in pointing out cause and effect, indicating the timing of an event, or modifying information about the main clause in the sentence. Furthermore, clauses may also modify individual nouns or verbs. Clauses include *noun clauses, adjective clauses,* and *adverb clauses* – all named for their *function* within the sentence.

Phrases modify nouns, verbs, and, occasionally, adverbs; they may also convey relationships in time or space. Phrases include *prepositional phrases, gerund, participle,* and *infinitive phrases* – all named for the type of grammatical object that begins them. (For more on these ominous-sounding things, see below.)

1. *Dangling modifiers*: we say that a modifier *dangles* when its subject isn't included in the sentence, or when its subject isn't the subject of the sentence. Most dangling modifiers are phrases, not individual words. To correct a dangling modifier, rewrite the modifier as a minor clause or rewrite the main clause so that the subject is modified by the phrase:

   Wrong!
   Do not sit in the chair without being fully assembled.

   Correct versions:
   Do not sit in the chair without its being fully assembled.

   Do not sit in the chair unless it is fully assembled.

   Wrong!
   Strolling down Fifth Avenue, the Empire State Building came slowly into view.

   Correct versions:
   While we were strolling down Fifth Avenue, the Empire State Building came slowly into view.

   Strolling down Fifth Avenue, I watched the Empire State Building come slowly into view.

2. *Misplaced modifiers* are words, clauses, or phrases that crop up far from the thing their writer intended them to modify. The resulting sentence not only fails to convey your intended meaning; it usually also implies something unintentionally funny. At this point, the old Strunk and White dictum to "put related things together" actually comes in handy:

Wrong! [from the *London Review of Books*, no less]:

The rare exchange of letters between Vita Sackville-West and Virginia Woolf was found, of all places, in the morning room of Sissinghurst by a Dutch graduate student curled up in a drawer.

Correct version:
A Dutch graduate student discovered the rare exchange of letters between Vita Sackville-West and Virginia Woolf curled up in a drawer in, of all places, the morning room of Sissinghurst.

Wrong!
Two cars were reported stolen by the Gainesville police yesterday. [This version is accurate if the police run a stolen-car ring, which would merit a screaming headline, not a "just the facts, ma'am," report in the local paper.]

Correct version: *Yesterday, the Gainesville police reported two cars stolen.* [Tip: If you try to rely on people or tangible objects as your subjects, you'll find it nearly impossible to write dangling or misplaced modifiers.]

3. *Split infinitives* result when you place an adverb or phrase between the *to* portion of the infinitive and the verb. According to the trusty *Oxford English Dictionary*, split infinitives are now officially kosher, provided you don't work for (a) anyone born prior to 1957 or (b) anyone British or (c) professors of English who haven't checked the changing rules in the past fifteen years. As Irish playwright George Bernard Shaw once put it in a letter to the London *Times*:

There is a busybody on your staff who devotes a lot of time to chasing split infinitives ... I call for the immediate dismissal of this pedant. It is of no consequence whether he decides to go quickly or to quickly go or quickly to go. The important thing is that he should go at once.

4. The same ruling applies to prepositions at the ends of sentences. The old rule states: "A preposition is something you should never end a sentence with." My advice: if the writer stating the rule can't follow the rule, neither should you. The rule mainly evolved to prevent the awkward rhythm created by a preposition dangling at the very end of a sentence, and prepositions certainly can waste the all-important stress position of sentences, but, ultimately, the correctness judgment call is yours to make.

A phrase is a phrase: or, what the hell's a preposition/participle/gerund/appositive/infinitive?

Prepositions indicate relationships in space or time. Prepositions link nouns or pronouns to other words in a sentence and include words like: *to, from, in, out, on top of, behind, before, during, under, beneath, after, since. Prepositional phrases* consist of prepositions and nouns or pronouns. Common prepositional phrases modify or provide additional information about nouns, pronouns, verbs, or adverbs:

On Tuesday, the market plummeted to its lowest point <u>in eight years.</u>

The incentive package included four days vacation <u>at my choice of Caribbean resort.</u>

WHY YOU SHOULD CARE ABOUT PREPOSITIONAL PHRASES:

1. By identifying prepositions and prepositional phrases correctly, you minimize the possibility of confusing your subject with the pronoun or noun in the prepositional phrase – which can result in your using the wrong form of a verb.

2. You may use a comma after a prepositional phrase that begins a sentence. If the phrase is seven words or longer, however, you should follow it with a comma to avoid your reader sifting through the string for likely subject–verb combinations.

3. You should NOT use a comma before a prepositional phrase that ends a sentence.

4. You rarely need to use commas to set off prepositions or prepositional phrases from the rest of the sentence.

Participles are forms of a verb that end in either -*ed* or -*ing* and act like adjectives. Participles can stand alone in a sentence, functioning strictly as an adjective, or they can begin participle phrases, which simply modify a noun or pronoun.

> *Munching slowly, the employees worked their way through the retirement buffet.*

WHY YOU SHOULD CARE ABOUT PARTICIPLE PHRASES:

1. Participle phrases *cannot* be preceded by possessive pronouns.

2. Participle phrases should generally be set off with commas, wherever they appear, to avoid your reader stumbling down the garden path by seizing on the participle as your sentence's or clause's verb. One comma should separate the participle phrase from the main clause if the phrase begins or ends the sentence. Use two commas to bracket the phrase if it occurs anywhere else in the sentence.

Gerunds are not noxious forms of tropical diseases, despite the image this word conjures up. Instead, gerunds are forms of a verb that end in -*ing* and act like nouns. Gerunds are true grammatical shape-shifters. A gerund can act alone as the subject of the sentence, begin a phrase that acts as the grammatical subject, act as an indirect or direct object, or even serve as the object of a preposition. Gerunds can also begin gerund phrases, which also act as either subjects, indirect or direct objects, or objects of prepositions.

WHY YOU SHOULD BOTHER KNOWING ANYTHING ABOUT
GERUND PHRASES:

1. Gerund phrases *must* be preceded by possessive pronouns:

   *I was annoyed by the employees' munching slowly as they
   worked their way through the retirement buffet.*

2. Because gerund phrases are integral parts of the sentences they
   occur in, you should *never* set them off with commas:

   Partying hearty requires great endurance. [Gerund phrase
   acting as a subject.]

   We enjoyed <u>partying hearty.</u> [Gerund phrase acting as a direct
   object.]

   We objected to everyone's <u>partying so heartily.</u> [Gerund phrase
   acting as the object of a preposition.]

Appositives are nouns, pronouns, or a short phrase that renames
another noun or pronoun; they most commonly rename the subject
of the sentence. Appositive phrases modify nouns or pronouns and
should appear as close as possible to the items they modify. They
are also great stylistic devices because they can help you to create
more graceful sentences, eliminate repetition, create a rhythm in
your writing, and make your sentences more interesting.

WHY YOU SHOULD GIVE A DAMN ABOUT APPOSITIVES (ASIDE FROM
THE NUMEROUS ADVANTAGES LISTED ABOVE):

1. Appositives and appositive phrases are *always* set off by commas, usually bracketed off from the rest of the sentence by two
   commas:

   *Bob's car, <u>an utter wreck</u>, died a grisly death by the side of
   I-75.*

   Do you know my friend, <u>Bill</u>?

   *David Prowse, <u>the guy in the Darth Vader suit in the Star
   Wars movies</u>, did not find out that his lines were going to
   be dubbed over by James Earl Jones until he attended the
   premiere screening of the film.*

Phineas T. Barnum, the great American showman, was near death in 1891 when the New York World *asked if he'd like to have his obituary published while he could still read it.*

Infinitives are the equivalent to baseball's utility infielders: they can act as nouns, adjectives, or adverbs, either by themselves or as part of a longer phrase. Infinitives are formed by the word *to* and the form of the verb that accompanies *to*: *to be, to succeed, to yield, to promote.*

WHY YOU SHOULD WORRY ABOUT INFINITIVES:
You should punctuate infinitives, either by themselves or as part of a phrase, according to their function within the sentence.

1. If they function as a noun, they're usually essential to the sentence and should NOT be set off from it by commas.

   To succeed takes courage, foresight, and a hefty dose of luck. [Infinitive acting as noun and subject of the sentence.]

   Alone in her cubicle, she wanted only to survive. [Infinitive acting as noun and direct object of sentence.]

2. If the infinitive or infinitive phrase functions as an adverb but *not* as an essential part of a sentence, you usually set it off from the sentence with a comma or pair of commas.

   Afraid to move, he froze in terror. [Infinitive modifying *afraid*, acting as adverb.]

3. Most commonly, infinitives and infinitive phrases acting as adjectives are also acting as essentials within the sentence, usually as *appositives* (see above definition) or as *predicate adjectives*, adjectives that rename the subject of the sentence, always following a non-action verb.

   The firm's hope was to grow the business enough to warrant an IPO within two years. [Infinitive phrase acting as a predicate adjective.]

   His goal, to break into Fort Knox, was, of course, never achieved. [Infinitive phrase acting as an appositive.]

A rule that will guide you in punctuating both infinitive phrases and just about anything else in a sentence: **Never place <u>a single</u> comma between the subject and verb. <u>Always use either two</u> – to bracket off a phrase or word – or <u>none</u>.**

Adverb, adjective, and noun clauses

Clauses come in three forms – adverb, adjective, and noun – and differ from phrases in that clauses always have a subject and verb, while phrases lack both, having only an object. Major clauses can stand on their own; minor clauses, not surprisingly, cannot (see first page of this Supplement, p. 164, above).

Adverb clauses tend to convey relationships in time and space, results or causation, choices, conditions, contrast, and locations, although they can also sometimes modify or hedge the statement in the main clause. Adverb clauses begin with words like: *when, since, whenever, because, although, until, as soon as, while, once, as, for, unless, provided that, even if, rather than, in order that.*

WHY YOU SHOULD PAY ATTENTION TO ADVERB CLAUSES:

1. They enable you to put sentences together smoothly, giving the illusion of cause and effect, even when none exists.
2. They enable you to demonstrate concisely complex relationships between items or situations by relying on the sentence structure to establish part of the relationships.
3. They allow you to vary the rhythm of your sentences radically and easily, as an adverb clause beginning a sentence provides the most stark contrast possible with the usual subject–verb–object of standard written English sentences.
4. Adverb clauses are governed by especially quirky rules concerning punctuation:

    a. *Always* set an adverb clause off from the main clause when it begins a sentence:

       <u>Whenever Microsoft introduces a product with a zero at the end of the version number,</u> I avoid it completely.

b. While you don't always need to punctuate adverb clauses in the middles of sentences, placing commas around the clause can help distinguish the clause from your all-important subject and verb. And, since Americans tend to prefer more punctuation over less punctuation – enabling them to better control the way readers interpret their writing – when in doubt, plug in a comma. Just remember to use either *two* or *none*, never just *one:*

We looked at the product, and, <u>since it was water-damaged,</u> marked it down steeply.

c. You should insert commas in adverb clauses at the ends of sentences *only* when they begin with the words *as, for,* or *since* when they are used to mean *because*. You should NOT punctuate adverb clauses that begin with *because* or with *for* or *since* used merely to indicate time or location. This rule probably originated in the need to distinguish causation from time/spatial relationships:

We marked the product down, <u>since it was water-damaged</u>. [*Since* here is synonymous with *because*.]

We deep-discounted the product <u>because it was water-damaged.</u> [When *because* begins an adverb clause, you never use a comma.]

I enjoyed Hearts of Darkness, A Filmmaker's Apocalypse <u>*more than I enjoyed* Apocalypse Now.</u> [All other kinds of adverb clauses are also not set off with a comma when they end the sentence.]

Rob had watched the Francis Ford Coppola film more than 200 times <u>since its first release.</u> [*Since* here indicates a relationship in time, not a causal relationship.]

Adjective clauses exclusively modify a noun or pronoun within a sentence, sometimes merely providing supplementary information about it, occasionally identifying the noun absolutely.

WHY YOU SHOULD PAY ATTENTION TO ADJECTIVE CLAUSES:

1. While the distinction is no longer observed in the *Oxford English Dictionary*, some grammarians still insist *that* should be used only for defining adjective clauses, while *which* should be used solely for non-defining adjective clauses.

    a. In a *defining* clause, the clause identifies the object being modified absolutely, nailing its identity down to a single thing:

        The book that I had laid on the table has been stolen.

    b. In a *non-defining* clause, the clause only provides more information about the object being modified:

        The book, which has grease spots on its dust cover, is one I consult frequently.

2. The only rule that still does legitimately refer to the difference between the two is: **never place commas around a defining clause; always place commas around a non-defining clause.**

Noun clauses are minor clauses that act like nouns. We seldom set noun clauses off with a comma or set of commas, since they can function as essential parts of sentences – subjects, direct and indirect objects, objects of prepositions, or predicate nouns (which restate the subject and always follow an non-action verb).

Noun clause as subject:
How the accountant managed to dredge up those profit and loss figures is a mystery.

Noun clause as direct object:
No one understands why a reputation is something people usually bother about only when it's in shreds.

Noun clause as appositive:
Adolescent males, the members of the population who most want to control their lives and, arguably, feel least in control, represent 80 percent of the market for US video games.

WHY YOU SHOULD CARE ABOUT NOUN CLAUSES FOR
PUNCTUATION'S SAKE:

> Noun clauses can also function as appositives, requiring
> two commas to bracket them off from the subjects and
> verbs of sentences (see above).

Where do you put the ___? Punctuation made painless

In addition to the punctuation principles we've covered above,
you should be aware of some weird or particular usages for the
common elements of punctuation: the period, question mark,
comma, semicolon, colon, and dashes.

Periods, of course, are the workhorses of the punctuation stable.

1. Always use them after a complete sentence, but also after
2. a command or a request disguised as a command:

Can you please return this report to me as soon as possible.

3. Use periods after most abbreviations: *Dr. Ms. Jr.*
4. But not after individual letters in an acronym: *NATO.*
5. Use a period after an initial: *John F. Kennedy.*
6. Always place a period inside a quotation mark that ends a
   sentence:

The sign read: "A pest is a friend in need."

Question marks tend to be underused, as writers forget that questions require question marks, just as a rising inflection in a spoken
sentence indicates a query or uncertainty.

1 Always use a question mark to end a question.
2. Place a question mark *inside* of closing quotation marks *if the
   question mark belongs in the original quotation:*

*In a dream I heard someone asking, "Isn't atheism a
non-prophet organization?"*

3. Place the question mark *outside* the closing quotation marks if
   the question mark is *not* part of the quotation:

Didn't your mother say, "I knew I shouldn't have sold my Coca-Cola shares in 1958"?

Commas control how your readers interpret your writing, indicating when they should pause and which clusters of words should be read separately from the major clause. When in doubt, you're usually better to over-punctuate than to under-punctuate as long as you avoid separating the subject and verb with a single comma – the big comma error – or use a comma to separate two major clauses.

1. Use a comma to show contrast between phrases:

   The neighbors returned home at all hours, often falling-down drunk.

2. Use a comma to stand in for a word that has been omitted:

   To err is human, to forgive, divine. [Since your reader can easily infer the second *is*, you can leave it out but must indicate its absence with the comma.]

3. Use two commas to bracket off appositives and appositive phrases (see above).

4. Use a comma to set off *direct address*, or words that express to whom a remark is addressed:

   <u>Gary,</u> are you with us on this one?

5. Use a comma to set off *parenthetical expressions*, or phrases and expressions that interrupt a sentence:

   The issue, <u>as you well know</u>, is a potentially explosive one.

6. Use a comma to separate items in a series:

   We purchased an entirely new suite of office equipment, including <u>a digital video camera, two digital still cameras, and a digital editing suite.</u>

7. Use a comma to set off a direct quotation:

   "Lawyers are the larval forms of politicians," he said.
   [Quote occupies the beginning of a sentence.]

He said, "Lawyers are the larval forms of politicians."
[Quote occupies the end of a sentence.]

"Lawyers," he said, "are the larval forms of politicians."
[Split one-sentence quote, with the attribution (*he said*) in the middle.]

"Lawyers are the larval forms of politicians," he said. "Why else do you think I suffered through three years at NYU's College of Law?" [Split two-sentence quote.]

8. Use a comma to separate two major clauses joined by *and, or, but, for, so,* and *yet*:

   Our management strategies failed to work, and we ran out of money.

9. Use a comma after or commas around coordinate conjunctions like *however, consequently, conversely, nevertheless, moreover, furthermore, therefore*:

   The wide-body plane lumbered down the runway, seeming far too heavy to ever take flight, however, its thrust lifted the heavy aircraft rapidly away from the ground.

10. DO NOT use a comma to separate two clauses when they share the same subject. If you use a comma between two verbs referring to the same grammatical subject, you sever one verb from the subject it refers to:

    We stopped thinking about an IPO and started worrying about staying solvent.

Semicolons are halfway between a comma and period in terms of their emphasis. While semicolons don't cement the ends of sentences the way periods do, they indicate totally major clauses, not subordination. They also, however, have a variety of uses.

1. Use a semicolon between closely related major clauses:

   Bigamy is one spouse too many; monogamy is the same idea.

2. Semicolons can also flag contrasting relationships between major clauses:

The man appeared to be begging us for help; he was threatening us with outspread hands.

3. Use a semicolon to separate items in a series when they contain internal punctuation:

   When Cunard decided to take its fleet upmarket, the company's ships consisted of several transatlantic class mid-sized ships, which had mostly seen their better days; a few mid-sized, flashy ships that were flat-bottomed and therefore restricted to the Caribbean; and the venerable Queen Elizabeth 2, *the most powerful name brand at sea.*

4. Place semicolons outside quotation marks:

   The team acknowledged they were "psyched about the profit sharing agreement"; they still, however, held out for more vacation time.

Colons receive more abuse than any other form of punctuation, usually by academics who seem to hate ending a sentence with a period and insist on seeing everything as endlessly connected.

1. Use a colon before a list:

   In the Thoroughbred industry, you can make money in several ways: through breeding and selling as weanlings or yearlings; through breeding and selling as two-year-olds; or through buying weanlings or yearlings and selling as two-year-olds.

2. Use a colon before a long quotation:

   Abraham Lincoln said: "Fourscore and seven years ago, our fathers brought forth upon this continent a new nation, conceived in liberty and dedicated to the proposition that all men are created equal."

3. Use a colon before a part of a sentence that restates the subject of the sentence:

   I know only one certain way to make a small fortune from horse racing: start with an extremely large one.

4. Use a colon after the salutation of a business letter:

Dear Chancellor:

Dashes enable you to break some of the monotony that can accompany one too many sentences bristling with loads of commas. Dashes can replace any form of punctuation, save for the period. If you're in doubt about what piece of punctuation to use, use the trusty dash. Just remember that dashes are obtrusive bits of punctuation, excellent for emphasis, but sufficiently "loud" that you should restrict yourself to using them only once per paragraph.

1 Dashes are distinct from *hyphens*, which link words together or which link nouns together to indicate they're being used as an adjective: two-year-olds, age-related illness.

2. Dashes represent changes of thought, show emphasis, and stand in for both commas and semicolons:

An archeologist – of course, I'm not referring to
Dr. Montebello – is someone whose career lies in ruins.

Ahead lay our choice – to do or die.

We made up our minds – tomorrow we were going to begin
rowing between Australia and New Zealand.

ENDNOTES

1 So much advice, so much lousy writing

1   Richard Marius, *A Writer's Companion*. 4th edn (New York: McGraw-Hill, 1999).
2   William Strunk, Jr. and E. B. White, *The Elements of Style* (Boston: Allyn & Bacon, 1979).
3   Sheridan Baker, *The Practical Stylist* (New York: Longman, 1997).
4   Knoblauch and Brannon (1984): 163.
5   The sentence in the California Penal Code, Chapter 1.5, Section 631a, reads: Any person who, by means of any machine, instrument, or contrivance, or in any other manner, intentionally taps, or makes any unauthorized connection, whether physically, electrically, acoustically, inductively, or otherwise, with any telegraph or telephone wire, line, cable, or instrument, including the wire, line, cable, or instrument of any internal telephonic communication system, or who willfully and without the consent of all parties to the communication, or in any unauthorized manner, reads, or attempts to read, or to learn the contents or meaning of any message, report, or communication while the same is in transit or passing over any wire, line, or cable, or is being sent from, or received at any place within this state; or who uses, or attempts to use, in any manner, or for any purpose, or to communicate in any way, any information so obtained, or who aids, agrees with, employs, or conspires with any person or persons to unlawfully do, or permit, or cause to be done any of the acts or things mentioned above in this section, is punishable by a fine not exceeding two thousand five hundred dollars ($2,500), or by imprisonment in the county jail not exceeding one year, or by imprisonment in the state prison, or by both a fine and imprisonment in the county jail or in the state prison. If the person has previously been convicted of a violation of this section or Section 632, 632.5, 632.6, 632.7, or 636, he or she is punishable by a fine not exceeding ten thousand dollars ($10,000), or by

imprisonment in the county jail not exceeding one year, or by imprisonment in the state prison, or by both a fine and imprisonment in the county jail or in the state prison.

6 Scott Adams, qtd. in Lepore (2014): 73.

2 The new science of writing

1 Moore (1965): 114–117.
2 These daunting equations form the basis of the three bibles of readability formulas:

 1. Flesch (1974).
 2. Flesch (1979).
 3. Gunning and Kallan (1994).

3 David Denby, "A Famous Man: The Collected Works of James Agee," *The New Yorker,* January 9, 2006: 85.
4 Lynne Truss, *Eats, Shoots & Leaves: The Zero Tolerance Approach to Punctuation* (London: Profile Books, 2003): 71.
5 Dehaene (2009): 15–16.
6 Perfetti (1999).
7 Zwaan *et al.* (1995); Zwaan (1996); Zwaan and Radvansky (1998).
8 Fleischman (1990).
9 Bruner (1986): 16–25.
10 Leslie and Keeble (1987).
11 Rumelhart (1975); Anderson *et al.* (1978).
12 The Egyptians relied on a schema to represent important people as large (and nonentities as small). In contrast, during the 1817 exhibition at the Royal Academy of Arts, an entirely different schema prompted one critic to describe painter John Constable's now-classic painting *Wivenhoe Park, Essex*, as "that nasty green thing." See Gombrich (1961).
13 Oliver Sacks, *An Anthropologist on Mars: Seven Paradoxical Tales* (New York: Vintage, 1996).

3 Choosing words and structuring sentences: The first C: Clarity

1 Heider and Simmel (1944).
2 Michotte (1963).

3 Leslie and Keeble (1987).
4 Michael *et al.* (2001).
5 Anderson *et al.* (1978).
6 Fleischman (1990); Norman *et al.* (1991); Noordman *et al.* (1992); Zwaan (1996); Ferreira *et al.* (2002); Ferreira (2003).
7 F. Ferreira and J. Stacey, unpublished manuscript, 2000.
8 Evans (2014): 75.
9 McWhorter (2001): 158–159.
10 Rhodes (1997).
11 Olson and Filby (1972).
12 Stelzner (1966).
13 Wydick (1998); Cordes (2002).
14 Anthony (2007).
15 Olson (1991).
16 Eisenstein (1979).
17 Ferreira and Clifton (1986); Ferreira (2003).
18 Greene and McKoon (1995); Bornkessel *et al.* (2005).
19 Clifton *et al.* (1984).
20 Clifton *et al.* (1984).
21 Bornkessel *et al.* (2005).
22 Klee and Legge (1976).
23 K. Kearns, unpublished manuscript, 1988; Bornkessel *et al.* (2002).
24 Berk and Whalen (1992); Billig (2008).
25 Van Dijk (2008).
26 Stallings *et al.* (1998).
27 Clark and Sengul (1979).
28 Frazier *et al.* (1984).
29 Researchers use the term *NP shift* or *Heavy NP shift* to indicate sentences that begin with noun phrases and are also left-branching, embedding complexity to the left of the main verb in the major clause. Noun Phrase (NP) shift and left-branching sentences make readers' brains work overtime: Hagoort *et al.* (1993); Just *et al.* (1996); Gibson (1998); Culicover and Levine (2001); Lieberman (2001); Clifton *et al.* (2007); Temperly (2007).
30 Schank (1982).
31 Ferreira and Clifton (1986); Michael *et al.* (2001).
32 Pluchino *et al.* (2003): 688.
33 Steinman (2003): 671.

4 Putting sentences together: The second C: Continuity

1 Britt (1994); Miyake *et al.* (1994); Ferreira *et al.* (2002); Baddeley (2004).

2 The term *cognitive overload* crops up as a research topic with the emergence of hyper- and multimedia. New technologies gave researchers multiple lenses on these new media – as a curse, as an everyday challenge, and as fodder for understanding how brains cope with multiple demands. Unsurprisingly, studies through the 1990s focused on the downside of increased competition for our attention, while studies after 2000 simply seized opportunities for understanding our brains' peak attentional capacity: Landauer (1995); Mackay (2000); Fox *et al.* (2007).

3 Schank and Abelson (1977); Spiro (1980).

4 Smith (2012).

5 Anderson *et al.* (1978).

6 Bain (1890): 11; Atkinson and Shiffrin (1968); Glanzer (1972); Baddeley and Hitch (1993); Thapar and Greene (1993); Davelaar *et al.* (2005).

7 Murdock (1962); Just and Carpenter (1980); Williams *et al.* (1981); Graesser *et al.* (1997).

8 This approximation of working memory avoids the impact of predictability, syntactic, or inferential difficulty, as well as the abilities of the subjects doing the recalling: Miller (1956); Schnotz and Kürschner (2007).

9 Daneman (1982).

10 Graesser *et al.* (2001).

11 Daneman and Carpenter (1983).

12 Garnham *et al.* (1982).

13 Just and Carpenter (1980); Trabasso and van den Broek (1985); King and Just (1991).

14 Black and Bower (1979); Zwaan (1996).

15 Coulson *et al.* (1998); Mason *et al.* (2003); Davis (2005); Temperly (2007); Smith (2012).

16 Chafe (1974).

17 Mayer (1976).

18 Sperber and Wilson (1985, 2002, 2004).

19 Just and Carpenter (1980); Daneman and Carpenter (1983); Fahnestock (1983); Sloan (1988).

20 Garnham *et al.* (1982).
21 Dee-Lucas *et al.* (1982).
22 Daneman (1982).
23 Lupker (1984); Nicholas (1998); Chang *et al.* (2000).
24 Graf and Schacter (1985).
25 Kintsch and van Dijk (1978); Kintsch and Vipond (1979).
26 Tversky and Kahneman (1973).
27 Rayner *et al.* (2001).
28 Frazier and Rayner (1982); Rayner *et al.* (1983); Ferreira and Clifton (1986).

5 Organizing paragraphs and documents: The third C: Coherence

1 DeKay (2010).
2 Nielsen (2006).
3 Samuels and Kamil (1984).
4 Brown (1982).
5 Spiro (1980).
6 Yore and Shymansky (1985).
7 Chang *et al.* (2000).
8 Graesser *et al.* (1997).
9 Van Dijk (1988).
10 Dor (2003).
11 Duggan and Payne (2011). See earlier research on inferential processing and comprehension: Kintsch and van Dijk (1978); Bower *et al.* (1979); Miller and Kintsch (1980); Masson (1982).
12 Williams *et al.* (1981).
13 McCarthy *et al.* (2008).
14 Britton (1994); Kintsch (2002).
15 Cutrell and Guan (2007).
16 Cirilo (1981).
17 McCarthy *et al.* (2008).
18 Miller and Kintsch (1980).
19 Wikborg (1985).
20 Hakala and O'Brien (1995).
21 Miller and Kintsch (1980).
22 Williams (1995).
23 Anderson *et al.* (1978); Kintsch (2002).

24 Fredric Jameson in the *London Review of Books* 23 (19) October 4, 2001.

25 Pickering and Branigan (1998); Pickering and Garrod (2013).

26 Baddeley (2004): 81. For the particularly strong impact of recency on recall, see Glenberg and Swanson (1986); Baddeley and Hitch (1993).

27 McCarthy *et al.* (2008).

28 Kintsch and van Dijk (1978).

29 Kintsch and van Dijk (1978).

30 Frase (1969).

31 Kintsch and van Dijk (1978).

32 Graesser *et al.* (1997).

33 Zwaan (1994).

34 Kintsch (1988).

35 Graeme Wood, "The Future of College?" *The Atlantic*, September 2014: 50–60.

36 Spyridakis and Fukuoka (2002).

37 Lorch and Lorch (1985); Kintsch (1988); Murray and McGlone (1997); Therriault and Raney (2002); Ritchey (2011).

38 Higgins *et al.* (2004).

39 Diederich *et al.* (1961).

40 Spyridakis and Fukuoka (2002); Therriault and Raney (2002); Ritchey (2011).

41 Murdock (1962).

42 Spiro (1980); Brown (1982); Yore and Shymansky (1985).

43 Van den Broek *et al.* (2001).

44 Luchins (1958).

45 Kieras (1978).

46 Moreno and Mayer (2000).

47 Paivio (1990).

48 Van den Broek *et al.* (2001).

49 Pickering and Ferreira (2008).

6 Maximizing efficiency: The fourth C: Concision

1 Transcript of a recording of a meeting among the President, H. R. Haldeman, and John Dean, on September 15, 1972, from 5:27 to 6:27 pm. Mary Ferrell Foundation, Watergate Recording Transcripts. Available as of 2014 from www.maryferrell.org/mffweb/archive/docset/getList.do?docSetId = 1923.

2 Ron Grossman, "In May 1974, Tribune Delivered 2 Watergate Bombshells," *Chicago Tribune*, April 27, 2014.

3 Grice (1975); Limaye and Cherry (1987).

4 Britton (1982); Nell (1988); Bazerman (2003).

5 Plato (1973).

6 Grice (1975).

7 Ong (1982).

8 Limaye and Cherry (1987); Hyland and Tse (2004); Lebovits (2006); Matsuda and Tardy (2007); Dermer *et al.* (2010).

9 Crystal (2004).

10 McCrum *et al.* (1992); Crystal (2004).

11 Clanchy (1979).

12 McCrum *et al.* (1992).

13 Crystal (2004).

14 Eisenstein (1979).

15 Bryson (1990).

16 Locker (1987).

17 Wydick (1998).

18 Costello and Keane (2000).

19 Crystal (2004).

20 Baddeley (2004).

21 Williams (1995).

22 Hyland and Tse (2004).

23 Handlin *et al.* (2003).

24 Hyland and Tse (2004). Metadiscourse is alive and everywhere in academic medicine: Salager-Meyer (1994).

25 Harwood (2005).

26 Matsuda and Tardy (2007).

27 See the *Oxford English Dictionary*'s entry for *intent*, under Phrases (2): www.oed.com. The abbreviation first crops up in Joseph Addison's essay for *Tatler* (Number 96): "Whoever resides in the World without having any Business in it...is to me a Dead Man to all Intents and Purposes." Addison, an elegant prose stylist, at least takes us from the triplet of meaningless, cover-your-ass-ness to a doublet of meaningless, cover-your-ass-ness.

28 Fowler (1965).

29 *The Oxford New French Dictionary* (New York: Berkley Books, 2003).

30 Herbert (1967).

31 Baddeley *et al.* (1975).

7 Making music with words: The fifth C: Cadence

1 Erasmus (1978).
2 Fowler (1965): 526.
3 Qtd. in Manguel (1996): 42.
4 Fischer (2005).
5 Cobban (1975); Pedersen (1997).
6 Schwinges (1996).
7 Dehaene (2009).
8 Paulesu *et al.* (1993).
9 For a highly readable layperson's guide to the brain and neuroanatomy, look no further than Rita Carter, *Mapping the Mind* (1998). For one of the most informative guides you'd never imagined existed on what the most minute and insignificant aspects of our language says about us – and an equally engaging transcription of Broca's and Wernicke's aphasiacs in conversation, see James W. Pennebaker, *The Secret Life of Pronouns: What Our Words Say about Us* (2011).
10 Horwitz *et al.* (1998); Bernal and Ardila (2009).
11 Horwitz *et al.* (1998).
12 Büchel *et al.* (1998).
13 Nishimura *et al.* (1999).
14 Ernest Hemingway, "Three Shots," *The Nick Adams Stories* (New York: Scribner, 1972): 13.
15 Henry James, "The Aspern Papers," *The Great Short Novels of Henry James*. Ed. Philip Rahv (New York: Skyhorse Publishing, 2014): 453.
16 "Ernest Hemingway at 100: *Star* Style and Rules for Writing," *The Kansas City Star*, June 26, 1999. Available as of 2014 at www.kcstar.com/hemingway/ehstarstyle.shtml.
17 Sean Michaels, "Rihanna and Michael Jackson Sued by African Singer," *Guardian*, February 4, 2009.
18 Heilman *et al.* (2004).
19 Ramachandran (2011).
20 Speedie *et al.* (1993).
21 Patel (2010).
22 Carpenter (1999).
23 Gordon *et al.* (2002).
24 Research on the role of reading in fostering better writing is surprisingly scarce. However, some studies have made convincing

cases for the unquestionable impact of reading on writing in elementary education. In this area, the most worthwhile findings stem from a largely one-man crusade by researcher Timothy Shanahan: Shanahan (1984); Shanahan and Lomax (1986); Crowhurst (1990); Fitzgerald and Shanahan (2000); Shanahan (2006).

25 Pennebaker (2011).

26 Coh-Metrix, an automated tool for assessing the quality of writing, contains some admirable features correlated with the principles tied to readability outcomes we've explored throughout *The Reader's Brain*. Most significantly for cadence, Coh-Metrix tied perceptions of the quality of the writing directly to its syntactic complexity. This outcome is unsurprising, given that some of the brains behind Coh-Metrix include Arthur Graesser, Philip McCarthy, and Danielle McNamara, all of whom published insightful research on many aspects of cognition, reading, and readability. See McNamara *et al.* (2010).

27 Pennebaker (2011).

SELECT BIBLIOGRAPHY

Anderson, Richard C., Rand J. Spiro, and Mark C. Anderson. (1978). "Schemata as Scaffolding for the Representation of Information in Connected Discourse," *American Educational Research Journal* 15/3: 433–440.

Anthony, Ted. (2007). *Chasing the Rising Sun: The Journey of an American Song*. New York: Simon & Schuster.

Atkinson, R. C. and R. M. Shiffrin. (1968). "Human Memory: A Proposed System and Its Control Processes," in K. W. Spence and J. T. Spence (eds.), *The Psychology of Learning and Motivation: Advances in Research and Theory*. New York: Academic Press: 89–195.

Baddeley, Alan. (2004). *Your Memory: A User's Guide*. Buffalo, NY: Firefly Books.

Baddeley, Alan D. and Graham Hitch. (1993). "The Recency Effect: Implicit Learning with Explicit Retrieval?" *Memory & Cognition* 21/2: 146–155.

Baddeley, Alan D., Neil Thomson, and Mary Buchanan. (1975). "Word Length and the Structure of Short-Term Memory," *Journal of Verbal Learning and Verbal Behavior* 14/6: 575–589.

Bain, Alexander. (1890). *English Composition and Rhetoric*. Enlarged edn. London: Longmans, Green, and Company.

Bazerman, Charles. (2003). "Speech Acts, Genres, and Activity Systems: How Texts Organize Activity and People," in Charles Bazerman and Paul Prior (eds.), *What Writing Does and How It Does It: An Introduction to Analyzing Texts and Textual Practices*. New York: Routledge: 309–339.

Berk, Robert N. and Elizabeth Whalen. (1992). "Impediments to Clarity: An Annotated Glossary of Rhetorical Pratfalls and Pitfalls," *AJR: American Journal of Roentgenology* 159/5: 1115–1121.

Bernal, Byron and Alfredo Ardila. (2009). "The Role of the Arcuate Fasciculus in Conduction Aphasia," *Brain* 132/9: 2309–2316.

Billig, Michael. (2008). "The Language of Critical Discourse Analysis: The Case of Nominalization," *Discourse & Society* 19/6: 783–800.

Black, John B. and Gordon H. Bower. (1979). "Episodes as Chunks in Narrative Memory," *Journal of Verbal Learning and Verbal Behavior* 18: 309–318.

Bornkessel, Ina, Matthias Schlesewsky, and Angela D. Friederici. (2002). "Beyond Syntax: Language-related Positivities Reflect the Revision of Hierarchies," *NeuroReport* 13/3: 361–364.

Bornkessel, Ina, Stefan Zysset, Angela D. Friederici, D. Yves von Cramon, and Matthias Schlesewsky. (2005). "Who Did What to Whom? The Neural Basis of Argument Hierarchies during Language Comprehension," *NeuroImage* 26/1: 221–233.

Bower, Gordon H., John B. Black, and Terrence J. Turner. (1979). "Scripts in Memory for Text," *Cognitive Psychology* 11/2: 177–220.

Britt, M. Anne. (1994). "The Interaction of Referential Ambiguity and Argument Structure in the Parsing of Prepositional Phrases," *Journal of Memory and Language* 33/2: 251–283.

Britton, Bruce K. (1994). "Understanding Expository Text: Building Mental Structures to Induce Insights," in Morton Ann Gernsbacher (ed.), *Handbook of Psycholinguistics*. San Diego, CA: Academic Press: 641–674.

Britton, James. (1982). "A Reader's Expectations," in Gordon M. Pradl (ed.), *Prospect and Retrospect: Selected Essays of James Britton*. Montclair, NJ: Boynton/Cook: 130–138.

Brown, Ann L. (1982). "Learning How to Learn from Reading," in Judith A. Langer and M. Trika Smith-Burke (eds.), *Reader Meets Author/Bridging the Gap: A Psycholinguistic and Sociolinguistic Perspective*. Newark, DE: International Reading Association: 26–54.

Bruner, Jerome. (1986). *Actual Minds, Possible Worlds*. Cambridge, MA: Harvard University Press.

Bryson, Bill. (1990). *The Mother Tongue: English and How It Got That Way*. New York: William Morrow.

Büchel, Christian, Cathy Price, R. S. Frackowiak, and Karl Friston. (1998). "Different Activation Patterns in the Visual Cortex of Late and Congenitally Blind Subjects," *Brain* 121/3: 409–419.

Carpenter, Ronald H. (1999). *Choosing Powerful Words: Eloquence That Works*. Needham Heights, MA: Allyn & Bacon.

Carter, Rita. (1998). *Mapping the Mind*. Berkeley, CA: University of California Press.

Chafe, Wallace L. (1974). "Language and Consciousness," *Language* 50/1: 111–133.

Chang, Franklin, Gary S. Dell, Kathryn Bock, and Zenzi M. Griffin. (2000). "Structural Priming as Implicit Learning: A Comparison of Models of Sentence Production," *Journal of Psycholinguistic Research* 29/2: 217–230.

Cirilo, Randolph K. (1981). "Referential Coherence and Text Structure in Story Comprehension," *Journal of Verbal Learning and Verbal Behavior* 20/3: 358–367.

Clanchy, Michael T. (1979). *From Memory to Written Record 1066–1307*. Cambridge, MA: Harvard University Press.

Clark, Herbert H. and C. J. Sengul. (1979). "In Search of Referents for Nouns and Pronouns," *Memory & Cognition* 7/1: 35–41.

Clifton, Charles, Lyn Frazier, and Cynthia Connine. (1984). "Lexical Expectations in Sentence Comprehension," *Journal of Verbal Learning and Verbal Behavior* 23/6: 696–708.

Clifton, Charles, Adrian Staub, and Keith Rayner. (2007). "Eye Movements in Reading Words and Sentences," in Roger P. G. van Gompel (ed.), *Eye Movements: A Window on Mind and Brain*. Amsterdam: Elsevier: 341–372.

Cobban, Alan B. (1975). *The Medieval Universities: Their Development and Organisation*. London: Methuen.

Cordes, Jason L. (2002). "When Liability Can Attach for Remaining Passive: Construction of the Term 'Disposal' under Cercla: Crofton Ventures Limited Partnership v. G & H Partnership 1," *Missouri Environmental Law & Policy Review* 9: 67–154.

Costello, Fintan J. and Mark T. Keane. (2000). "Efficient Creativity: Constraint-guided Conceptual Combination," *Cognitive Science* 24/2: 299–349.

Coulson, Seana, Jonathan W. King, and Marta Kutas. (1998). "Expect the Unexpected: Event-related Brain Response to Morphosyntactic Violations," *Language & Cognitive Processes* 13/1: 21–58.

Crowhurst, Marion. (1990). "Reading/Writing Relationships: An Intervention Study," *Canadian Journal of Education* 15/2: 155–172.

Crystal, David. (2004). *The Stories of English*. New York: Overlook Press.

Culicover, Peter W. and Robert D. Levine. (2001). "Stylistic Inversion in English: A Reconsideration," *Natural Language & Linguistic Theory* 19/2: 283–310.

Cutrell, Edward and Zhiwei Guan. (2007). "What Are You Looking For?: An Eye-Tracking Study of Information Usage in Web Search," in *Proceedings of the SIGCHI Conference on Human Factors in Computing Systems*. New York: Association for Digital Machinery (ACM).

Daneman, Meredyth. (1982). "The Measurement of Reading Comprehension: How Not to Trade Construct Validity for Predictive Power," *Intelligence* 6/4: 331–345.

Daneman, Meredyth and Patricia A Carpenter. (1983). "Individual Differences in Integrating Information between and within Sentences," *Journal of Experimental Psychology: Learning, Memory, and Cognition* 9/4: 561–584.

Davelaar, Eddy J., Yonatan Goshen-Gottstein, Amir Ashkenazi, Henk J. Haarmann, and Marius Usher. (2005). "The Demise of Short-term Memory Revisited: Empirical and Computational Investigations of Recency Effects," *Psychological Review* 112/1: 3–42.

Davis, Kirsten. (2005). "Persuasion through Organization: The Final Installment – Transitions," *Arizona Attorney*: 31–33.

Dee-Lucas, Diana, Marcel Adam Just, Patricia A. Carpenter, and Meredyth Daneman. (1982). "What Eye Fixations Tell Us about the Time Course of Text Integration," in Rudolf Groner and Paul Fraisse (eds.), *Cognition and Eye Movements*. Leipzig: North-Holland: 155–168.

Dehaene, Stanislas. (2009). *Reading in the Brain: The Science and Evolution of a Human Invention*. New York: Viking.

DeKay, Sam H. (2010). "Focus on Business Practices: Designing Email Messages for Corporate Readers: A Case Study of Effective and Ineffective Rhetorical Strategies at a Fortune 100 Company," *Business Communication Quarterly* 73/1: 109–119.

Dermer, Marshall L., Shannon L. Lopez, and Paul A. Messling. (2010). "Fluency Training a Writing Skill: Editing for Concision," *The Psychological Record* 59/1: 3–20.

Diederich, Paul, John W. French, and Sydell T. Carlton. (1961). "Factors in Judgments of Writing Quality," Princeton, NJ: Educational Testing Service: ERIC ED 002 172.

Dor, Daniel. (2003). "On Newspaper Headlines as Relevance Optimizers," *Journal of Pragmatics* 35/5: 695–721.

Duggan, Geoffrey B. and Stephen J. Payne. (2011). "Skim Reading by Satisficing: Evidence from Eye Tracking," in *Proceedings of the SIGCHI Conference on Human Factors in Computing Systems*. New York: Association for Digital Machinery (ACM): 1141–1150.

Eisenstein, Elizabeth L. (1979). *The Printing Press as an Agent of Change: Communications and Cultural Transformations in Early Modern Europe*. 2 vols. Cambridge: Cambridge University Press.

——(1983). *The Printing Revolution in Early Modern Europe*. New York: Cambridge University Press.

Erasmus, Desiderius. (1978). *Copia: Foundations of the Abundant Style* (De Duplici Copia Verborum ac Rerum Commentarii Duo). Trans. Betty Knott. In Craig R. Thompson (ed.), *Collected Works of Erasmus*. Vol. xxiv. Toronto: University of Toronto Press.

Evans, Vyvyan. (2014). *The Language Myth: Why Language Is Not an Instinct*. Cambridge: Cambridge University Press.

Fahnestock, Jeanne. (1983). "Semantic and Lexical Coherence," *College Composition and Communication* 34/4: 400–416.

Ferreira, Fernanda. (2003). "The Misinterpretation of Noncanonical Sentences," *Cognitive Psychology* 47: 164–203.

Ferreira, Fernanda, Karl G. D. Bailey, and Vittoria Ferraro. (2002). "Good-enough Representations in Language Comprehension," *Current Directions in Psychological Science* 11/1: 11–15.

Ferreira, Fernanda, and Charles Clifton. (1986). "The Independence of Syntactic Processing," *Journal of Memory and Language* 25: 348–368.

Ferreira, Fernanda and Janis Stacey. (2000). "The Misinterpretation of Passive Sentences," unpublished manuscript.

Fischer, Steven Roger. (2005). *A History of Reading*. Amsterdam: Reaktion Books.

Fitzgerald, Jill and Timothy Shanahan. (2000). "Reading and Writing Relations and Their Development," *Educational Psychologist* 35/1: 39–50.

Fleischman, Suzanne. (1990). *Tense and Narrativity: From Medieval Performance to Modern Fiction*. Austin, TX: University of Texas Press.

Flesch, Rudolf. (1974). *The Art of Readable Writing*. New York: Harper.

——(1979). *How to Write in Plain English: A Book for Lawyers and Consumers*. New York: Harper.

Fowler, H. W. (1965). *A Dictionary of Modern English Usage*. 2nd edn. New York: Oxford University Press.

Fox, Julia R., Byungho Park, and Annie Lang. (2007). "When Available Resources Become Negative Resources: The Effects of Cognitive

Overload on Memory Sensitivity and Criterion Bias," *Communication Research* 34/3: 277–296.

Frase, Lawrence T. (1969). "Paragraph Organization of Written Materials: The Influence of Conceptual Clustering upon the Level and Organization of Recall," *Journal of Educational Psychology* 60/5: 394–401.

Frazier, Lyn and Keith Rayner. (1982). "Making and Correcting Errors during Sentence Comprehension: Eye Movements in the Analysis of Structurally Ambiguous Sentences," *Cognitive Psychology* 14/2: 178–210.

Frazier, Lyn, Lori Taft, Tom Roeper, Charles Clifton, and Kate Ehrlich. (1984). "Parallel Structure: A Source of Facilitation in Sentence Comprehension," *Memory & Cognition* 12/5: 421–430.

Garnham, Alan, Jane Oakhill, and P. N. Johnson-Laird. (1982). "Referential Continuity and the Coherence of Discourse," *Cognition* 11/1: 29–46.

Gibson, Edward. (1998). "Linguistic Complexity: Locality of Syntactic Dependencies," *Cognition* 68: 1–76.

Glanzer, M. (1972). "Storage Mechanisms in Recall," in G. H. Bower and J. T. Spence (eds.), *The Psychology of Learning and Motivation*. New York: Academic Press: 129–193.

Glenberg, Arthur M. and Naomi G. Swanson. (1986). "A Temporal Distinctiveness Theory of Recency and Modality Effects," *Journal of Experimental Psychology: Learning, Memory, and Cognition* 12/1: 3–15.

Gombrich, E. H. (1961). *Art and Illusion: A Study in the Psychology of Pictorial Representation*. New York: Bollingen Foundation.

Gordon, Peter C., Randall Hendrick, and William H. Levine. (2002). "Memory-load Interference in Syntactic Processing," *Psychological Science* 13/5: 425–430.

Graesser, Arthur C., Keith K. Millis, and Rolf A. Zwaan. (1997). "Discourse Comprehension," *Annual Review of Psychology* 48/1: 163–189.

Graesser, Arthur C., Ashish B. Karnavat, Frances K. Daniel, Elisa Cooper, Shannon N. Whitten, and Max Louwerse. (2001). "A Computer Tool to Improve Questionnaire Design," paper presented at the Funding Opportunity in Survey Research Seminar, June 11, Bureau of Labor Statistics, Washington, DC.

Graf, Peter, and Daniel L. Schacter. (1985). "Implicit and Explicit Memory for New Associations in Normal and Amnesic Subjects,"

Journal of Experimental Psychology: Learning, Memory, and Cognition 11/3: 501–518.

Greene, Steven B. and Gail McKoon. (1995). "Telling Something We Can't Know: Experimental Approaches to Verbs Exhibiting Implicit Causality," *Psychological Science* 6/5: 262–270.

Grice, H. Paul. (1975). "Logic and Conversation," in P. Cole and J. L. Morgan (eds.), *Speech Acts*. New York: Academic Press: 41–58.

Gunning, Robert and Richard A. Kallan. (1994). *How to Take the Fog out of Business Writing*. Chicago: Dartnell.

Hagoort, Peter, Colin Brown, and Jolanda Groothusen. (1993). "The Syntactic Positive Shift (SPS) as an ERP Measure of Syntactic Processing," *Language & Cognitive Processes* 8/4: 439–483.

Hakala, Christopher M. and Edward J. O'Brien. (1995). "Strategies for Resolving Coherence Breaks in Reading," *Discourse Processes* 20/2: 167–185.

Handlin, Amy, Joseph B. Mosca, Dana A. Forgione, and Dennis Pitta. (2003). "DTC Pharmaceutical Advertising: The Debate's not Over," *Journal of Consumer Marketing* 20/3: 227–237.

Harwood, Nigel. (2005). "'Nowhere Has Anyone Attempted … in This Article I Aim to Do Just That': A Corpus-based Study of Self-Promotional I and We in Academic Writing across Four Disciplines," *Journal of Pragmatics* 37/8: 1207–1231.

Heider, Fritz and Marianne Simmel. (1944). "An Experimental Study of Apparent Behavior," *American Journal of Psychology* 57/2: 243–259.

Heilman, Kenneth M., Susan A. Leon, and John C. Rosenbek. (2004). "Affective Aprosodia from a Medial Frontal Stroke," *Brain and Language* 89/3: 411–416.

Herbert, A. S. (1967). *Historical Catalogue of Printed Editions of the English Bible 1525–1961*. New York: American Bible Society.

Higgins, Derrick, Jill Burstein, Daniel Marcu, and Claudia Gentile. (2004). "Evaluating Multiple Aspects of Coherence in Student Essays," paper Presented at the Higher Learning/Teaching-NAACL, Boston, MA. Available as of 2014 via download at www.ets.org/Media/Research/pdf/erater_higgins_dis_coh.pdf.

Horwitz, B., J. M. Rumsey, and B. C. Donohue. (1998). "Functional Connectivity of the Angular Gyrus in Reading and Dyslexia," *Proceedings of the National Academy of Sciences USA* 95: 8939–8944.

Hyland, Ken. (2004). "Disciplinary Interactions: Metadiscourse in L2 Postgraduate Writing," *Journal of Second Language Writing* 13/2: 133–151.

Hyland, Ken and Polly Tse. (2004). "Metadiscourse in Academic Writing: A Reappraisal," *Applied Linguistics* 25/2: 156–177.

Just, Marcel Adam and Patricia A. Carpenter. (1980). "A Theory of Reading: From Eye Fixations to Comprehension," *Psychological Review* 87/4: 329–354.

Just, Marcel Adam, Patricia A. Carpenter, Timothy A. Keller, William F. Eddy, and Keith R. Thulborn. (1996). "Brain Activation Modulated by Sentence Comprehension," *Science* 274: 114–116.

Kieras, David E. (1978). "Good and Bad Structure in Simple Paragraphs: Effects on Apparent Theme, Reading Time, and Recall," *Journal of Verbal Learning and Verbal Behavior* 17/1: 13–28.

King, Jonathan and Marcel Adam Just. (1991). "Individual Differences in Syntactic Processing: The Role of Working Memory," *Journal of Memory and Language* 30/5: 580–602.

Kintsch, Walter. (1988). "The Role of Knowledge in Discourse Comprehension: A Construction-Integration Model," *Psychological Review* 95/2: 163–182.

——(2002). "On the Notions of Theme and Topic in Psychological Process Models of Text Comprehension," *Thematics: Interdisciplinary Studies* 3: 157–170.

Kintsch, Walter and Teun A. van Dijk. (1978). "Toward a Model of Text Comprehension and Production," *Psychological Review* 85/5: 363–394.

Kintsch, Walter and Douglas Vipond. (1979). "Reading Comprehension and Readability in Educational Practice and Psychological Theory," in Lars-Göran Nilsson (ed.), *Perspectives on Memory Research: Essays in Honor of Uppsala University's 500th Anniversary*. Hillsdale, NJ: Lawrence Erlbaum Associates: 329–365.

Klee, Hilary and David Legge. (1976). "Estimates of Concreteness and Other Indices for 200 Transitive Verbs," *Journal of Experimental Psychology: Human Learning and Memory* 2/4: 497–507.

Knoblauch, C. H. and Lil Brannon. (1984). *Rhetorical Traditions and the Teaching of Writing*. Portsmouth, NH: Boynton/Cook.

Landauer, Thomas. (1995). *The Trouble with Computers*. Cambridge, MA: MIT Press.

Lebovits, Gerald. (2006). "The Department of Redundancy Department: Concision and Succinctness – Part II," *New York State Bar Association Journal* 78/7: 44–54.

Lepore, Jill. (2014). "Away from My Desk," *The New Yorker*, May 12: 72–74.

Leslie, Alan and Stephanie Keeble. (1987). "Do Six-month-old Infants Perceive Causality?" *Cognition* 25: 265–288.

Lieberman, Philip. (2001). "Human Language and Our Reptilian Brain: The Subcortical Bases of Speech, Syntax, and Thought," *Perspectives in Biology and Medicine* 44/1: 32–51.

Limaye, Mohan R. and Roger D. Cherry. (1987). "Pragmatics, 'Situated' Language, and Business Communication," *Journal of Business and Technical Communication* 1/1: 68–88.

Locker, Kitty O. (1987). "'As Per Your Request': A History of Business Jargon," *Journal of Business and Technical Communication* 1/1: 27–47.

Lorch, Robert F. and Elizabeth P. Lorch. (1985). "Topic Structure Representation and Text Recall," *Journal of Education Psychology* 77/2: 137–148.

Luchins, Abraham S. (1958). "Definitiveness of Impression and Primacy–Recency in Communications," *Journal of Social Psychology* 48/2: 275–290.

Lupker, Stephen J. (1984). "Semantic Priming without Association: A Second Look," *Journal of Verbal Learning and Verbal Behavior* 23/6: 709–733.

Mackay, Wendy E. (2000). "Responding to Cognitive Overload: Co-adaptation between Users and Technology," *Intellectica* 30/1: 177–193.

Manguel, Alberto. (1996). *A History of Reading*. New York: Viking.

Mason, Robert A., Marcel Adam Just, Timothy A. Keller, and Patricia A. Carpenter. (2003). "Ambiguity in the Brain: What Brain Imaging Reveals About the Processing of Syntactically Ambiguous Sentences," *Journal of Experimental Psychology: Learning, Memory, and Cognition* 29/6: 1319–1338.

Masson, Michael E. (1982). "Cognitive Processes in Skimming Stories," *Journal of Experimental Psychology: Learning, Memory, and Cognition* 8/5: 400–417.

Matsuda, Paul Kei and Christine M. Tardy. (2007). "Voice in Academic Writing: The Rhetorical Construction of Author Identity in Blind

Manuscript Review," *English for Specific Purposes* 26/2: 235–249.

Mayer, Richard E. (1976). "Integration of Information during Problem Solving due to a Meaningful Context of Learning," *Memory & Cognition* 4/5: 603–608.

McCarthy, Philip M., Adam M. Renner, Michael G. Duncan, Nicholas D. Duran, Erin J. Lightman, and Danielle S. McNamara. (2008). "Identifying Topic Sentencehood," *Behavior Research Methods* 40/3: 647–664.

McCrum, Robert, William Cran, and Robert MacNeil. (1992). *The Story of English*. New York: Penguin.

McNamara, Danielle S., Scott A. Crossley, and Philip M. McCarthy. (2010). "Linguistic Features of Writing Quality," *Written Communication* 27/1: 57–86.

McWhorter, John. (2001). *The Power of Babel: A Natural History of Language*. New York: HarperCollins.

Michael, Erica B., Timothy A. Keller, Patricia A. Carpenter, and Marcel Adam Just. (2001). "fMRI Investigation of Sentence Comprehension by Eye and by Ear: Modality Fingerprints on Cognitive Processes," *Human Brain Mapping* 13: 239–252.

Michotte, A. (1963). *The Perception of Causality*. New York: Basic Books.

Miller, George A. (1956). "The Magical Number Seven, Plus or Minus Two: Some Limits on Our Capacity for Processing Information," *Psychological Review* 63: 81–97.

Miller, James R. and Walter Kintsch. (1980). "Recall and Readability of Short Prose Passages." paper presented at the American Educational Research Association Conference, Boston, MA. April 7–11: 32pp.

Miyake, Akira, Marcel Adam Just, and Patricia A. Carpenter. (1994). "Working Memory Constraints on the Resolution of Lexical Ambiguity: Maintaining Multiple Interpretations in Neutral Contexts," *Journal of Memory and Language* 33/2: 175–202.

Moore, Gordon E. (1965). "Cramming More Components onto Integrated Circuits," *Electronics*, April 19: 114–117.

Moreno, Roxana and Richard E. Mayer. (2000). "A Learner-centered Approach to Multimedia Explanations: Deriving Instructional Design Principles from Cognitive Theory," *Interactive Multimedia Electronic Journal of Computer-enhanced Learning* 2/2: 12–20.

Murdock, Bennet B. (1962). "The Serial Position Effect of Free Recall," *Journal of Experimental Psychology* 64/5: 482–488.

Murray, John D. and Chadd McGlone. (1997). "Topic Overviews and Processing of Topic Structure," *Journal of Educational Psychology* 89/2: 251–261.

Nell, Victor. (1988). *Lost in a Book: The Psychology of Reading for Pleasure*. New Haven, CT: Yale University Press.

Nicholas, Serge. (1998). "Perceptual and Conceptual Priming of Individual Words in Coherent Texts," *Memory* 6/6: 643–663.

Nielsen, Jakob. (2006). "F-shaped Pattern for Reading Web Content," *Alertbox: Current Issues in Web Usability*. Available as of 2014 from http://www.useit.com/alertbox/reading_patternhtml.

Nishimura, Hiroshi, Kazuo Hashikawa, Katsumi Doi, Takako Iwaki, Yoshiyuki Watanabe, Hideo Kusuoka, Tsunehiko Nishimura, and Takeshi Kubo. (1999). "Sign Language 'Heard' in the Auditory Cortex," *Nature* 397: 116.

Noordman, Leo, Wietske Vonk, and Henk J. Kempff. (1992). "Causal Inferences during the Reading of Expository Texts," *Journal of Memory and Language* 31/5: 573–590.

Norman, Suzanne, Susan Kemper, Donna Kynette, Hintat Cheung, and Cheryl Anagnopoulos. (1991). "Syntactic Complexity and Adults' Running Memory Span," *Journal of Gerontology* 46/6: 346–351.

Olson, David R. (1991). "Literacy and Objectivity: The Rise of Modern Science," in David R. Olson and Nancy Torrance (eds.), *Literacy and Orality*. New York: Cambridge University Press: 149–164.

Olson, David R. and Nikola Filby. (1972). "On the Comprehension of Active and Passive Sentences," *Cognitive Psychology* 3/3: 361–481.

Ong, Walter J. (1982). *Orality and Literacy: The Technologizing of the Word*. New York: Methuen.

Orwell, George. (1986). "Politics and the English Language," in M. H. Abrams (ed.), *The Norton Anthology of English Literature*. London: W. W. Norton: 2260–2270.

Paivio, Allan. (1990). *Mental Representations: A Dual Coding Approach*. New York: Oxford University Press.

Patel, Aniruddh D. (2010). *Music, Language, and the Brain*. New York: Oxford University Press.

Paulesu, Eraldo, Christopher D. Frith, and Richard S. J. Frackowiak. (1993). "The Neural Correlates of the Verbal Component of Working Memory," *Nature* 362/25: 342–345.

Pedersen, Olaf. (1997). *The First Universities: Studium Generale and the Origins of University Education in Europe*. Trans. Richard North. Cambridge: Cambridge University Press.

Pennebaker, James W. (2011). *The Secret Life of Pronouns: What Our Words Say about Us*. New York: Bloomsbury Press.

Perfetti, Charles A. (1999). "Comprehending Written Language: A Blueprint of the Reader," in C. M. Brown and P. Hagoort (eds.), *The Neurocognition of Language*. Oxford: Oxford University Press: 167–208.

Pickering, Martin J. and Holly P. Branigan. (1998). "The Representation of Verbs: Evidence from Syntactic Priming in Language Production," *Journal of Memory and Language* 39: 633–651.

Pickering, Martin J. and Victor S. Ferreira. (2008). "Structural Priming: A Critical Review," *Psychological Bulletin* 134/3: 427–459.

Pickering Martin J. and Simon Garrod. (2013). "Forward Models and Their Implications for Production, Comprehension, and Dialogue," *Behavioral and Brain Sciences* 36/4: 377–392.

Pinker, Steven. (1994). *The Language Instinct: How the Mind Generates Language*. New York: Harper.

Plato. (1973). *Phaedrus*. Trans. Walter Hamilton. London: Penguin.

Pluchino, Stefano, Angelo Quattrini, Elena Brambilla, Angela Gritti, Giuliana Salani, Giorgia Dina, Rossella Galli *et al.* (2003)."Injection of Adult Neurospheres Induces Recovery in a Chronic Model of Multiple Sclerosis," *Nature* 422: 688–694.

Ramachandran, V. S. (2011). *The Tell-Tale Brain: A Neuroscientist's Quest for What Makes Us Human*. New York: W. W. Norton.

Rayner, Keith, Marcia Carlson, and Lyn Frazier. (1983). "The Interaction of Syntax and Semantics during Sentence Processing: Eye Movements in the Analysis of Semantically Biased Sentences," *Journal of Verbal Learning and Verbal Behavior* 22/3: 358–374.

Rayner, Keith, Barbara R. Foorman, Charles A. Perfetti, David Pesetsky, and Mark S. Seidenberg. (2001). "How Psychological Science Informs the Teaching of Reading," *Psychological Science in the Public Interest* 2/2: 31–74.

Rhodes, Susan. (1997). "The Active and Passive Voice Are Equally Comprehensible in Scientific Writing," PhD thesis, University of Washington, 1997. Available as of 2014 at https://digital.lib.washington.edu/researchworks/bitstream/handle/1773/9033/9819294.pdf?sequence = 1&isAllowed = y.

Richards, I. A.(1930). *Practical Criticism: A Study of Literary Judgment*. London: Kegan Paul Trench Trubner.

Ritchey, Kristin A. (2011). "How Generalization Inferences Are Constructed in Expository Text Comprehension," *Contemporary Educational Psychology* 36/4: 280–288.

Rumelhart, David. (1975). "Notes on a Schema for Stories," in David G. Bobrow and Alan Collins (eds.), *Representation and Understanding*. New York: Academic Press: 211–235.

Salager-Meyer, Françoise. (1994). "Hedges and Textual Communicative Function in Medical English Written Discourse," *English for Specific Purposes* 13/2: 149–170.

Samuels, S. Jay and Michael L. Kamil. (1984). "Models of the Reading Process," *Handbook of Reading Research* 1: 185–224.

Schank, Roger C. (1982). *Dynamic Memory: A Theory of Reminding and Learning in Computers and People*. Cambridge: Cambridge University Press.

Schank, Roger and Robert Abelson. (1977). *Scripts, Plans, Goals and Understanding*. Hillsdale, NJ: Lawrence Erlbaum Associates.

Schnotz, Wolfgang and Christian Kürschner. (2007). "A Reconsideration of Cognitive Load Theory," *Educational Psychology Review* 19: 469–508.

Schwinges, Rainer Christoph. (1996). "Student Education, Student Life," in Hilde de Ridder-Symoens (ed.), *Universities in Early Modern Europe, 1500–1800*. Cambridge: Cambridge University Press: 195–243.

Shanahan, Timothy. (1984). "Nature of the Reading–Writing Relation: An Exploratory Multivariate Analysis," *Journal of Educational Psychology* 76/3: 466–477.

——(2006). "Relations among Oral Language, Reading, and Writing Development," in C. A. MacArthur, S. Graham, and J. Fitzgerald (eds.), *Handbook of Writing Research*. New York: Guildford Press: 171–186.

Shanahan, Timothy and Richard G. Lomax. (1986). "An Analysis and Comparison of Theoretical Models of the Reading–Writing Relationship," *Journal of Educational Psychology* 78/2: 116–123.

Sloan, Gary. (1988). "Relational Ambiguity between Sentences," *College Composition and Communication* 39/2: 154–165.

Smith, Frank. (2012). *Understanding Reading: A Psycholinguistic Analysis of Reading and Learning to Read*. 6th edn. New York: Routledge.

Speedie, Lynn J., Eliahu Wertman, Judy Ta'ir, and Kenneth M. Heilman. (1993). "Disruption of Automatic Speech Following a Right Basal Ganglia Lesion," *Neurology* 43/9: 1768–1774.

Sperber, Dan and Deirdre Wilson. (1985). "Loose Talk," *Proceedings of the Aristotelian Society* 86/1: 153–171.

——(2002). "Pragmatics, Modularity and Mind Reading," *Mind & Language* 17/1–2: 3–23.

——(2004). "Relevance Theory," in Laurence Horn and Gregory Ward (eds.), *Handbook of Pragmatics*. Oxford: Blackwell: 607–632.

Spiro, Rand J. (1980). "Prior Knowledge and Story Processing: Integration, Selection, and Variation," *Poetics* 9/1: 313–327.

Spyridakis, Jan H. and Waka Fukuoka. (2002). "The Effect of Inductively versus Deductively Organized Text on American and Japanese Readers," *IEEE Transactions on Professional Communication* 45/2: 99–114.

Stallings, Lynne M., Maryellen C. MacDonald, and Padraig O'Seaghdha. (1998). "Phrasal Ordering Constraints in Sentence Production: Phrase Length and Verb Disposition in Heavy-NP Shift," *Journal of Memory and Language* 39: 392–417.

Steinman, Lawrence. (2003). "Collateral Damage Repaired," *Nature* 422: 671–672.

Stelzner, Hermann G. (1966). "'War Message,' December 8, 1941: An Approach to Language," *Communications Monographs* 33/4: 419–437.

Temperly, David. (2007). "Minimization of Dependency Length in Written English," *Cognition* 105: 300–333.

Thapar, Anjal and Robert L. Greene. (1993). "Evidence against a Short-term Store Account of Long-Term Recency Effects," *Memory & Cognition* 21/3: 329–337.

Therriault, David J. and Gary E. Raney. (2002). "The Representation and Comprehension of Place-on-the-Page and Text-Sequence Memory," *Scientific Studies of Reading* 6/2: 117–134.

Trabasso, Tom and Paul van den Broek. (1985). "Causal Thinking and the Representation of Narrative Events," *Journal of Memory and Language* 24/5: 612–630.

Tversky, Amos and Daniel Kahneman. (1973). "Availability: A Heuristic for Judging Frequency and Probability," *Cognitive Psychology* 5: 207–232.

Van den Broek, Paul, Robert F. Lorch, Tracy Linderholm, and Mary Gustafson. (2001). "The Effects of Readers' Goals on Inference Generation and Memory for Texts," *Memory & Cognition* 29/8: 1081–1087.

Van Dijk, Teun A. (1988). *The News as Discourse*. Hillsdale, NJ: Lawrence Erlbaum Associates.

——(2008). "Critical Discourse Analysis and Nominalization: Problem or Pseudo-Problem?" *Discourse & Society* 19/6: 821–828.

Wikborg, Eleanor. (1985). "Unspecified Topic in University Student Essays," *Text – Interdisciplinary Journal for the Study of Discourse* 5/4: 359–370.

Williams, Joanna P., Maravene B. Taylor, and Sonia Ganger. (1981). "Text Variations at the Level of the Individual Sentence and the Comprehension of Simple Expository Paragraphs," *Journal of Educational Psychology* 73/6: 851–865.

Williams, Joseph M. (1995). *Style: Toward Clarity and Grace*. Chicago: University of Chicago Press.

Wydick, Richard C. (1998). *Plain English for Lawyers*. 4th edn. Durham, NC: Carolina Academic Press.

Yore, Larry D. and James A. Shymansky. (1985). "Reading, Understanding, Remembering and Using Information in Written Science Materials," in *Association for the Education of Teachers in Science*. Cincinnati, OH: ERIC: 1–59.

Zwaan, Rolf A. (1994). "Effect of Genre Expectations on Text Comprehension," *Journal of Experimental Psychology: Learning, Memory, and Cognition* 20/4: 920–933.

——(1996). "Processing Narrative Time Shifts," *Journal of Experimental Psychology: Learning, Memory, and Cognition* 22/5: 1196–1207.

Zwaan, Rolf A., Mark C. Langston, and Arthur Graesser. (1995). "The Construction of Situation Models in Narrative Comprehension: An Event-Indexing Model," *Psychological Science* 6: 292–297.

Zwaan, Rolf A. and Gabriel A. Radvansky. (1998). "Situation Models in Language Comprehension and Memory," *Psychological Bulletin* 123/2: 162–185.

INDEX